With friendship,

Harry

Educational Theory and Jewish Studies in Conversation

Educational Theory and Jewish Studies in Conversation

From Volozhin to Buczacz

Harvey Shapiro

LEXINGTON BOOKS
Lanham • Boulder • New York • Toronto • Plymouth, UK

Published by Lexington Books
A wholly owned subsidiary of The Rowman & Littlefield Publishing Group, Inc.
4501 Forbes Boulevard, Suite 200, Lanham, Maryland 20706
www.rowman.com

10 Thornbury Road, Plymouth PL6 7PP, United Kingdom

British Library Cataloguing in Publication Information Available

Library of Congress Cataloging-in-Publication Data
Shapiro, Harvey, 1952–
Educational theory and Jewish studies in conversation : from Volozhin to Buczacz / Harvey Shapiro.
pages cm.
Includes bibliographical references and index.
ISBN 978-0-7391-7531-6 (cloth : alk. paper)—ISBN 978-0-7391-7532-3 (electronic)
1. Jews—Education—Philosophy. 2. Jewish religious education—Philosophy. I. Title.
LC719.S485 2013
371.82924—dc23
2012037351

™ The paper used in this publication meets the minimum requirements of American National Standard for Information Sciences Permanence of Paper for Printed Library Materials, ANSI/NISO Z39.48-1992.

Printed in the United States of America

In memory of Frayda Shapiro
and
Debi Shapiro Partouche

Contents

Acknowledgments

A version of chapters 3 and 5 originally appeared as Harvey Shapiro, "Contingency, Inquiry, and Effort: The Educational Thought of R. Ḥayyim of Volozhin," *International Journal of Jewish Education Research* 2 (2010): 7–48. A version of chapter 4 originally appeared as Harvey Shapiro, "Rabbi Ḥayyim of Volozhin's Non-Messianic Theory of the Present and Future," *Journal of Jewish Thought and Philosophy* 15 (2007): 27–57. A version of chapter 6 originally appeared as Harvey Shapiro, "Multivocal Narrative and the Teacher as Narrator: The Case of Agnon's 'Two Scholars Who Were in Our Town,'" *Shofar: An Interdisciplinary Journal of Jewish Studies*, 29 (2011): 23–45. Portions of chapter 7 originally appeared as Harvey Shapiro, "Double-voice in S. Y. Agnon's 'The Outcast' (*Hanidaḥ*): Overtures to a Developing Style," *Journal of Modern Jewish Studies*, 10 (2011): 285–306. A version of chapter 2 was delivered at the 2012 annual conference of the Network for Research in Jewish Education as Harvey Shapiro, "Educational Theory and Jewish Studies in Conversation: Engaging the Discourses."

Part 1

Introducing the Discourses: Education, Jewish Studies, and Interdisciplinarity

In his analysis of recent dramatic changes in higher education, Louis Menand notes a significant and valuable tendency:

> The most important intellectual development in the academy in the twenty-first century has to do with the relationship between the life sciences—particularly neurobiology, genetics, and psychology—to fields outside the natural sciences, such as philosophy, economics, and literary studies. So far, contention and collaboration in this area seem robust. The system is doing what it was designed to do. It is helping people think better by helping them think together.[1]

In this book, I consider what is at stake when students and faculty think and communicate together across discourses. Specifically, I suggest the potential for expanding and deepening the relationships between Jewish studies and education. Though focusing on these particular fields, this book's import can extend to virtually all relationships between the humanities and professional education when disciplines and their discourses illuminate and challenge one another—when "contention and collaboration" are "robust."

Education and Jewish studies have a decades-old relationship in professional education programs for Jewish educators. And the number of academic and programmatic partnerships between Jewish studies and education is growing in universities, most significantly in doctoral studies.[2] With this growth, I suggest that the relationship is in need of further philosophical articulation and conceptual differentiation in order for each field to realize increasingly meaningful, mutually beneficial engagement. I further suggest that, notwithstanding significant intermittent efforts to connect education and Jewish studies, there are many lost opportunities to do so, resulting in limited interaction and infrequent reciprocal influence (See figure 1.1). I therefore wish to present a broader universe of alternatives for the relationship between these disciplines and discourses in higher education, professional education, and scholarship—beyond a generic "bringing Jewish studies and education together."

Crossing disciplinary boundaries is, of course, a ubiquitous feature of the academy today. The successes and controversies surrounding border-breaching interdisciplinarity and relatively recently constructed fields such as gen-

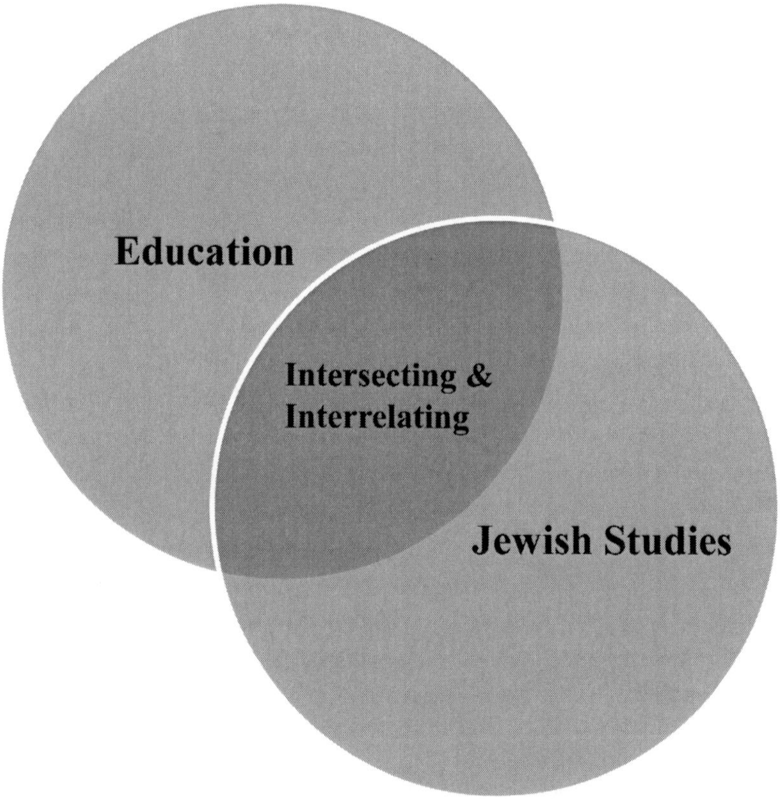

Figure 1.1. When considered as the sum total of the student's formal learning experiences, "bringing Jewish studies and education together" often results in limited intersecting relationships between the respective disciplines.

der studies and cultural studies attest to the displacibility of traditional disciplinary limits. In chapter 1, I note how the proliferation of Jewish studies in the last few decades has relied on new disciplinary assemblages and their inevitable displacements,[3] as scholars have given increasing attention to the aporias and possibilities of defining the field's particularities, conceptual frameworks, terminologies, definitions, and interdisciplinarity.[4] While I will show how different concepts of interdisciplinarity afford certain kinds of relationships between Jewish studies and the study of education, I will maintain that an alternative concept of *interdiscursivity* has more potential for enhancing these fields' relationships and their "interillumination."[5]

In another sense, this book builds upon an emergent literature that, implicitly and explicitly, seeks to articulate and illustrate potential interdisciplinary connections. Jewish educational theorists have been renewing suggestions to "bridge" Jewish studies and education and have offered curricular innovations to address "the divide" between them.[6] This literature has gained significant momentum since Michael Rosenak first compellingly presented the need for conversation between the languages and literatures of Jewish philosophy, theology, and educational theory, and since Seymour Fox first proposed ways to translate scholarship into Jewish educational experience.[7]

In chapter 2, I differentiate this literature, suggesting its implicit philosophical bases for engaging Jewish studies with education. In doing so, I introduce conceptual language that may inform, broaden, frame, and advance our deliberation on these fields' relationships. The growth of this hybrid discourse invites consideration on the meta-levels of its nature and assumptions. For the appearance of a common scholarly agenda may belie different, albeit intersecting, rationales that could influence how we address these theoretical and curricular relationships.

While full analyses of Jewish studies and education's constituent elements, contexts, and discourses are beyond this book's scope and purpose, it is first important to consider the nature of these fields' commensurability. Chapter 1 thus examines how modern academic Jewish studies are continuous or discontinuous with the educational aspirations of Jewish learning and growth and what is meant by the term "interdisciplinarity" and its various avatars.

NOTES

1. Louis Menand, *The Marketplace of Ideas: Reform and Resistance in the American University* (New York: Norton, 2010), 19.

2. In the United States, perhaps the most notable are the joint doctoral programs in Education and Jewish Studies at Stanford University and New York University. Stanford University School of Education, Concentration in Education and Jewish Studies (2012), http://

ed.stanford.edu/academics/doctoral/edandjewishstudies; New York University, Steinhardt School of Culture, Education, and Human Development, Education and Jewish Studies (EJST-PHD) Doctoral Program (2012), http://steinhardt.nyu.edu/graduate_admissions/guide/ejst/phd.

3. Leslie Morris, "Placing and Displacing Jewish Studies: Notes on the Future of a Field," *PMLA* 125, no. 3: 764–773.

4. Andrew Bush, *Jewish Studies: A Theoretical Introduction* (Piscataway, NJ: Rutgers University Press, 2011).

5. Mikhail Bakhtin, *The Dialogic Imagination*, translated by Michael Holquist, edited by Caryl Emerson and Michael Holquist, 259–422 (Austin, TX: University of Texas Press, 1981), 12, 17, 49, 362–363, 429–430.

6. Barry W. Holtz, "Across the Divide: What Might Jewish Educators Learn from Jewish Scholars?" *Journal of Jewish Education* 72 (2006): 5–28.

Jon Levisohn, "What Is Bridging Scholarship and Pedagogy?" In The Initiative on Bridging Scholarship and Pedagogy of Brandeis University, Mandel Center for Studies in Jewish Education and Jewish Studies. Working Paper 1 (Revised September 2006). http://www.brandeis.edu/mandel/research/bridging/bridginginitiative_docs.html.

7. Seymour Fox and Geraldine Rosenfield, eds. *From the Scholar to the Classroom: Translating Jewish Tradition Into Curriculum* (New York: Melton Research Center for Jewish Education, Jewish Theological Seminary of America, 1977).

Michael Rosenak, *Commandments and Concerns: Jewish Religious Education in Secular Society* (New York: Jewish Publication Society, 1987).

Chapter One

Engaging the Discourses

Academic Jewish studies is "non-doctrinal, non-parochial, and non-denominational scholarship and pedagogy about aspects of the Jewish experience using modern research tools,"[1] as Judith Baskin succinctly points out. How could such a seemingly objectivized Judaism become subjectivized in educators' professional conduct and deliberation? Can we affirm, in Andrew Bush's terms, that the academy is an appropriate context for those "many students who are not studying Jews as an external object, as *them*, but rather as *us*, seeking points of contact between their own lives and other Jewish experiences as the basis for grounding their sense of their own Jewish identity"?[2] How then can a relationship be emplaced across the apparent chasm between academic scholarship, on the one hand, and religious, cultural, communal, and personal commitment, on the other?

But if this assumed gulf presents such an obstacle, how are we to explain why rabbinic schools, Jewish education graduate programs, and communal institutions of higher Jewish learning continue to be ready hosts for modern Jewish studies scholarship and academic pedagogy? And how are we to interpret the long-standing practice "of credible scholars working side-by-side with influential rabbis and respected communal executives"[3] in Jewish community deliberation and education?

In a remarkable analysis and narrative of the development of Jewish studies in academia, Bush seeks to remove a veil that shrouds the conjunctions and continuities between the scholarly and the religio-cultural-educational realms. He notes substantial, perhaps counterintuitive, consistencies between traditional Jewish learning and modern Jewish studies, claiming that "the new does not supersede the old, but transforms it."[4] In maintaining this dual notion of continuity with transformation, Bush draws on sociologist of religion Danièle Hervieu-Léger, citing her argument for "*metaphorization*" as "an explicit alternative to the concept of *secularization*":

> Far from being an indication of the disintegration of religion in societies where politics, science, art, sexuality, and culture have gradually broken free from the control of traditional religions, metaphorization testifies to the fact that their new autonomy has made them available for a new kind of religious function; and it needs be asked how this function compares with that performed by traditional religions in premodern society.[5]

Bush points out how this notion of metaphorization informs aspects of the nineteenth-century Science of Judaism's historical method in as much as the latter "imports the ground concept of inner [historical] unity as its truth . . . from the Jewish reading of the Bible."[6] And, though perhaps in a somewhat overstated metaphor, he explains that "Jewish history is, metaphorically, the Scripture of Jewish science."[7]

Making the case for this immanence of the old in the new, Bush draws on Gershom Scholem's critique of the Science of Judaism.[8] Scholem was not objecting to that academic movement's apparent exclusion of the religious, political, and "conservative" dimensions of Jewish history and religion but rather its inability to recognize and "grapple with a set of inner contradictions," Bush notes.[9] In Scholem's words, these contradictions were (1) between "'a pure and objective science'" and "the political function which this discipline was intended to fulfill" as it affirmed Judaism's historical development and belonging; (2) between "rationalistic evaluations" and "the elevation of the aura and brilliance attached to the past by virtue of its being the past"; and (3) between "the conservative tendencies and destructive tendencies within this discipline."[10]

While Jewish studies has changed dramatically, it is not a stretch of the imagination to see how these kinds of contradictions are experienced by students and teachers of Jewish studies today. With all of its academic rigor, Jewish studies plays a constructive role; it "both constructs Jews as a people with a history and reconstructs Jewish memory."[11] Contemporary studies of identity—"a key word in the current state of Jewish Studies"—cannot avoid the potential of reflexive inquiry into the meaning of being a Jew today.[12] And like women's studies, feminist approaches to Jewish studies do not simply examine an objectified phenomenon, but also lend perspective to being a Jewish woman today.[13] History and memory are increasingly intertwined in the discourse of Jewish history, challenging the notion that history is a purely objective science, devoid of meaning for religiosity, belonging, and identity.[14] And, in its very displacement of a unified historical narrative, Jewish studies' pluralization of Jewish history, ideas, and cultures opens up academic, personal, and communal perspectives on Jewish alterities. Thus Bush affirms that "it is also possible to reconceive Jewish Studies on the basis of theories of alterity, heterogeneity, provinciality."[15]

Continuities between Jewish studies and Jewish education's aspirations are also evident in the increasingly questionable status of a clearly marked border between secular and religious aspects of textual interpretation, a phenomenon of great significance for this book.[16] The ambiguities of such a demarcation are implicit in Roskies's declaration of the mission of the Jewish literary journal, *Prooftexts*: "We are creating a thickness of description, a marketplace of voices, a cultural space of extraordinary density, an echo chamber in which all forms and all periods of Jewish self-expression miraculously reverberate."[17]

To be sure, there are substantial disjunctions between traditional and modern Jewish studies. Learning Torah does not coincide seamlessly with the academy's study of Jews, Jewish lives, and narratives; there are many profound sources of tension. Yet Bush and others make compelling arguments for considering modern Jewish studies in a more nuanced, broader context: "not a break with the past of Jewish learning, but rather its extension," even as it develops "more complex interrelationships of togetherness" and often "reads-in"—against the grain—new perspectives on being a Jew. As Rachel Adler suggests with regard to feminist relationships to traditions, it is important to consider the potential for broader, more inclusive, and reflexive renderings, for "a tradition cannot be reduced to a shelf of books or an argument. It is a way groups of people live out stories and arguments in relationships, in ritual, in play, in work, and in love."[18]

Leslie Morris's apt metaphors for "placing and displacing" the "transdisciplinary work" of Jewish studies also suggest a range of potential relationships to educational theory and education studies.[19] Jewish studies today exposes a certain "porousness and entanglement" of "textual, philosophical, and cultural encounter," emerging in "fault lines" and "border zones" of "religion, culture, and media."[20] If what has been called "the new Jewish studies"[21] "moves between disciplines, drawing on but not bound by them, adding to them,"[22] then the field of education can and should be a welcomed destination, way station, and fellow traveler. Indeed, it would be difficult for educators to separate themselves from literary scholar Robert Alter's asserting the capacity of Jewish studies "to ventilate the tradition, illuminate its obscure and contradictory facets," and "[k]eep alive its ongoing claims on our most finely attentive faculties of understanding and reflection."[23]

The nature of education studies is also the subject of ongoing lively international discussion.[24] One theorist recently encapsulated the type of learning and scholarship required in education studies: "Education Studies require a 'trans' capacity based on an informed understanding that goes beyond formation of new boundaries."[25] New demarcations and defined recombinations of disciplines do "not serve the trans capacity that is required."[26]

Indeed, both education studies and Jewish studies require a kind of learning, teaching, thinking, reflecting, and researching that are informed by what contemporary philosopher Calvin Schrag calls "transversal rationality": "a convergence without coincidence, an interplay without synthesis, an appropriating without totalization, and a unification that allows for difference."[27] The key to transversality is communication and dialogue across disciplines and groups, resisting synthesis while engendering an interrogative spirit, engaging in inquiry and meaningful conversation. In this book, I wish to illustrate how Jewish studies and education are well-suited for such transversal discourse.

There have been other significant and valuable approaches to relating Jewish studies and education. And the literature on interdisciplinarity in higher education is extensive and shows no signs of abatement. It is therefore important to distinguish this particular project. First, I am not here suggesting a process of translation that would seek to render one disciplinary language in another. As will be evident, I am promoting the educational goal of achieving a substantial facility with both Jewish studies and education discourses.[28] Achieving this goal and the interdiscursive conversation that can ensue involves a respect for the particularity of each discourse as well as its *conversability* with another. I therefore seek neither a synthesis nor an amalgam. No reduction or dilution is implied. And I am not suggesting a combining of two fields to address each's insufficiency. Similarly, this is not a process of filtering one discourse through the lens of another.[29] A metaphor of "filter" would connote screening out some aspects of Jewish studies in order to recognize those that are most transparently convergent with educational discourse. As I will argue, such a process can limit the scope of engagement. At the same time, there is no privileging of one discourse over another in this approach. Instead, I maintain that educational theory is enriched by participating in different discourses rather than by seeing one as necessarily primary.[30] Finally, I am not here developing an explicit, particular philosophy of Jewish education, nor am I suggesting a primary source for such a philosophy. As I argue in these studies, Jewish educational philosophy and theory today call for engaging multiple sources and discourses.[31]

In the next chapter, I will suggest particular kinds of relationships between Jewish studies and education. Before doing so, however, it is important to make a distinction between two terms. *Interdisciplinarity* refers to the collaborative and integrative effort of multiple disciplines to address particular issues or problems, to critique existing understandings, and to articulate new conceptual frameworks. In Jewish education, for example, these issues might relate to teaching prayer, creating meaningful Jewish communal experiences, engaging youth with improved relationships to Israel, or developing more effective adult education programs and curricula. Critiques could address suppressions or expressions of Jewish women's voices in particular hermeneutic modalities and texts, considering ways to foster discoveries and encounters with these voices. And new articulations might express relationships between textuality and history in Jewish thought and consider how these relationships might inform curricular design and educational theory. Whether these kinds of inquiries emerge from interdisciplinary engagement or are starting points that call for such engagement, these examples suggest the need for sustained conversation and communication among the fields of Jewish studies, the humanities, social sciences, and education to address a particular set of issues, to develop critique, or to articulate new understandings.

Interdiscursivity, in contrast, involves the reciprocal influence and interaction of different discourses.[32] Each discourse has its own set of language games, vocabularies, norms of reasoning, modes of argument, rules, and rhetorical styles. But discourses are also living languages, the grammatical, lexical, syntactic, and semantic dimensions of which speak in texts, conversations, and conduct. Thus, discourse includes language, literature, idioms, and ideas *in use*.[33] It exists in sentences, statements, propositions, queries, and most importantly, dialogue.[34] Interdiscursivity is concerned with questions such as: What does it mean to converse across discourses, to share meaning, to respond to one another? What kind of communication among disciplines is efficacious—and for what purposes? Let us, then, consider these meanings of interdisciplinarity and interdiscursivity further in order to provide a conceptual context for the kinds of exchanges illustrated in part 2 (chapters 3, 4, and 5) and part 3 (chapters 6 and 7).

In his preface to the 2010 second edition of his important book, *Interdisciplinarity*, Joe Moran notes a change in the eight years since its first publication in 2002:

> Interdisciplinarity is even more of a buzzword than it was when I completed the first edition of this book . . . Almost all academic journals, in their mission statement, now claim to be "interdisciplinary": so do many academic departments . . . and even entire universities.[35]

If we trace the literature back even further, we see that, in the last forty years, interdisciplinarity has become increasingly prominent. Journal articles, books, commissioned studies, and doctoral dissertations abound with theoretical approaches to interdisciplinarity, criteria for assessing its efficacy, evaluations of its influence on institutional and cultural contexts, and historical studies of its development.[36]

Articulations of interdisciplinarity's definitions and purposes continue to be ubiquitous, recurring, in particular, to the themes of integration, holism, and pragmatic problem solving. The Committee on Facilitating Interdisciplinary Research[37] recently offered this definition of "interdisciplinary research":

> Interdisciplinary research (IDR) is a mode of research by teams or individuals that integrates information, data, techniques, tools, perspectives, concepts, and/or theories from two or more disciplines or bodies of specialized knowledge to advance fundamental understanding or to solve problems whose solutions are beyond the scope of a single discipline or field of research practice.[38]

Expanding on this definition, the committee report continues: "Research is truly interdisciplinary when it is not just pasting two disciplines together to create one product but rather is an integration and synthesis of ideas and methods."[39] These notions of integration and synthesis also extend to recent definitions of "interdisciplinary learning" by scholars and higher education commissions:

> Interdisciplinary learning is a process by which individuals and groups integrate insights and modes of thinking from two or more disciplines or established fields, to advance their fundamental or practical understanding of a subject that stands beyond the scope of a single discipline.[40]

Each of these definitions emphasizes integration, incorporation in a broader "scope," and achieving a more "fundamental understanding" with a greater panoptic vision. Also emphasized is the need to "solve problems." Interdisciplinarity, thus, is considered a unifier of knowledge and a way to address the modern world's problems. Let us seek to explain the bases for these recurring themes and how they influence the prevailing interest in interdisciplinarity.

The western philosophical tradition provides one ideational context.[41] This tradition is not only commensurate with interdisciplinarity, but in some ways demands it. The European enlightenment's legacy to higher education was "the notion of reason as the regulatory ideal of the modern university and the *ratio* between disciplines."[42] This universal human reason was soon replaced by the German idealists with "a concept and a content of culture."[43] Thus, the university became "a model of unification legitimating the political containment of conflictual diversity, whether that of social relations or that involved in historical transformations."[44] The ideology of centralization and unification of the modern nation-state was thus complicit with the university's seeking to integrate all knowledge and to develop an all-encompassing cultural character ideal (*Bildung*).[45]

So calls for interdisciplinarity, in this sense, can be rendered as begging the question. For their ubiquity

> suggests precisely what has to be in doubt, namely that there is a unity to the university; that across institutions, disciplines and academic activities, there remains a set of ideas or hopes through which the university might live as a coherent human project.[46]

It is not surprising, then, that the university theoretically embraces the notion of interdisciplinarity. The modern tendencies toward holism, integration, and synthesis constitute this strong thread of its justifications. The discourse on interdisciplinarity is replete with references to "the holistic complex of interrelationships"[47] "the promise of . . . overarching synthesis"[48] "conceptual frameworks which claim to transcend the narrow scope of disciplinary world views,"[49] in which disciplines are "subordinate . . . to a particular issue, problem, or holistic scheme,"[50] "forging new overriding paradigms,"[51] in "a comprehensive integrative curriculum design,"[52] "to unify knowledge beyond disciplines"[53] in "comprehensive frameworks."[54]

So in a certain sense, these calls for interdisciplinarity result from the university's very universality having gone awry, as characterized by Whitehead:

> Effective knowledge is professionalised knowledge, supported by a restricted acquaintance with useful subjects subservient to it. This situation has its dangers. It produces minds in a groove. Each profession makes progress, but it is progress in its own groove. Now to be mentally in a groove is to live in contemplating a given set of abstractions. The groove prevents straying across country, and the abstraction abstracts from something to which no further attention is paid. But there is no groove of abstractions which is adequate for the comprehension of human life.[55]

Transcending these "grooves of abstractions," a pragmatic motivation is another impetus for interdisciplinarity.[56] As noted by James Lee Welch, a significant portion of the literature

> is focused upon practical problem solving . . . As such, it possesses a strong pragmatic impetus, a goal orientation that seeks to enhance social and academic progress, along with the implicit need to organize value systems to direct this progress.[57]

When academic disciplines are enjoined to work together for the sake of professional and social utility, particular problems and their resolutions tend to function as interdisciplinary common denominators.[58]

Despite these integrative and pragmatic rationales for interdisciplinarity, there continue to be significant sources of resistance. For some, the resistance comes from the term's ambiguity and self-justification, its "unreflexive use."[59] A leading literary theorist characterizes interdisciplinarity as a superficial amalgam—a "Polonius-like religious-historical-philosophical-cultural overview."[60] And significant scholarly critiques claim interdisciplinarity's lack of internal discursive and ideational rigor: its lack of "intellectual coherence,"[61] its "distractive eclecticism"[62] that "slights the immanent intelligibility of disciplines."[63] Perhaps the strongest claim against the assumptions of the above mentioned integrative and pragmatic rationales for interdisciplinarity is what Bill Readings calls "suspicion of the implicit harmonic convergence" of disciplines.[64] In Reading's critique of "the university in ruins," he argues "that in thinking about the university we should lay aside the automatic privileging of unity and synthesis, without however simply making disharmony and conflict into a negative goal."[65]

Yet interdisciplinary thinking is said to be a response and alternative to the very intellectual virtues and research habits that the disciplines afford to themselves. The modern demarcations of disciplines are grounded in two seemingly contradictory principles—foundationalism and delimitation. In his landmark work, *The Culture of Professionalism*, Burton Bledstein explains the first principle as the assumed rootedness of specialized disciplines and professions in a natural order: "Through a special understanding of a segment of the universe, the professional person released nature's potential and rearranged reality . . . Such was the august basis for the authority of the professional."[66] Such foundational authority extended to individual university departments and their professors.

The second principle is that of demarcation or delimitation. Samuel Weber explores this notion of borders or limits in his important essay, "The Limits of Professionalism."[67] As he explains, throughout the development of the university and professionalism in modern society, "limits have been conceived as provisional markers in a process of continuous expansion, much like record performances in sports, which are there only to be surpassed at the next best occasion." It is in this expansive tendency that limits seek their connection to foundationalism. Yet despite valuing a certain notion of foundations, disciplines continue to guard their borders.

These dual efforts of foundationalism and delimitation are characteristic of what Robert Wiebe calls late-nineteenth-century America's "search for order."[68] A driving force for these demarcations of disciplinary specializations was "the need to devise a system of beliefs, habits, and practices capable of anticipating, ordering, and responding to those challenges"[69] presented by changing, expanding, and seemingly unstable economic, social, technological, political, industrial, and scientific realities. This was the soil from which the culture of professionalism grew. As Weber explains, this culture:

> was the collective effort of a significant part of the middle class to establish a measure of self-control, of status and standing, in face of rapid economic and social change . . . the development of this "culture" entailed the transformation of a particular institution: the American university, which was fashioned into the privileged social instrument of professionalization.[70]

More than simply specialization, the professional ethos was based on autonomy and incommensurability:

> Such autonomy, however, does not derive simply from the specialized skills involved; the 'services' rendered by a doctor, lawyer, or research scientist are not merely specialized (as are those of the auto mechanic), they are, in a crucial sense, *incommensurable*, and upon this incommensurability the distinctive autonomy and authority of the professional is founded.[71]

Autonomy and incommensurability thus have shaped "the techniques and the attitudes of professionalism":

> [T]he professional disposes over a body of systematic, esoteric knowledge, inaccessible to the layman and yet in itself coherent, self-contained, reposing on founding *principles*. These principles form the cognitive basis of laws, rules, and techniques, which constitute a *discipline*, and a praxis requiring a long period of training and initiation.[72]

Yet, at the same time, this bounded autonomy and incommensurability are foundational as they are "based on an equally self-contained 'natural' state of things."[73]

This type of autonomous, incommensurable praxis is consistent with Bledstein's characterization of professional "genius" as "an act of concentration"[74] entailing

> self-discipline as subjective condition for the mastery of a discipline, itself separated—isolated—from other disciplines. Limits and limitation were indispensable for the demarcation of the professional field.[75]

Thus these delimitations took place, "within carefully established spaces"[76] as "the university, itself divided into more or less isolated, self-contained departments, was the embodiment of that kind of limited universality that characterized the cognitive model of professionalism."[77] This seemingly oxymoronic concept of "limited universality" became an apt characterization of the academic culture that emplaced foundationalism within demarcated disciplines and departments.

In an important sense, then, the university has not been a comfortable place for transdisciplinary scholarship or interdisciplinary teaching. As Weber notes: "the very notion of academic 'seriousness' came increasingly to exclude reflection upon the relation of one 'field' to another."[78] This ethos of exclusivity is perhaps the source of the well-known opposition toward Cambridge University's bestowing an honorary degree on Jacques Derrida.[79] In a letter to the *Times*, a group of philosophers challenged Derrida's standing in the discipline of philosophy:

> M. Derrida describes himself as a philosopher, and his writings do indeed bear some of the marks of writing in that discipline. Their influence, however, has been to a striking degree almost entirely in fields outside philosophy—in departments of film studies, for example, or of French and English Literature . . . We submit that, if the works of a physicist [say] were similarly taken to be of merit primarily by those working in other disciplines, this would in itself be sufficient grounds for casting doubt upon the idea that the physicist in question was a suitable candidate for an honorary degree.[80]

Though disciplinary rigor was perhaps a self-conscious motivation, this exclusivity was also part of a larger effort to maintain an insularity not only between departments, but between disciplines and the broader marketplace of services and commodities. As Weber notes, it was felt that scholarship and professionalism were able "to transcend the self-interest of business and market relations" and operate "outside of the pale of ordinary commodity relationships."[81] Many critics continue to blame interdisciplinarity for weakening this barrier between the special, self-contained, limited universality of academic disciplinarity, on the one hand, and broader political, economic, and social relations, on the other.[82]

A different network of ideas and critiques gained substantial momentum and influence in the last quarter of the twentieth century, responding to this weakening as well as to the dynamics and presumptions of foundational self-containment and integration just described, Under the names of deconstruction, post-structuralism, and postmodernism, these critiques have thus been sources for calls to "deconstruct" the modern culture of professionalism and the purportedly foundational universalism of the university. In a very different key, these postmodern perspectives have criticized, as well as promoted certain notions of interdisciplinarity, transdisciplinarity, and even post-disciplinarity.

Thus, deconstructionists have called for disciplines "to reconsider the status of their own limits, and to revise the previously prevailing view of them as borders to be extended, or as external boundaries serving merely to establish the integrity of the areas they demarcate."[83] As Weber describes this "revision in our thinking about limits," "we have come to conceive of them not as neutral and stable entities, but rather as active, volatile, and constraining factors that can no longer be taken for granted, factors that menace as much as they protect or contain."[84] In this kind of post-structural discourse all disciplinary demarcations and boundaries are in play.

So deconstructionists avoid creating newly bounded, seemingly integrated amalgams that reconstitute or recombine different specializations into a presumed whole. To do so would simply extend and reconstitute the culture of professionalism and disciplinarity into new supervening structures. As an alternative, Weber suggests a "deconstructive pragmatics" that "would work from the 'inside' of the various disciplines":

> in order to demonstrate concretely, in each case, how the exclusion of limits from the field organizes the practice it makes possible, but in a way that diverges from the self-consciousness of the practitioners, as dictated by the ethos of professional competence. One way of exploring such limitations might be precisely to demonstrate how the apparently objective, denotative language of individual disciplines entails, necessarily but implicitly, a precise series of prescriptive "speech acts," involving injunctions and commands such as those that comprise the professional ethos in general.[85]

What Weber refers to here as "denotative language of individual disciplines" and "speech acts" are features of discourse. It is in the notion of discourse that we see an alternative to more characteristically modern (i.e., integrative and pragmatic) interdisciplinarity. Let us then consider what we mean by discourse.

Discourse is not just speaking or writing in a language nor is it simply citing or grafting excerpts from a literature.[86] Among discourse's necessary qualities is that it is eventful—it is what Ricoeur calls the "very event of speaking."[87] As such, it is communicative. It has speakers and hearers, writers and readers, as well as senses that it carries. Discourse invokes both language and literature but can never be reduced to one or the other.[88] Every aspect of discourse is laden with a tradition of literature, gestures, values, concepts, and outlooks. In living discourse, a culture or community responds and recurs to such a tradition. In doing so, discourse is critical as well as creative, interpreting texts, experiences, structures, and relations while generating new ones. Interpretation, creative expression, and conversation are partners in discursive activity as "linguistic competence actualizes itself in performance."[89]

When we think of discourse in relation to interdisciplinarity, we are less concerned with a specific supposed referent or what Derrida calls a "finished signified beneath a textual surface."[90] Rather, we are focused on the function of language in what Moran succinctly calls "dialogue or interaction between two or more disciplines."[91] Hence Derrida and other postmodernists are concerned with "the *discourse* of the human sciences"[92] rather than their disciplinarity.

Yet discourse is anything but a neutral, purely linguistic category. It refers not only to collectivities and their communication styles and patterns, but, equally important, to relations of power, to legitimations and delegitimations of individuals, groups, and languages; it suppresses as well as expresses. This relation to power is why Michel Foucault invokes military and political language when referring to discourse: "discursive formations"[93] and "discursive regimes."[94] And discourse does not stand in isolation from its usages; strategically or habitually, it is both appropriated and expropriated.

Thus, Foucault "remains within the dimension of discourse,"[95] challenging some of the presumptions of disciplinarity. Discourse does not simply convey a particular preexisting meaning or context. For Foucault, it is "a system of regularities with no reference to a prior exteriority (a historical context) or interiority (a human meaning)."[96] Yet as Colebrook explains, Foucault's notion of discourse is not a purely textual phenomenon, separated from relationships, events, conduct, dispositions, and societal structures:

> Remaining within the dimension of discourse cannot be equated with a crude "textualism" (the idea that outside language there is no world). Rather, the "world" is itself part of the system of discourse. Non-linguistic phenomena (the housing of the insane in asylums for example) are discursive in so far as they are part of a system of relations. Actions are discursive: the position of a king in a masque, the architecture of a prison, the geography of eighteenth-century London are part of, not external or prior to, a system of relations in which texts are produced and consumed.[97]

It would therefore be important for the academy to consider the relations among its discourses, their influences on one another, and their capacities to both limit or liberate.[98]

What is important for this inquiry is that the academy's discourses have the capacity to interact, contradict, reinforce, and challenge one another in a dynamic, multi-voiced assemblage. At the "crossroads" or "trading zones"[99] of transversal conversation and exchange, new phenomena emerge (such as the "textuality of history and the historicity of the text"),[100] the result of what Bakhtin calls "interillumination."[101] Thus, the academy is a living matrix of "communicative praxis" in which different discourses mix, mingle, and converse. This is certainly the case for graduate programs that combine Jewish studies and education. Calvin Schrag explains this interwoven praxial, discursive "texture":

> [C]ommunication and praxis intersect within a common space. Communication is a qualification of praxis. It is the manner in which praxis comes to expression. But praxis is also a qualification of communication in that it determines communication as a *performing* and an *accomplishing*.[102]

In this conception, the academy is constituted in an interlaced "performing" and "accomplishing" of discourses and conduct.[103] In this book, I consider and illustrate such interdiscursivity between Jewish studies and education and rationales for its being supported, sustained, and expanded.

To be sure, all discourse stands in relation to other discourses, in as much as each recognizes and responds to different discursive tendencies, conceptual boundaries, and paradigms of inquiry. No discourse, then, is completely exclusive and insulated from the multiplicity of discourses. It anticipates and reacts to imagined or real interlocutors.[104] In the academy, interdiscursivity emerges when there is communication and conversation in multiple discursive styles and disciplinary frameworks. The study of Jewish education, of course, is no exception, being comprised of variegated discourses, concepts, and modes of conduct. Thus, a single discourse will hardly coincide with the full range of Jewish education's discursive multiplicity.

As we will see in chapter 7, much of the conceptual, linguistic rationale for such interchange draws on the work of Russian linguist Mikhail Bakhtin, who articulates a tension between the centripetal and centrifugal forces of discourse. Bakhtin argues that there is inevitably "constant interaction between meanings, all of which have the potential of conditioning others."[105] So "alongside the centripetal forces" that give discourse its internal coherence and social cohesion, "the centrifugal forces of language carry on their uninterrupted work; alongside verbal-ideological centralization and unification, the uninterrupted processes of decentralization and disunification go forward."[106] Thus, in the reciprocal interplay of meanings, the internally unifying (centripetal) and the externally influential (centrifugal) forces of discourse exist in a dynamic interactive tension. In Parts Two and Three of this book, we seek to be mindful of both of these discursive forces, recognizing both the centripetal integrity and the centrifugal potentiality for interactive influence between Jewish studies and education.

Anthropologist Clifford Geertz sees this discursive interaction as the necessary alternative to an integration of disciplines:

> The hard dying hope that there can again be (assuming there ever was) an integrated high culture . . . has to be abandoned in favor of the much more modest sort of ambition that scholars, artists, scientists, professionals, and (dare we hope?) administrators . . . can begin to find something circumstantial to say to one another again . . . one in which econometricians, epigraphers, cytochemists, and iconologists can give a credible account of themselves to one another.[107]

The modes and rationales for exchanging these "accounts" form the background landscape of this book. To the extent that these interdiscursive exchanges' purposes are, in Geertz's terms, "modest," "ambitious," or both is left to the reader's judgment. As we will see, the significance of discourse across disciplines is of a different "sort" than what often are interdisciplinarity's integrative and purely pragmatic purposes.

NOTES

1. Judith R. Baskin, "Academic Jewish Studies in North America," in *International Handbook of Jewish Education*, ed. Helena Miller, Lisa Grant, and Alex Pomson. (New York: Springer, 2011), Abstract.

2. Bush, 67. Baskin also notes Rabbi Alfred Jospe's assertion that "the purpose of Jewish studies in the university" is exclusively "the study of Judaism and the Jewish people and not the Judaization of young Jews, the stimulation of their Jewish commitment, or the strengthening of their Jewish identification." As quoted in Baskin, 662. She also points out that to maintain "academic respectability," Jewish studies scholars have been enjoined to avoid what Rabbi Irving Greenberg characterizes as "too close an identification with the concerns of the Jewish community and the Jewish civilization." Greenberg as quoted in Baskin, 662.

3. H. M. Lewis, "The Jewish Studies Professor as Communal Leader," *Shofar: An Interdisciplinary Journal of Jewish Studies* 24, no. 3 (2006): 131–132, as quoted in Baskin, 664.

4. Bush, 2.

5. As quoted in Bush, 2. As Bush notes, this "metaphorization" resonates with Rabbi Mordecai Kaplan's characterization of "the transformation of mitzvoth, commandments, in modern Jewish life a generation earlier." Kaplan's "metaphorical sense" of divine commandments is a kind of "metaphorical extension" that displaces their divine organ with their promoting "solidarity within Jewish communities and between the present and the past." Bush, 5.

6. Bush, 25. *Wissenschaft des Judentums* was the movement of Jewish scholars that began in the first half of the nineteenth century in Germany. Its official mission was to pursue a comprehensive "knowledge of Judaism through its literary and historical documentation, and . . . a statistical knowledge of Judaism in relation to the Jews of our time in all the countries of the world." *Zeitschrift fuer die Wissenschaft des Judentums* (1822), as quoted in Benzion Dinur, "*Wissenschaft des Judentums*," in *Encyclopaedia Judaica*, ed. Michael Berenbaum and Fred Skolnik. 2nd ed. Vol. 21 (Detroit: Macmillan Reference USA, 2007), 105–114. Consistent with a modern scientific outlook, the movement maintained the importance of open, disciplined critique of the traditional Jewish languages, texts, ideas, norms, patterns of conduct, and history. The movement is considered the progenitor of the academic study of Judaism in universities and seminaries, though both its objectification of Jews and Judaism and its apologetics have been criticized often.

7. Bush, 25.

8. Gershom Scholem, "Reflections on Modern Jewish Studies," in *On the Possibility of Jewish Mysticism in Our Time and Other Essays*, ed. Avraham Shapira, trans. Jonathan Chipman (Philadelphia: Jewish Publication Society, 1997), 51, 54–55.

9. Bush, 31.

10. Scholem, "Reflections," as quoted in Bush, 31.

11. Bush, 56.

12. Bush, 57.

13. As Bush points out, "Adler lays claim simultaneously to identity positions as a woman and a Jew, and thus to an intellectual base in both Jewish Studies and Women's Studies." Bush, 65.

14. Yosef Hayyim Yerushalmi, *Zakhor: Jewish History and Jewish Memory* (New York, 1989). Also see special issue of *The Jewish Quarterly Review* 97, no. 4, (2007), devoted to the twenty-fifth anniversary of the book's first publication.

15. Bush, 92.

16. See Morris, "Placing and Displacing"; Among the many examples are Geoffrey Hartman and Sanford Budick, *Midrash and Literature* (New Haven: Yale University Press, 1986), and David Stern, *Midrash and Theory: Ancient Jewish Exegesis and Contemporary Literary Studies* (Evanston, IL: Northwestern University Press, 1996).
17. David G. Roskies, "The Task of the Jewish Translator: A Valedictory Address," *Prooftexts* 24, no. 3 (Fall 2004), 270.
18. Rachel Adler, *Engendering Judaism: An Inclusive Theology and Ethics* (Boston: Beacon Press, 1999), 50.
19. Morris, "Placing and Displacing," 765.
20. Morris, "How Jewish Is," x.
21. Scott Heller, "The New Jewish Studies: Defying Tradition and Easy Categorization," *Chronicle of Higher Education* (January 29, 1999): 39.
22. Morris, "Placing and Displacing," 772
23. Robert Alter, "What Jewish Studies Can Do," *Commentary* (Oct. 1974): 71–76, as quoted in Morris, 771.
24. S. Barlett and D. Burton, "The Evolution of Education Studies in Higher Education in England." *Curriculum Journal* 17, no. 4 (2006): 383–396. Lisa Murphy, Emmanuel Mufti, and Derek Kassem, *Education Studies: An Introduction* (Berkshire, GBR: Open University Press, 2008). Noblit, "Walls of Jericho." Ioanna Palaiologou, "The Death of a Discipline or the Birth of a Transdiscipline: Subverting Questions of Disciplinarity within Undergraduate Courses," *Education Studies* 36, No. 3 (July 2010): 269–282.
25. Palaiologou, 276.
26. Palaiologou, 276.
27. Calvin O. Schrag, *The Resources of Rationality: A Response to the Postmodern Challenge* (Indianapolis: Indiana University Press, 1992), 158–159.
28. Of course, the capacity for translating is also a necessary and valuable goal.
29. See Rosenak, *Roads to the Palace*, xiv, and Isa Aron, "What Is Philosophy of Jewish Education?" review of *Roads to the Palace: Jewish Texts and Teaching*, by Michael Rosenak, *Religious Education* 94, no. 1 (1999): 126–132.
30. For a different approach see Dinah Laron and Asher Shkedi, "Between Two Languages: Student-Teachers Teach Jewish Content," *Religious Education* 102, no. 2 (Spring 2007).
31. For a more integrative approach to philosophy of Jewish education, see Jonathan Cohen, "Hartman, Rosenak and Schweid on Maimonides' Introduction to Helek: The Beginnings of a Tradition in the Philosophy of Jewish Education," *Studies in Jewish Education* 13 (2008/2009): 15–46.
32. On the distinction between "integration" and "interaction" in Jewish day schools, see Michael Zeldin, "Integration and Interaction in the Jewish Day School," in *The Jewish Educational Leader's Handbook*, ed. R. E. Tornberg (Denver: A.R.E. Publishing, 1998), 579–590 and David Ellenson, "An Ideology for the Liberal Jewish Day School: A Philosophical-Sociological Investigation," *Journal of Jewish Education* 74 (2008): 245–263.
Some philosophers of education and Jewish education place strong emphasis on the distinction between language and literature. This distinction is helpful and significant. Discourse may be said to include aspects of both language and literature. See Michael Rosenak, *Roads to the Palace: Jewish Texts and Teaching* (New York: Berghahn Books, 1995), and *Commandments and Concerns.*
33. Paul Ricoeur, *Interpretation Theory: Discourse and the Surplus of Meaning* (Fort Worth: Texas Christian University Press, 1976), 7.
34. Ricoeur, 14.
35. Joe Moran, *Interdisciplinarity* Second Edition (New York: Routledge, 2010), viii.
36. Because of higher education's rapidly increasing interest in interdisciplinarity, the Association for the Study of Higher Education's *Higher Education Report* devoted a special 2009 issue to the topic. *ASHE Higher Education* Report "Special Issue: Understanding Interdisciplinary Challenges and Opportunities in Higher Education," 35, no. 2 (2009). Some other examples are Tracie Marcella Addy, "Epistemological Beliefs and Practices of Science Faculty with Education Specialties: Combining Teaching Scholarship and Interdisciplinarity," Dissertation (North Carolina State University, Raleigh, North Carolina, 2011). Lisa Rose Lattuca, "Envi-

sioning Interdisciplinarity: Processes, Contexts, Outcomes," Dissertation (University of Michigan, 1996). Lisa R. Lattuca, "Learning Interdisciplinarity: Sociocultural Perspectives on Academic Work," *The Journal of Higher Education* 73, no. 6 (November/December 2002): 711–739. Julie T. Klein, *Interdisciplinarity: History, Theory, and Practice* (Detroit: Wayne State University Press, 1990); Julie T. Klein, *Humanities, Culture, and Interdisciplinarity: The Changing American Academy* (Albany: State University of New York, 2005); Julie T. Klein, *Crossing Boundaries: Knowledge, Disciplinarities, and Interdisciplinarities* (University Press of Virginia, 1996).

37. Committee on Facilitating Interdisciplinary Research, Committee on Science, Engineering, and Public Policy, *Facilitating Interdisciplinary Research* (Washington, DC.: National Academy of Sciences, National Academy of Engineering, and Institute of Medicine, National Academies Press, 2004).

38. *Facilitating Interdisciplinary Research*, 26.

39. *Facilitating Interdisciplinary Research*, 27.

40. Veronica Boix Mansilla, "Learning to Synthesize: A Cognitive-Epistemological Foundation for Interdisciplinary Learning http://www.pz.harvard.edu/interdisciplinary/pdf/VBM_Synthesize_2009.pdf. Also see Veronica Boix Mansilla, "Assessing Student Work at Disciplinary Crossroads," *Change* 37, no. 1 (January/February 2005): 14–21.

41. James Lee Welch, "Interdisciplinarity and the History of Ideas, Dissertation (The University of Texas at Dallas, August, 2009).

42. Simon Wortham, "'To Come Walking': Reinterpreting the Institution and the Work of Samuel Weber," *Cultural Critique*, 48 (Spring, 2001): 164–199.

43. Wortham, 181.

44. Samuel Weber, "The Future of the Humanities: Experimenting," *Culture Machine* 2 (2000). http://www.culturemachine.net/index.php/cm/rt/printerFriendly/311/296.

45. *Bildung* here refers to the organic character ideal as it developed in eighteenth- and nineteenth-century German educational ideology and philosophy. The term suggests an integrated idea of education, culture, and character. In its varied usages, it also connotes personal, spiritual, intellectual, natural, and physical formation.

46. Ronald Barnett, "Recapturing the Universal in the University," *Educational Philosophy and Theory* 37, no. 6 (2005): 785.

47. Marilyn Stember, "Advancing the Social Sciences Through the Interdisciplinary Enterprise," *Social Science Journal* 28, no. 1 (1991): 8.

48. Julie T. Klein, *Interdisciplinarity: History, Theory, and Practice* (Detroit: Wayne State University Press, 1990), 65–66.

49. Raymond Miller, "Varieties of Interdisciplinary Approaches in the Social Sciences," *Issues in Integrative Studies* 1 (1982): 11.

50. Klein, *Interdisciplinarity*, 65–66.

51. Julie T. Klein, "Education," in *Handbook of Transdisciplinary Research*, ed. G. Hirsch Hadorn, et al. (Springer, 2008), 400.

52. Julie Thompson Klein, "A Taxonomy of Interdisciplinarity," in *The Oxford Handbook of Interdisciplinarity*, ed. Robert Frodeman, Julie Thompson Klein, and Carl Mitcham, (Oxford: Oxford University Press, 2010), 24. (15–30).

53. Palaiologou, *Death of a Discipline*, 277.

54. Julie T. Klein, *Creating Interdisciplinary Campus Cultures: A Model for Strength and Sustainability* (Hoboken, NJ, USA: Jossey-Bass, 2010), 182.

55. Alfred North Whitehead, *Science and the Modern World* (Cambridge: Cambridge University Press, 1953), 245.

56. I use the word, "pragmatic," in the conventional, rather than philosophical sense. To be sure, the philosophical movement known as "pragmatism" is more complex and diverse than the adjective "pragmatic." With this latter term, I wish to emphasize a problem-solving progressivism.

57. Welch, 185.

58. Related to this pragmatic focus, interdisciplinarity can be understood in the context of complexity theory: See Michael Finkenthal, *Complexity, Multi-Disciplinarity, and Beyond* (New York: Peter Lang, 2008): "At a closer look, we discover that the inter-disciplinarian

approach was always a technique used to cope, intellectually, with complexity . . . the concept of interdisciplinarity had been (and it still is) extensively used as a synonymous term for "multifaceted approach to difficult problems." 2–3.

59. Moran, viii.

60. Helen Vendler, "Presidential Address," *PMLA* 96, no. 3 (May, 1981): 346. (344– 48) Also quoted in Marjorie Garber, *Academic Instincts* (Princeton, NJ: Princeton University Press).

61. Edward Said, "Restoring Intellectual Coherence," *MLA Newsletter* 3, no. 38 (Spring 1999).

62. Y. Lenoir, Y. Geoffroy, and A. Hasni, "Entre le trou noir et la dispersion évanescente: Quelle cohérence épistemologique pour l'interdisciplinarité? Un essai de classification des différentes conceptions de l'interdisciplinarité," in *Les Fondements de L'interdisciplinarité dans La Formation á L'Enseignement,* edited by Y. Lenoir, B. Rey, and I. Fazenda, 85–110 (Sherbrooke: Éditions du CRP. 2001). As translated and quoted in Ioanna Palaiologou, "Death of a Discipline," 275.

63. "In doing justice to the relationships between disciplines it slights the immanent intelligibility of disciplines." Stanley Fish, *Professional Correctness: Literary Studies and Political Change,* (Cambridge, MA: Harvard University Press, 1995), 80.

64. Bill Readings, *The University in Ruins* (Cambridge, Massachusetts and London, England: Harvard University Press, 1996), 201.

65. Readings, 201.

66. Burton Bledstein, *The Culture of Professionalism: The Middle Class and the Development of Higher Education in America* (New York: W.W. Norton & Co., 1978), 89–90.

67. Samuel Weber, *Institution and Interpretation* (Minneapolis: University of Minnesota Press, 1987), 18–32. Jacques Derrida refers to Weber's article, "The Limits of Professionalism," as "a remarkable essay" in his "The Principle of Reason: The University in the Eyes of Its Pupils," *Diacritics* 13, no. 3 (Autumn, 1983), 9.

68. Robert Wiebe, *The Search for Order* (New York: Hill & Wang, 1967), as quoted in Weber, *Institution and Interpretation*, 24.

69. Weber, *Institution and Interpretation*, 24.

70. Weber, *Institution and Interpretation*, 25.

71. Weber, *Institution and Interpretation*, 26 (original italics).

72. Weber, *Institution and Interpretation*, 26.

73. Weber, *Institution and Interpretation*, 26–27.

74. Bledstein, 267, as quoted in Weber, *Institution and Interpretation*, 29–30.

75. Weber, *Institution and Interpretation*, 30.

76. Bledstein, 95, as quoted in Weber, *Institution and Interpretation*, 30.

77. Weber, *Institution and Interpretation*, 32.

78. Weber, *Institution and Interpretation*, 32.

79. Barry Smith with Jeffrey Sims, "Revisiting the Derrida Affair With Barry Smith," *Sophia* 138, no. 2 (September-October, 1999): 142–68. On this incident, see also John D. Caputo, *The Prayers* and *Tears of Jacques Derrida: Religion Without Religion* (Bloomington: Indiana University Press, 1997) and *Deconstruction in a Nutshell: A Conversation with Jacques Derrida* (New York: Fordham University Press, 1997).

80. Letter from Professor Barry Smith, et. al., *The Times* (London, Saturday, May 9, 1992). *Internationale Akademie für Philosophie*, Obergass 75, 9494S Schaan, Liechtenstein.

81. Weber, *Institution and Interpretation*, 25.

82. See Readings, *University in Ruins*, 38, 113, 121.

83. Weber, *Institution and Interpretation*, 18–19.

84. Weber, *Institution and Interpretation*, 18. On this subject of frames and framing, also see Jacques Derrida, "Le Parergon" in *The Truth in Painting*, trans. Geoff Bennington and Ian McLeod (Chicago: Univ. of Chicago Press, 1987), 59.

85. Weber, *Institution and Interpretation*, 32.

86. Ricoeur, 7.

87. Ricoeur, 7.

88. See Rosenak, *Roads to the Palace* and *Commandments and Concerns.*

89. Ricoeur, 11.
90. Jacques Derrida, *Positions*, trans. Alan Bass. (London: Athlone Press, 1981), 63.
91. Moran, 14.
92. Jacques Derrida, "Structure, Sign, and Play in the Discourse of the Human Sciences," Alan Bass (trans.) in *Writing and Difference* (Chicago: University of Chicago Press, 1978). 427.
93. Michel Foucault, *The Archaeology of Knowledge*, trans. A. M. Sheridan Smith (New York: Pantheon Books, 1972), 34.
94. Michel Foucault, "Truth and Power," in *Power: Essential Works of Foucault 1954–1984*, ed. James D. Faubion, trans. Robert Hurley (New York: New Press, 2000), vol. 3, 114.
95. Michel Foucault, *Archaeology of Knowledge*, 76.
96. Claire Colebrook, *New Literary Histories: New Historicism and Contemporary Criticism* (Manchester, UK: Manchester University Press, 1997), 50.
97. Colebrook, *New Literary Histories*, 50
98. Colebrook, 50.
99. Klein, *Humanities, Culture, and Interdisciplinarity: The Changing American Academy* (Albany: State University of New York, 2005), 79, 174.
100. Sacvan Bercovitch, *The Cambridge History of American Literature*, Volume 1, Introduction, ed. Sacvan Bercovitch and Cyrus R. K. Patell (1994), 3–4: "The matter of nationhood here becomes a focal point for exploring the two most vexed issues today in literary studies: the historicity of the text and the textuality of history."
101. M. M. Bakhtin, *The Dialogic Imagination: Four Essays*, Michael Holquist, ed., trans. By Caryl Emerson and Michael Holquist (Austin: University of Texas Press, 1981), 12, 17, 49, 362–363, 429–430.
102. Calvin O. Schrag, *Communicative Praxis and the Space of Subjectivity* (Bloomington and Indianapolis: Indiana University Press, 1986), 22–23.
103. Schrag, *Communicative Praxis,* 31.
104. This point will be the focus of part 3.
105. These kinds of interactive multivoiced narratives and their import for teaching are explored in chapter 7. Mikhael Bakhtin, *Speech Genres and Other Late Essays*, eds. Caryl Emerson and Michael Holquist, trans. V. W. McGee (Austin, TX: University of Texas Press, 1986), 95. See also B. Hannah Rockwell, "An Ethics of Dialogue and Community: Reflections on Interdisciplinary Gender Scholarship," *Women and Language* 31, no. 2 (2008): 22.
106. Bakhtin, *Dialogic Imagination*, 272. Wittgenstein, *Philosophical Investigations*, trans. G. E. M. Anscombe, P.M.S. Hacker, and Joachim Schulte, ed. P.M.S. Hacker, and Joachim Schulte (Oxford, UK: Wiley Blackwell, 2009), xxxix, 171.
As Colin Grant explains: "Wittgenstein began to investigate language as forms of life and games: language could no longer be seen as an invariable essence. 'Meaning' is generated in games amounting to complexes of elements of discourse and other action forms." Colin B. Grant, *Rethinking Communicative Interaction: New Interdisciplinary Horizons* (Philadelphia: John Benjamins B.V., 2003), 9.
107. Clifford Geertz, "The Way We Think Now: Toward an Ethnography of Modern Thought," *Bulletin of the American Academy of Arts and Sciences* 35, no. 5 (February 1982): 31.

Chapter Two

Differentiating and Deepening the Relationships

John Dewey, Justus Buchler, and Michael Oakeshott

In this chapter, I suggest three approaches to interdiscursive relationships between Jewish studies and education. To do so, I draw on the work of twentieth-century philosophers John Dewey, Justus Buchler, and Michael Oakeshott, each of whom had an abiding interest in the relationships between theory and practice, and between liberal arts discourses and the field of education. Each implicates distinctive, compelling perspectives on interdisciplinarity and interdiscursivity in the study of education. And, significant for our purposes, each would contest a dualist separation between the liberal arts and professional education.[1]

Following Dewey, I suggest how Jewish studies might function as a vital "source," among others, for educational theory.[2] Buchler's notion of "trans-ordinal," "cooperative judgment" across disciplines (what he refers to as "complexes" or "orders") provides further language for exploring the relationships between Jewish studies and educational theory.[3] In Oakeshott's notion of "conversation" I present yet another rationale for putting these two broad fields into sustained dynamic interdiscursive communication.[4] As we will see, each of these kinds of relationships has implications for how we pursue concurrent or convergent scholarship and for how we articulate rationales for curricular hybridity. Let us briefly examine these conceptual perspectives and how they might inform these fields' interdiscusive relations.

JOHN DEWEY'S "SOURCES FOR A SCIENCE OF EDUCATION"

For Dewey, the word *science* in "The Sources of a Science of Education" has a broad range.[5] For our purposes, we can here consider science as *theory*, as this latter term coincides with a wide spectrum of Dewey's uses of the former. I thus here consider Jewish studies as a *source* for Jewish educational theory. It is, of course, but one of a number of sources, including, for example, developmental and social psychology, sociology, anthropology, philosophy, personal experience, as well as the cumulative wisdom of the field. It is therefore necessary to consider what it means to function as a *source* for theory.

A theory of education, for Dewey, emerges when we weave together elements from multiple sources "to form a relatively coherent system."[6] The sources enter into meaningful relationship with educational theory, then, when these elements provide each other with "added significance and illumination" while being articulated together to serve educational aspirations.[7] An effective educational theory would draw on multiple sources to provide an "intellectual ground for alertness"[8] to educational phenomena and to increase an educator's capacities to interpret them. So deliberating on these sources and relating them to each other and to educational concerns, educational theory renders an educator's practice "more intelligent, more flexible and better adapted to deal effectively with concrete phenomena of practice."[9]

The concept of "sources" is vital to Dewey's notion of educational theory. For him, the latter has no discrete, intrinsically demarcated content.[10] Selected subject matters and experiences serve as *sources* for its content to the extent that they enable the educator to have a clearer, more comprehensive, penetrating vision of her practice.[11] And even as he articulates the relationship between sources for theory and theory itself, Dewey emphasizes that a viable theory of education is included *within* the field of education. The latter is not something separated from theory. Yet it is a special kind of inclusion without prescribed borders. Since education is an ongoing, dynamic process, theory, as part of education, is never final or complete; it "is never made" but "it is always making," as it functions in "an endless circle or spiral"[12] with educational praxis.

Furthermore, Dewey is ambitious and demanding when it comes to the study of sources for educational theory, suggesting that their proper use "would compel attempt at *mastery* of what they [these sources] have to offer."[13] Considering what Dewey means here by "mastery," then, will suggest certain "ends-in-view" for the study of disciplines within Jewish studies as sources for educational theory.[14] Such mastery would allow the educational theorist to draw on discourses of multiple disciplines "so that there shall be steady and cumulative growth of intelligent, communicable insight and power of direction."[15] This growth implies that the study of a source for educational theory requires treating that source as dynamic and intricate discourse, rather than as a static body of knowledge. Such study of sources, then, should be of the kind that gives the educational theorist "command of . . . systematized subject matter."[16] Mastery does not only involve becoming familiar with a specific corpus of information and updated findings, to be taken off the shelf, as it were, and applied to a particular curriculum, educational problem, or situation. Rather, "command" of a discursive "system" requires fluid understandings of how one aspect of a system affects another, how foregrounding one dimension of Jewish history inevitably conceals another dimension, how asserting one mode of biblical interpretation influences understandings of prayer and theology, how teaching modern Hebrew influences understandings of traditional Jewish texts. To function as a source, Jewish studies requires students' systemic understanding of its constituent disciplines. Such an understanding is akin to scholarship in those disciplines. The ability to draw upon Jewish studies systemically and dynamically, then, is different in kind from having an encyclopedic knowledge of Jewish studies. The former involves having a command of the disciplines that, according to Dewey, "liberates individuals" to the extent that it allows them to "make new integrations" of Jewish studies as a source and "turn it to new and previously unfamiliar and unforeseen uses."[17]

Contrary to widespread misconceptions of his pragmatism, Dewey maintains that such capacities for educational theorists would allow them to engage in inquiry that is *not* limited to questions of how those sources might function in "familiar practical experience."[18] For Dewey, this kind of reduction eclipses more fluid, systemic inquiry into sources of educational theory. Intellectual and discursive independence in particular disciplines can be liberating in that it avoids what Dewey calls the "dangers of slavish imitation partisanship, and such jealous devotion to" particular points of view, modes of argument, and interpretations.[19] Without a capacity to transcend imitation of Jewish studies scholarship, educational theorists may "become impervious to other problems and truths" as "they incline to swear by the words of their master and to go on repeating his thoughts after him, and often without the spirit and insight that originally made them significant."[20]

Jewish studies functions as a source for the intelligent direction of Jewish education to the extent that it liberates educators, allowing them to be sensitive to new kinds of problems and create diverse means of understanding, addressing, and communicating them.[21] So, for Dewey, relevant questions would be: How might Jewish studies function as a source for intelligent professional conduct and educational theorizing? How might it contribute to "steady and cumulative growth of intelligent, communicable insight and power of direction in education"?[22]

As Michael Rosenak points out, the observations and arguments that emerge from studying these transdisciplinary relationships do not serve educational purposes until they interact with multiple sources of Jewish educational theory, contributing to a broader sense of purpose, sensitivity to certain types of problems, or rendering the practice of Jewish education more intelligent.[23] The value of Jewish studies as a source for Jewish educational theory, then, is not simply that it provides the content knowledge for the practice of Jewish education. For example, Jewish studies is not a source for Jewish education so educators will know *about* Jewish history or literature before they teach it. Rather, it functions as a source so that, in the study of Jewish history and literature, we consider how a discipline's discourse might converge with multiple sources of educational theory to change and enhance the latter.

This Deweyan rationale appears to be the premise and framework for Brandeis University's recent initiative on bridging Jewish studies scholarship and pedagogy.[24] There Jewish studies scholarship functions as a source for pedagogical thinking and conduct. As a source for pedagogy, scholarship in Jewish studies would help the educator "make decisions about what approaches to use and how to defend ideas."[25] Examples of that initiative's working papers' titles illustrate this function: "How Can Teachers of Rabbinics Use the Mishnah for Moral Education,"[26] "Helping Students Get a Foot in the Door Through the Use of Academic Scholarship in the Teaching of Rabbinic Texts,"[27] "The Pedagogical Implications of Shifting Paradigms in the Study of Rabbinic Narratives."[28] Similarly, this functioning as a source is reflected in Barry Holtz's article's title, "What Might Jewish Educators Learn from Jewish Scholars?" and in his noting that "resources of Judaica scholarship" for Jewish educational research and practice need to consider the "tension" that exists between academic content scholarship and professionalism in Jewish education.[29]

Michael Rosenak, whose modes of engaging Jewish scholarship and education traverse the conceptual frameworks that I will be suggesting, operates in a Deweyan mode when he states: "The great complexity of Judaism, as both an historical and 'national' phenomenon, on the one hand, and a 'religious' one, on the other hand, invites diverse approaches to Jewish education."[30] In this formulation, the study of these historical, national, and religious dimensions of Judaism present "challenges that (may) undermine . . . or . . . 'reconstruct' Jewish life and education."[31] Here again, Jewish studies serves as a vital source for Jewish educational theory.[32]

Yet it is important to emphasize that, for Dewey, narratives, normative principles, or historical understandings do not constitute sources because they may be *about* education. More often than not, they are not *referring* specifically to pedagogical dynamics and principles. The educational theorist must not limit her study of a source simply by searching for educational referents or metaphors. Dewey's notion of mastery would demand that educational theorists achieve a kind of understanding of Jewish studies that goes deeply and fluidly into the discourses and disciplines in order to achieve "steady cumulative" "insight" and "direction," not just the ability to recognize educational issues in Jewish sources and to apply them. The educational theorist, thus, deepens her capacities for thoughtful inquiry within Jewish studies disciplines and engages in those disciplines' discourses. In doing so, she allows Jewish studies to reveal its language, literatures, modes of thinking, analogies, and aporias in ways that resonate with and attune educational theorists in new ways to Jewish educational thought and practice.

This type of cumulative insight is what Israel Scheffler, drawing on R. S. Peters, calls "cognitive perspective": "Cognitive perspective not only requires breadth; it demands also that the knowledge of the educated person be active . . . should enter into the educated person's perception and commerce with the environment."[33] Active, ongoing Jewish studies scholarship and discursive practice would thus be a necessary quality of Jewish educational theorizing. A systemic facility with Jewish studies disciplines is necessary for their discourses to serve as "sources for a science of education," in Dewey's sense.

JUSTUS BUCHLER AND THE RELATIONSHIP BETWEEN JEWISH STUDIES AND EDUCATIONAL THEORY

A different, more reciprocal relationship between Jewish studies discourse and education is suggested by the philosophy of Justus Buchler. Though departing from, and sometimes critiquing, his Columbia University elder and predecessor, Buchler was substantially influenced by Dewey, often responding to him. Whereas Dewey helps us consider how Jewish studies might function as a *source* for Jewish educational theory, Buchler provides a conceptual language and perspective that lets us suggest how Jewish studies and educational theory might function *relationally* and *reciprocally*.

Buchler was considered by his colleagues to be among the most important American philosophers of the second half of the twentieth century,[34] though today he is lesser known than other influential philosophers. Unlike many of his contemporaries, Buchler was interested in a metaphysics and an epistemology that construct "categories to frame one's thinking about a particular subject matter."[35] Though offering intricate and systematic categories of human judgment, Buchler maintains that his categories do not suggest *a priori* conditions. They are, rather, ways of interpreting reality and experience. He is particularly interested in articulating a metaphysics of judgment that "should be able to encompass aspects of human life reflected by the sciences and arts, by moral and religious attitudes, and by what takes place psychologically, socially, technologically."[36] Table 2.1, on page 35, reflects the following explanation of Buchler's terms and the organizing structure of his notion of judgment.

Drawing on Buchler's language and distinctions, we can consider Jewish studies and educational theory as "complexes" or "orders" that bear and share certain "traits."[37] For Buchler, disciplines are "complexes" and indeed, so is "whatever is, in whatever way":

> Relations, structures, processes, societies, human individuals, human products, physical bodies, words and bodies of discourse, ideas, qualities, contradictions, meanings, possibilities, myths, laws, duties, feelings, illusions, reasonings, dreams—all are natural complexes. All of these terms bespeak discriminations of some kind, and whatever is discriminated in any respect or in any degree is a natural complex.[38]

Equally important, any complex is intricately related to some other complexes:

> Every complex (complex of traits) is thus a constituent of some other complex and includes other complexes as constituents of it . . . every complex is an order of complexes and belongs to an order of complexes.[39]

These relationships among complexes occur as a result of our "producing" "judgment." Thus, there is a kind of paradox when considering the relationship between complexes and judgment. On the one hand, these complexes or orders are essential to understanding. Yet, on the other hand, they are the products of human judgment. They are metaphysical *and* epistemological. This duality is felicitously characterized by one interpreter of Buchler as "systematic nonfoundationalism."[40] It is rigorously systematic but inventive in its categories and their relationships. If Dewey helps us see how Jewish studies can function as a source for educational theory, Buchler provides us with a way of recognizing and articulating these fields' (i.e., these "complexes'") shared traits and possibilities for mutual edification.

Buchler's philosophy centers on the concept of "ordinality." Ordinality connotes that everything that exists has an internal and external relational complexity—never fully definable. Everything that "is" is a complex (often called a "natural complex" and used interchangeably with "order") in that it can be identified as made up of traits that have a certain order, a certain interrelationship. In addition, any complex is located in some *other* orders or complexes. And because we can never reduce nor fully delimit the complexity of an order, it is not possible to define absolute boundaries between or within them. For Buchler, anything that "is" is a complex (or "order") bearing traits: "Whatever is, in whatever way, is an order of constituents and a constituent of other orders" and "[w]hatever is, in whatever way, is a natural complex and a trait of other complexes."[41] It is important to clarify that the notion of trait here does not connote an adjectival characterization of an order or complex. Rather, it refers to a component, constituent, or feature of a complex: "Not only entities, but qualities, quantities, and relations, possibilities, potentialities, and powers, ideas, feelings, and values are natural complexes and orders of traits."[42]

Though every trait is shared with some other complexes, every complex has a particular "sphere of relevance which obtains," a "definite character, an integrity."[43] The character of a complex is defined by a particular order of traits that allows its specific character to "prevail."[44] Thus, every complex has an "order of prevalence"[45] that gives it particularity, even as it shares traits with different complexes.[46] Equally important for Buchler, there are no simple, isolated traits or complexes, for each one is comprised of multiple complexes and each is related to other complexes.[47] There are then two principles of Buchler's ordinality: *There are no simple, fully reduced complexes or traits that are not made up of others, and there is no such thing as an isolated complex that has no relation to others.*

Following Buchler, certain traits shared by the discourses of Jewish studies and educational theory can be made explicit even as we seek to preserve the distinctiveness of the prevailing order—the discursive, disciplinary integrity—that obtains in each area. Any product of human judgment can acquire new relationships, new ways of being relevant to other products. Any product has a dynamic relationality and therefore can transcend its prior delimitations that may have marked off its initial instantiations.

Let us consider how Buchler suggests we might engage these intersecting traits and complexes with each other. For him, such engagement would involve applying ways of judging, absorbing, and changing complexes (i.e., orders of prevalence, disciplines).

Product and Producer

Human beings have two types of relationships to complexes. (In our case, we should be thinking of Jewish studies, educational theory, and their constituent fields as complexes or orders of prevalence.) For some complexes, human beings are "products";[48] that is to say, one's sense of self, identity, and basis for relating to others are functions of being part of a complex; one is, in part, a product of that complex. Examples of complexes that "produce" human beings are families, languages, frameworks of meaning, societal contexts, and professional norms. The second type of relationship is one in which an individual is a "producer"[49] of a complex, an active shaper and creator of a complex. Buchler calls such shaping and creating "judging"[50]: "To the extent that a man can be said to be the product of other natural complexes, he does not judge. To the extent that any complexes can be said to be his product, he judges."[51] When we judge a field, a realm of discourse, or an idea, we are, in a sense, producing. We are producing ways of interpreting it, of using it, of adapting, or changing it and its relations. Though "a judgment presupposes a set of limiting conditions, a perspective, within which it functions to define properties of . . . natural complexes which establish a perspective or limiting order for each judgment,"[52] Buchler emphasizes the *productive* quality of judgment.

A Jewish educational theorist's or an educator's thought and practice, then, are not only the *products* of theory and prior practices; rather, the theorist or educator *produces*. The same holds true for scholarship in Jewish studies. When we say that we judge by producing, this means that in producing judgments and understandings, in extending knowledge and changing it, we are committing ourselves to discriminating, selecting, and interpreting in certain ways characteristic or even constitutive of our respective fields and their discourses of which we are also products. But if we wish to consider an interdiscursive relationship between Jewish studies and educational theory, educational theorists would judge not only in an educational theoretical way, but also, for example, in an historical or literary way. In this sense, we are engaging (judging) Jewish studies as a producer. So Jewish studies is more than a content source; it involves ways of judging in which the educational theorist participates, critiques, and produces discourse.

Next I will examine Buchler's categories of judgment and how they might inform productive interdiscursive relationships between Jewish studies and education. (See table 2.1, page 35)

Assimilating and Manipulating

There are two broad modes of productive judgment: "assimilating" and "manipulating."[53] In judging Jewish studies, for example, educational theorists can both assimilate *and* manipulate[54] complexes of Jewish studies. Usually we only think of manipulating the complexes with which we are the most experienced, comfortable, and knowledgeable. Typically, educational theorists manipulate the concepts of education and its philosophies, goals and aspirations, assessment principles, teaching strategies, curriculum theories, etc. But if there is a program of higher learning or scholarship in which Jewish studies, as a complex or set of complexes, interacts with educational theory, then educational theorists need to do more than *assimilate* Jewish studies discourse; they must also *manipulate* it, work with it, and shape it, producing further judgments within it. Active production requires discursive manipulation as well as assimilation.

Analysis and Coordination

For Buchler, the judgment within and between complexes occurs in two ways. The first he calls "analysis":

> Analysis is the process whereby a given natural complex is explored with respect to its integrity as a complex rather than with respect to its possible bearing upon the integrity of another complex. It is the emphasis upon the exploration of a complex in so far as other complexes are relevant to it rather than in so far as it is relevant to other complexes.[55]

Scholarship tends to be conducted as analysis (in Buchler's sense of the term). The scholar judges the constituent traits of a discipline, responds to its prevailing issues and questions, and participates in its discursive styles. In as much as analytical judgment is interested in complexes outside of it, such judgment focuses primarily on how those other complexes may be relevant to it.

"Analytical" judgment is to be contrasted with "coordinative" judgment. The latter is concerned not simply with how other complexes may contribute to or influence the discipline in which one has acquired expertise (as would be the case with analytical judgment). Rather, coordinative judgment involves the reverse direction, considering how one's complex has import for other complexes or how it may be part of a broader, more comprehensive complex: "Where, on the other hand, the same complex is judged as contributing to or bearing upon (i.e., as constituting) another, our concern may be not only with its relevance to the integrity of another, but with another which is more extensive or inclusive than it."[56]

Thus, coordinative judgment is reciprocally relational. This relational interdiscursivity is implicit in Buchler's metaphysics:

> Whatever is, is in some relation: a given complex may be unrelated to another given complex, but not unrelated to any other . . . There is no end to the relational "chain" of a complex; and there is no end to the explorability of a complex, whether in respect to its relational traits or any other.[57]

Coordinative judgment is therefore "transordinal."[58] As such, coordinative judgment considers "how the various facets of human invention can *accent and augment one another* in the interest of human betterment."[59] In our case, this accenting and augmenting are in the interest of Jewish educational theory and practice *and* in the interest of Jewish studies disciplines with which they are engaged.

Examples in the Literature

There are clear examples in recent discourse on Jewish educational theory and philosophy that, while not necessarily intentionally so, could be associated with Buchler's notions of intersecting complexes and coordinative, transordinal judgment. These concepts appear to be operative in Michael Rosenak's effort "to show not only how Jewish law, the halakhah, draws the commandments on the Torah into the concrete circumstances of life, but also how the laws' internal controversies reflect diverse philosophical and educational positions."[60] Buchler's categories also resonate with Rosenak's demonstrating the common traits—what Buchler would call the "transordinality"—between philosophy of Jewish law, political philosophy, and "educational concerns."[61]

When Jonathan Cohen notes that "Maimonides is important to Rosenak . . . for the more fundamental claim that a systematic philosophy of education can indeed be derived from Jewish sources," there is really more to it than *derivation*.[62] If it is to be only derivation, this conception would be strictly Deweyan. But in Buchler's terms, Maimonides' philosophy and Jewish educational thought share common traits and complexes. The "character ideals" expressed in Maimonides writings are *shared* with "the final end. . . and successful outcome of the educational process."[63] This transordinal potential of Jewish studies and education is also exemplified in Cohen's noting how Rosenak demonstrates a commonality of traits between Joseph Schwab's commonplaces (i.e., "the learner, the teacher, the milieu and the subject matter") and Maimonidean categories.[64]

Yet another example of an interdiscursive approach that could be informed by Buchler's categories is some of the work of Avinoam Rosenak. In the following passage, his opening premise is distinctively Buchlerian: "Jewish Law (halakhah) is not solely a legal text; it is also—if not primarily—an educational text."[65] As he points out, this premise influences how we understand "halakhah itself" and "the analytical tools to be applied to it."[66] What Buchler would call a transordinal relationship allows us to examine the "philosophy of halakhah," and to consider its potential for interdiscursive exchange with education. A. Rosenak's "educational figure," "halakhic decisor," and "jurist,"[67] in Buchler's terms, would be complexes or orders that share certain traits. There is thus a "correspondence between the purpose of educational activity and the purpose of the halakhic system" that "provides fertile ground for a further connection."[68]

Buchler's paradigm is also evident in Ari Ackerman's demonstration of how "[David] Hartman's theology is shot through with educational concerns."[69] Similarly, Elie Holzer could be read in a Buchler-like spirit in that he demonstrates common concerns shared by Gadamer and Ricoeur, teacher educators, and features of *ḥevruta* learning,[70] as these complexes share a view of "understanding as an interpretive and dialogical process.[71] He even makes the point that this shared trait is the "central issue" of "how people understand."[72]

Finally, there is an aspect of Levisohn's writing that, though largely Deweyan (see above), demonstrates an implicit concern with aspects of Buchler's discourse. This is particularly the case when he notes that Jewish studies and education share a kind of epistemology—an "epistemological isomorphism," or "similar structure of the knowledge of the subject as held by the scholar and the teacher—not that they *know* the same things, exactly, but that they do the same things, that they pursue parallel cognitive or intellectual practices." He thus rejects a "dichotomy between scholarship and pedagogy itself."[73]

Inquiry and Query

Buchler uses the term "query" to characterize judgment that has human betterment in view.[74] Query is distinct from inquiry, though it can include it. In query, we are not guided by a need to solve a problem or to restore an equilibrium to an indeterminate situation. Instead, query is extensive and continually interrogative, seeking to understand and transcend the limits of currently understood meanings. In query, Buchler exceeds Dewey's notion of "method of intelligence," and what he considers to be Dewey's methods of problem-solving. While he would agree with Dewey that methodical activity involves "intelligence in operation,"[75] he insists that we "guard against characterizing the interrogative situation as the 'problematic' situation."[76] And, in explaining query, he avoids using the Deweyan term, "indeterminacy," as this too "suggests a dilemmatic urgency that awaits mitigation."[77] For these reasons, "query is not limited to inquiry."[78] Rather than purely "remedial," query can "augment what there is no reason to be discontent with."[79] For Buchler, "[t]he spirit of query lies in the urge to make a work relevant in new ways—relevant to one's situation in life, *to one's disciplinary concerns*, and to one's sense of the world at large."[80]

So, in applying the notion of query, we consider how Jewish studies and education might "accent and augment one another in the interest"[81] of both and of Jewish education as a field. Such query "extends" the products of our judgment so they "pervade human experience."[82] Whereas inquiry will clarify and address a specific problem in Jewish education, query extends inquiry to a "wonder" that does not seek "appeasement" but rather promotes an interrogative spirit:

> When the ancient Greeks said that the pursuit of wisdom begins in wonder, they laid the foundation for the concept of query. But there are at least two kinds of wonder. There is the wonder that seeks to be appeased and the wonder to which appeasement is irrelevant. In the species of query exemplified by

> science, the former dominates; in that exemplified by poetry, the latter. Scientific wonder seeks to resolve the questions it provokes. Poetic wonder seeks no resolutions: its interrogativeness is not generated by vexations.[83]

Poetic wonder is thus a pursuit of knowledge and understanding that is not simply responding to a problem. For Buchler, this pursuit is what drives human judgment in all discourses:

> The principle that there always are questions beyond questions that have been asked, and complexes beyond and within the complexes that are known, besides being defensible as such, preserves the momentum of life and query. At least for man, absolute delimitation—perfect boundaries, incorrigible knowledge, total freedom from indecision (which is freedom from decision)—would be death.[84]

Thus, transcending conventional discourse and disciplinary knowledge enlivens and drives such pursuit. Each student, teacher, and researcher who pursues a wonder for which there is no appeasement "welcomes the extension of . . . boundaries in the direction of invention."[85]

Yet it is important to underscore that, for Buchler, we should not be concerned with an *a priori* overlap of traits. Rather, engaged in query, we seek to interrogate each field's or complex's order of relationships and discourse, producing transordinal, coordinative judgments. I suggest that the latter are important dimensions of the offices of educational theory *and* Jewish studies scholarship, just as Buchler suggests they are for office of philosophy:

> Philosophy effects a distinctive realization: that the categorial struggle to encompass structures of indefinitely greater breadth is both inevitable and valid. The philosopher comes to see that one perspective can excel or embrace but not annul another. Those who are most truly liberated by the philosophic spirit are likely to be most subject to the compulsion of other philosophies. Such compulsion does not entail literal cognitive acceptance but *greater articulative mastery* over one's own perspective and over the other, and greater conceptual endowment for the sense of encompassment.[86]

What he here claims for philosophy can thus extend to programs that join Jewish studies with educational theory. Those programs need to consider the nature and scope of the desired conceptual endowment and articulative (i.e., discursive) mastery in both fields and what type of interdiscursive relations should be attained.

Table 2.1. Buchler's categories of judgment as they relate to Jewish studies and education. Judgment by a student can be assimilative or manipulative. In relation to the disciplines, judgment can be analytical or coordinative. We can also differentiate the purpose and disposition of judgment as inquiry or query. Inquiry is that form of judgment that tends to assimilate and analyze with the intent of appeasing wonder. Query, in contrast, is driven by an interrogative spirit that can never be appeased and for which appeasement would be irrelevant. It therefore demands both manipulation and assimilation, often requiring both analytical and coordinative judgment.

	Category 1	Category 2
Judging by the student	Assimilative	Manipulative
Judgment's relation to disciplines	Analytical	Coordinative
Judgment's purpose and disposition	Inquiry	Query

MICHAEL OAKESHOTT: CONVERSATION

For British philosopher Michael Oakeshott, disciplines and discourses in academia are not simply "partners in a common undertaking, each with a role to perform . . . [serving as] suppliers of one another's wants."[87] Though neither Dewey's notion of inquiry nor Buchler's concept of query would contradict Oakeshott's point, his notion of "conversation" suggests additional important dimensions to interdiscursive relationships.

Each participant in such a conversation can be considered a "language" and "a manner of thinking," as distinct from a specific "literature" or set of texts, i.e., "what has been said from time to time in a 'language.'"[88] As "a manifold of different intellectual activities," a conversation is constituted by the engagement of different modes of thought and different living languages.[89] As Oakeshott explains, these living discursive modes may involve thinking and speaking "historically, mathematically, scientifically or philosophically . . . not as 'subjects' but as living 'languages.'"[90]

In this book, conversations include modes of discourse that can be called mystical, cosmological, theosophical, pragmatic, pedagogical and narratological. Each of these modes constitutes what Oakeshott would call "an authentic voice and idiom of its own."[91] Participants in conversation invoke their own language or authentic idiom of expression for the purpose of speaking it and articulating new insights and understandings in it, rather than simply employing a "language" as a "skill of using the information."[92]

But it is important to note that employing a language in conversation means that the language has a certain humble conversability. There is a sustained awareness of "the presence of ideas of another order" so that each field avoids having "an exclusive concern with its own utterance, which may result in its identifying the conversation with itself and its speaking as if it were speaking only to itself."[93] So as part of a genuine conversation, each separate discourse must be able to be comprehensible to another.[94] In other words, a field's particular language is not only for its own self-understanding, but rather for a fellow participant in the conversation who may not speak the same "language." This requires, particularly in our case, a kind of "recognition and accommodation" as we consider how discourses of such a disparate nature might communicate.

We should not confuse this relationship of "recognition and accommodation" with an extrinsic need "to inform, to persuade, or to refute" each other.[95] Rather, in a conversation, "each voice speaks in its own idiom . . . [F]rom time to time one voice may speak louder than others, but . . . none has natural superiority, let alone primacy."[96] Furthermore, the conversation does not necessarily seek improved technical understanding or specific, discrete skills, nor need it seek to develop a more encompassing strategy for change or improvement. Though not excluding them, pursuing know-how and experimentation are not necessarily the conversation's primary *modi operandi.*

In much of higher education, the liberal arts and professional education are not involved in a sustained conversation. Only a limited number of common themes or "applicable," intersecting content are admitted to the conversation as a much greater remainder's traces are left behind. Much is lost because the specific agenda is limited to the selected points of possible intersection between the fields. Similarly, the aspects of Jewish studies and education that do not appear to be mutually informing are often left by the wayside, perhaps to be revisited, perhaps remaining as background traces. (See figure 1.1.) A call for engagement, participation, and interpretation is thus often left unheeded.

Now lest we come to think of conversation as idle, tautological, or intellectually indulgent, Oakeshott helps us identify its anticipated outcomes:

> [C]ertainties are shown to be combustible, not by being brought in contact with other 'certainties' or with doubts, but by being kindled by the presence of ideas of another order; approximations are revealed between notions normally remote from one another. Thoughts of different species take wing and play round one another, responding to each other's movements and provoking one another to fresh exertions . . . [We] learn to recognize the voices, to distinguish the proper occasions of utterance, and . . . acquire the intellectual and moral habits appropriate to conversation.[97]

Conversations, then, have three ends-in-view. The first is to achieve a greater awareness and appreciation of "the presence of ideas of another order" so "approximations are revealed between notions normally remote from one another."[98] Second, this achievement of revealed approximations can result in "provoking one another to fresh exertions."[99] Finally, we come to "recognize the voices" of distinct discourses so that we can "distinguish the proper occasions" to invoke each of them.[100] This kind of conversation does not preclude the possibility or necessity of developing new skills, strategies, practical directions, and professional guidance. But in overemphasizing these latter ends, we can lose sight of the vitality of conversation, its capacity to cultivate recognition of distinctions and commonalities, to develop discernment of proper occasions for different discourses and a facility with interdiscursive exchange.

There are clear examples of this notion of conversation in Jewish educational theory. Interdiscursive conversation appears to be operative in Avinoam Rosenak's noting that:

> On the one hand, one may survey the various philosophical schools within Jewish thought and examine their educational implications; on the other, one may take examples from the philosophy of education, superimpose them back on the doctrines of Jewish thought, and consider the new philosophical insights that might be gained from such a procedure.[101]

As he notes, these dynamics involve "a conversation between the interpreter and the text" in "a progressive process of meaning making, which takes place between two horizons meeting each other."[102]

And this Oakeshottian mode of engagement appears to be at work in the way Michael and Avinoam Rosenak conduct a conversation between Soloveitchik's philosophy and his educational concerns.[103] They thus show that their presentation and explication of such a conversation is not simply identifying Soloveitchik's references to education. Rather, they maintain "that educational doctrine can be shown to arise from philosophical writings as such." There is thus a critical engagement between Soloveitchik's "thought" and "the philosophy of education." Such conversational engagement is of reciprocal benefit, illuminating "not only . . . his educational teachings but also . . . other aspects of his thought."[104]

This conversational paradigm is also evident in the way Jonathan Cohen characterizes Michael Rosenak's "lifelong academic pursuit" of creating a "meeting-ground"[105] between classical Jewish sources and the general philosophy of education literature. And Ari Ackerman operates in an Oakeshottian key when he places David Hartman's theology in conversation with his work in Jewish education.[106] He thus demonstrates that "Hartman sees the study of Talmud, with its dialectical style and multiple viewpoints, as a fruitful medium that can contribute to a dialogical approach to Jewish education."[107]

It is also significant that Brandeis's "Bridging Scholarship" initiative claims that it "promotes the improvement of the teaching of Jewish studies in multiple settings, through research by and critical dialogue among scholars and teachers."[108] Although it is distinctively Deweyan to engage Jewish studies in order to improve its being taught (as noted above), the notion of "critical dialogue among scholars and teachers" is particularly Oakeshottian. So Levisohn promotes this conversational paradigm when he says that "a better model is to bring people together to engage in shared discussion, common conversation, joint inquiry."[109] And in what could read as a gesture toward Oakeshott, he asserts that "conversation about the questions *across* settings and ages, but *within* the subject area, has the potential to be enlightening for all involved."[110]

Perhaps the quintessential interdiscursive conversation is what Joseph Lukinsky recalls of his working, as a young rabbi and educator, with Robert Cover on "a crazy idea that we called 'The American Talmud'":

> Our plan was to bring together outstanding authors and thinkers, along with stories from their lives and works. For starters, we identified Freud, Einstein, Marx, and Darwin (the irony of using these authors in our "American" Talmud was, I think, lost on us then)—people who significantly joined the great human issues. We would cluster them, with scissors and paste if necessary, in an interactive style bearing the hallmarks of Talmudic discourse and logic. That is, we did not plan to present these thinkers in the usual serial thematic anthology format (what each had to say about this or that topic), but rather in a constructed deliberation *with* one another. The essential idea was to present sources whose original formats were linear and univocal in a multiperspectival, dialogic, simultaneous debate on contemporary issues. We wanted to experience the deliberation, the inquiry itself, not the separate conclusions, as each of these greats hurled challenges at the others.[111]

Lukinsky uses this anecdote to illustrate some of the problems of bounded disciplines. I read what he here calls "synthesis" as more of a conversation than an undifferentiated amalgam: "This synthesis need not smooth out all differences, but rather must articulate the tensions that exist in a more total view; the experience should be one of participating in these tensions, of feeling the pushes and the pulls."[112] And as he successfully demonstrates, this mode of interdisciplinary, interdiscursive articulation and participation is grounded in a central Jewish hermeneutic and educational nomos:

> [T]o enter the study of Talmud is to enter the Jewish nomos in a participatory way, to engage in an inquiry that is taking place now. To be involved in the labyrinth of the discussion, of even rejected views, is to reexperience it in a very personal way, from inside the inquiry itself.[113]

Now, though this "labyrinth of discussion" is experienced "in a very personal way," it is important to note that the conversational paradigm does not assume that there is an independent "subject" (teacher or student) who objectively brings together separate fields to identify points of intersection and complementarity. As Oakeshott points out, "[a] conversation does not need a chairman,"[114] or a "symposiarch or arbiter, not even a doorkeeper to examine credentials."[115] The individual, as subject, does not serve as the foundation, but rather, the subject "moves about in a hermeneutical play of perspectival descriptions of the life of discourse and action," as Calvin O. Schrag asserts in an Oakeshottian key.[116] This "hermeneutical play" is what Israel Scheffler calls the "conversation" between "the traditions of imaginative thought."[117]

We seek a sustained conversation as the subject stands now within one field, now within another, as she shuttles and struggles to recognize, respect, and use the languages and idioms of each field as in a conversation. This kind of conversation is not concerned with selected points of intersection or opportunities for comprehensive, totalizing synthesis; rather, it is concerned with participation, engagement, and openness to conceptual and discursive concordance and dissonance. Instead of seeking to combine fields or to use one field to apply or explicate another, in conversation we assemble different disciplines for the purpose of expanding the way we think, to challenge perceptions, and to revisit prior assumptions. This challenging expansion of perception and thought is not the result of a new combination of disciplines or a new recognition of selected points of informing intersections. Rather, it is the result of a sustained conversation between discourses in which they affect each other. This kind of conversation lets the language and concepts of one discourse awaken what Merleau-Ponty calls "echoes . . . in the other" by a lateral traversing that communicates a type of meaning without presuming to merge them.[118]

I suggest that it is worth the effort to engage these multiple traditions in what Oakeshott calls conversation, what Buchler calls transordinal, coordinative query, and what Dewey calls sources for each other's efforts. We may then consider Jewish studies disciplines as sources for educational theory. We might also create a more interactive, reciprocal edification between what Buchler would call the different "complexes" or "orders of prevalence" in these fields. And we can invite distinct discursive languages into a conversation that is not reductive or subsumptive, while demonstrating its value and meaning.

NOTES

1. This dualism appears to be assumed by Louis Menand in his defining "liberal arts" as "subjects of disinterested inquiry rather than areas of professional or vocational education." Menand, *Marketplace of Ideas*, 18 n. 4.

2. John Dewey, *The Sources of a Science of Education* (New York: Horace Liveright, 1929).

3. Justus Buchler, *Toward a General Theory of Human Judgment* (New York: Columbia University Press, 1951). *Nature and Judgment* (New York: Columbia University Press, 1955); Buchler, *The Concept of Method* (New York: Columbia University Press, 1961); Buchler, *The Metaphysics of Natural Complexes* (New York: Columbia University Press, 1966); Buchler, *The Main of Light: On the Concept of Poetry* (New York: Oxford University Press, 1974).

4. Michael Oakeshott, "The Study of Politics in a University" and "The Voice of Poetry in the Conversation of Mankind," ed. T. Fuller, *Rationalism in Politics and Other Essays* (Indianapolis: The Liberty Fund, 1962/1991); Oakeshott, "The Idea of a University," "Learning and Teaching," and "A Place for Learning," ed. T. Fuller, *The Voice of Liberal Learning: Michael Oakeshott on Education* (New Haven, Yale University Press, 1975/1989).
5. Dewey, *Sources,* 8.
6. Dewey, *Sources,* 22.
7. Dewey, *Sources,* 33.
8. Dewey, *Sources,* 38.
9. Dewey, *Sources,* 20.
10. Dewey, *Sources,* 48.
11. Dewey, *Sources,* 75.
12. Dewey, *Sources,* 77.
13. Dewey, *Sources,* 42 (my italics).
14. John Dewey, *Human Nature and Conduct: An Introduction to Social Psychology* (New York: Holt, 1922), 223–25.
15. Dewey, *Sources,* 9–10.
16. Dewey, *Sources,* 12.
17. Dewey, *Sources,* 14.
18. Dewey, *Sources,* 14.
19. Dewey, *Sources,* 11.
20. Dewey, *Sources,* 12
21. Dewey, *Sources,* 12
22. Dewey, *Sources,* 10.
23. M. Rosenak, *Commandments and Concerns.*
24. Levisohn, "Bridging."
25. Levisohn, "Bridging."
26. Judd Kruger Levingston, "The Moral Mishnah: How Can Teachers of Rabbinics Use the Mishnah for Moral Education?" The Initiative on Bridging Scholarship and Pedagogy in Jewish Studies, Brandeis University Mandel Center for Studies in Jewish Education, Working Paper No. 21 (April 2010). http://www.brandeis.edu/mandel/research/bridging/bridginginitiative_docs.html
27. Gidon Rothstein, "Motivation Before Method: Helping Students Get a Foot in the Door through the Use of Academic Scholarship in the Teaching of Rabbinic Texts," The Initiative on Bridging Scholarship and Pedagogy in Jewish Studies, Brandeis University, Mandel Center for Studies in Jewish Education and Jewish Studies, Working Paper No. 22 (November 2009). http://www.brandeis.edu/mandel/research/bridging/bridginginitiative_docs.html
28. Jeffrey L. Rubenstein, "From History to Literature: The Pedagogical Implications of Shifting Paradigms in the Study of Rabbinic Narratives," The Initiative on Bridging Scholarship and Pedagogy in Jewish Studies, Brandeis University, Mandel Center for Studies in Jewish Education and Jewish Studies, Working Paper No. 26 (April 2010). http://www.brandeis.edu/mandel/research/bridging/bridginginitiative_docs.html
29. Holtz, "Across the Divide."
30. M. Rosenak, "Philosophy of Jewish Education."
31. M. Rosenak, "Philosophy of Jewish Education."
32. This Deweyan approach also appears to inform Jonathan Cohen's comments on "how insights from modern Jewish thought can enrich discourse and reflection on issues of principle in Jewish education." Jonathan Cohen, "Jewish Thought for Jewish Education: Sources and Resources," in *International Handbook of Jewish Education*, ed. Helena Miller, Lisa Grant, and Alex Pomson, (Springer, 2011). http://www.springerlink.com.ilsprod.lib.neu.edu/content/m377078611470749/.
33. Israel Scheffler, "The Concept of the Educated Person: With Some Applications to Jewish Education," in *Visions of Jewish Education*, ed. Seymour Fox, Israel Scheffler, and Daniel Marom (Cambridge University Press, 2003), 221.
34. In addition to Dewey, Buchler was influenced by fellow American scholars Charles Sanders Peirce, William James, Josiah Royce, and George Santayana.

35. Kathleen A. Wallace, "Justus Buchler," in *Dictionary of Literary Biography* (Thomson Gale, 2005–2006).
36. Buchler, *Theory of Human Judgment*, xxxix.
37. Buchler, *Metaphysics of Natural Complexes,* xvii, xviii, 1, 2, 5.
38. Buchler, *Metaphysics*, 1.
39. Buchler, *Metaphysics*, 13.
40. Beth Singer, "Systematic Nonfoundationalism: The Philosophy of Justus Buchler," *The Journal of Speculative Philosophy* 7, no. 3 (1993): 191–205.
41. "By metaphysics, Buchler means the construction of categories to frame one's thinking about a particular subject matter." Wallace, "Buchler."
42. Singer, *Systematic Nonfoundationalism.*
43. Buchler, *Main of Light*, 88.
44. Buchler, *Main of Light*, 131, 141.
45. Buchler, *Main of Light*, 170.
46. Buchler, *Metaphysics,* 52–92.
47. Buchler, *Metaphysics,* xxv, xxvi, 11, 17, 26.
48. Buchler, *Nature and Judgment,* 4, 7.
49. Buchler, *Metaphysics,* 126–28; *Nature and Judgment,* 6, 80; *Human Judgment,* 54, 58.
50. Buchler, *Human Judgment,* 86, 113; *Nature and Judgment,* 3–54.
51. Buchler, *Main of Light*, 92.
52. Buchler, *Nature and Judgment*, 17.
53. Buchler, *Human Judgment*, 20–21 ; *Metaphysics of Natural Complexes,* 25; *Nature and Judgment,* 142.
54. Buchler, *Human Judgment*, 20–21 ; *Metaphysics of Natural Complexes,* 25; *Nature and Judgment,* 142.
55. Buchler, *Main of Light*, 169.
56. Buchler, *Main of Light*, 170.
57. Buchler, *Metaphysic*, 24.
58. Buchler, *Main of Light*, 170.
59. Buchler, *Main of Light*, 101 (my italics).
60. M. Rosenak, *Tree of Life, Tree of Knowledge,* 138.
61. M. Rosenak, *Tree of Life*, *Tree of Knowledge,* 138.
62. Cohen, "Hartman, Rosenak and Schweid on Maimonides."
63. Cohen, "Hartman, Rosenak and Schweid on Maimonides."
64. Cohen, "Hartman, Rosenak and Schweid on Maimonides."
65. Avinoam Rosenak, "Styles of Halakhic Ruling: A Mapping in Light of Joseph Schwab's Philosophy of Education," *Journal of Jewish Education* 73 (2007): 81–106.
66. A. Rosenak, "Styles of Halakhic Ruling."
67. A. Rosenak, "Styles of Halakhic Ruling."
68. A. Rosenak, "Styles of Halakhic Ruling."
69. Ari Ackerman, "'Creating a Shared Spiritual Language': David Hartman's Philosophy of Jewish Education," *Studies in Jewish Education* 13 (2008/2009): 51–74.
70. Elie Holzer, "What Connects 'Good' Teaching, Text Study and *Hevruta* Learning? A Conceptual Argument," *Journal of Jewish Education* 72 (2006): 183–204.
71. Holzer, "Text Study and *Hevruta* Learning."
72. Holzer, "Text Study and *Hevruta* Learning."
73. Levisohn, "Bridging," 15.
74. Buchler, *Nature and Judgment,* 56–102.
75. Buchler, *The Concept of Method* (New York: Columbia University Press, 1961), 81.
76. Buchler, *Nature and Judgment,* 72.
77. Buchler, *Nature and Judgment,* 72.
78. Buchler, *Nature and Judgment,* 73.
79. Buchler, *Nature and Judgment,* 72–73.
80. Buchler, *Main of Light*, 127 (my italics).
81. Buchler, *Main of Light*, 101.
82. Buchler, *Nature and Judgment,* 92.

83. Buchler, *Main of Light*, 110.
84. Buchler, *Metaphysics*, 8.
85. Buchler, *Human Judgment*, 169.
86. Buchler, *Human Judgment*, 81 (my italics).
87. Oakeshott, "A Place for Learning," 30.
88. Oakeshott, "The Study of 'Politics' in a University," 192.
89. Oakeshott, "Study of 'Politics,'" 196.
90. Oakeshott, "Study of 'Politics,'" 196.
91. Oakeshott, "The Voice of Poetry in the Conversation of Mankind" 488.
92. Oakeshott, "Study of 'Politics,'" 192–193.
93. Oakeshott, "Voice of Poetry," 492.
94. Oakeshott, "Voice of Poetry," 535.
95. Oakeshott, "Voice of Poetry," 489.
96. Oakeshott, "Voice of Poetry," 534.
97. Oakeshott, "Voice of Poetry," 489–91.
98. Oakeshott, "Voice of Poetry," 489.
99. Oakeshott, "Voice of Poetry," 489.
100. Oakeshott, "Voice of Poetry," 490.
101. A. Rosenak, "The Concept of 'Image.'"
102. Holzer, "Text Study and *Hevruta* Learning," 191.
103. M. Rosenak and A. Rosenak, "Soloveitchik."
104. Michael Rosenak and Avinoam Rosenak, "Rabbi Joseph B. Soloveitchik and Aspects of Jewish Educational Philosophy: Explorations in his Philosophical Writings," *Journal of Jewish Education* 75 (2009): 114–129. Also see Lee S. Shulman, "Pedagogies of Interpretation, Argumentation, and Formation: From Understanding to Identity in Jewish Education," *Journal of Jewish Education* 74 (October 2008): 1–20.
105. Cohen, "Hartman, Rosenak and Schweid."
106. A. Ackerman, "Shared Spiritual Language."
107. A. Ackerman, "Shared Spiritual Language." Cohen shares this framework when he suggests that Schwab's commonplaces provide a language for seemingly "incommensurable conceptual frameworks," though Oakeshott would question the need for a kind of neutral Schwabian vocabulary to mediate these fields. Cohen, "Hartman, Rosenak and Schweid."
108. Brandeis University, Mandel Center for Studies in Jewish Education, "Bridging Scholarship and Pedagogy in Jewish Studies." Last modified August 15, 2011. http://www.brandeis.edu/mandel/projects/bridging/index.html
109. Levisohn, "Bridging."
110. Levisohn, "Bridging."
111. Joseph Lukinsky, "Law in Education: A Reminiscence with Some Footnotes to Robert Cover's Nomos and Narrative," *Yale Law Journal* 96 (1986–1987): 1836–1859
112. Lukinsky, "Law in Education."
113. Lukinsky, "Law in Education."
114. Oakeshott, "The Idea of a University," 109.
115. Oakeshott, "Voice of Poetry."
116. Schrag, *Communicative Praxis*, 214.
117. Scheffler, "Educated Person," 225, 230.
118. Maurice Merleau-Ponty, *Signs,* trans. R. C. McCleary (Evanston, IL: Northwestern University Press, 1964), 139.

Part 2

Educational Theory Meets Volozhin

Indeed, one should come to know, understand, and determine that each and every aspect of one's conduct, speech, and thoughts never perishes, God forbid, and that one's conduct becomes manifold, ascending to very exalted heights. (R. Ḥayyim of Volozhin, 1803)[1]

אמנם יבין וידע ויקבע במחשבותיו שכל פרטי מעשיו ודבוריו ומחשבותיו כל עת ורגע לא אתאבידו ח"ו, ומה רבו מעשיו ומאד גדלו ורמו. (ר' חיים מוולוזין, נפש החיים, א:ד).

When a sense of the infinite reach of an act physically occurring in a small point of space and occupying a petty instant of time comes home to us, the meaning of a present act is seen to be vast, immeasurable, unthinkable. (John Dewey, 1922)[2]

Where the mind is led forward
By thee into ever-widening
Thought and action—
Into that heaven of freedom,
My Father,
Let my country awake.
(Rabindranath Tagore, 1913, translated by Martha Nussbaum)[3]

R. Ḥayyim of Volozhin (1749–1821) holds an iconic place in traditional Jewish education, as does the Volozhin Yeshiva (*Yeshivat Ets Ḥayyim*) he founded in 1802. And it is widely recognized that his educational institution was the vanguard for a creative rejuvenation of traditional Jewish learning in

Lithuania and beyond.[4] Indeed, throughout the nineteenth century, the Yeshiva movement repeatedly claimed his paternity, as have many teachers and scholars who espouse the Volozhiner's[5] educational ethos.

Continents, cultures, and epochs apart, we would be hard-pressed to demonstrate lines of influence or relationships between R. Ḥayyim ("The Volozhiner") and modern American educational theorists. They are embedded within distinctive universes of discourse, conceptual vocabularies, and traditions. How, then, can we legitimately consider R. Ḥayyim's ideas in his own linguistic, cultural, spiritual framework while also striving to understand his educational thought in what he would surely consider an external, foreign vocabulary? Before proceeding, then, let us consider the appropriateness and value of an interdiscursive conversation between modern Western educational theory and R. Ḥayyim's rabbinic, kabbalistic framework.[6] As I will show, there is much to be revealed in this interdiscursive exchange. Reflected in the epigrams above, R. Ḥayyim's articulations of the enduring, exalted, far-reaching qualities of a student's and teacher's deeds, speech, and thoughts have a remarkable resonance with what John Dewey calls the "vast, immeasurable, unthinkable" qualities of the "infinite reach of an act,"[7] and with what Martha Nussbaum notes as Tagore's "ever-widening thought and action."[8]

My approach follows a recent trend that considers an educational theory in the context of the full range of ideas and conceptual frameworks of its proponent.[9] It is, thus, important to note that I am not simply identifying explicit references to education in R. Ḥayyim's thought, nor am I focusing on any one particular educational problem that can be addressed by direct application of one or another maxim within his writings. Rather, in Part Two's three chapters, I focus on how his thought can participate in a critical, interdiscursive exchange with modern educational thought. In doing so, I address these questions: Does the corpus of R. Ḥayyim's thought offer educators distinctive ways of looking at the world, themselves, their theorizing, and professional conduct? In what ways might his conceptions be commensurate with modern, progressive educational ideas, even as they do not coincide? Though a seemingly discomfiting conversation for some (on which I will comment further), I suggest that bringing together the worlds of the early-nineteenth-century Lithuanian Yeshiva and modern American educational thought might expand the concepts and narratives in which contemporary educators see themselves, their mission, and their work.

After leading the Volozhin Yeshiva for nearly twenty years, R. Ḥayyim composed a highly original and provocative treatise, the *Nefesh Ha-Ḥayyim* (NH), in which he articulates an innovative educational vision in kabbalistic and rabbinic language. He develops this vision through extensive consideration of how the meanings of one's deeds (*ma'aseh* מעשה), speech (*dibur*

דיבור), and thought (*maḥshavah* מחשבה) suggest modes and principles for Torah study, prayer, and performance of *mitsvot*. Closely correlated with this work is his commentary on *Pirke Avot*, the *Ru'aḥ Ḥayyim* (RH).[10]

While there have been a variety of characterizations of R. Ḥayyim of Volozhin in recent years, very little has been written from the vantage point of educational theory—an approach that could reveal vital dimensions of his thought and practice, especially considering his long tenure and profound accomplishments as an educator, scholar, and communal leader.[11]

In chapter 3, I consider these kinds of relationships between the discourses of R. Ḥayyim of Volozhin, John Dewey, and Martha Nussbaum. Despite the discursive dissonance in this engagement, I seek to show how Jewish intellectual history, American pragmatism, and modern political philosophy can serve as sources for each other and for educational theory. I will also illustrate what Buchler would call a coordinative, transordinal query in this interdiscursive exchange.

Chapter 4's focus is what I call R. Ḥayyim of Volozhin's non-messianic theory of the present and future, illustrating the potential for Jewish intellectual history to serve as a source for educational thinking regarding purposes, goals, and conduct. In chapter 5, R. Ḥayyim's and Dewey's conceptions of means, ends, and ideals are engaged in a conversation to articulate relationships among these educational commonplaces.

NOTES

1. R. Ḥayyim of Volozhin, *Nefesh Ha-Ḥayyim*, 1:4.
2. Dewey, *Human Nature and Conduct*, 263.
3. Martha Nussbaum, *The Clash Within: Democracy, Religious Violence, and India's Future* (Cambridge, MA: Harvard University Press, 2007), 301.
4. Esther Eisenman, "The Structure and Content of R. Ḥayyim of Volozhin's *Nefesh Ha-Ḥayyim*" (Hebrew), in Hallamish et al., 185–196; Dov Eliach, *Father of Yeshivot* (Hebrew) (Jerusalem: Mekhon Moreshet ha-yeshivot, 1990); Immanuel Etkes, "The Ideology and Activity of R. Ḥayyim of Volozhin as an Anti-Hasidic Response to Hasidism" (Hebrew) in *Proceedings of the American Academy of Jewish Research* (1972), 1–45; Etkes, "R. Ḥayyim of Volozhin's Response to Hasidism," in *The Gaon of Vilna*, 151–208; Benjamin Gross, "Rabbi Ḥayyim of Volozhin's Philosophical View" (Hebrew), *Annual of Bar-Ilan University. Studies in Judaica and the Humanities*, vol. 22–23 (1988), 121–160 [translated from original edition: *L'âme de la vie de Rabbi Ḥayyim de Volozhyn* (Paris: Verdier, 1986)]; Norman Lamm, "The Phase of Dialogue and Reconciliation," in *Tolerance and Movements of Religious Dissent in Eastern Europe*, ed. Béla K. Király (New York: Columbia University Press, 1975), 115–129; Norman Lamm, *Torah Lishmah: Torah for Torah's Sake in the Works of Rabbi Ḥayyim of Volozhin and His Contemporaries* (Hoboken, NJ: Ktav, 1989); Shaul Magid, "Deconstructing the Mystical: The Anti-Mystical Kabbalism in Rabbi Ḥayyim of Volozhin's *Nefesh ha-Ḥayyim*," *Journal of Jewish Thought and Philosophy* 9, no. 1 (1999): 21–67; Allan Nadler, *The Faith of the Mithnagdim: Rabbinic Responses to Hasidic Rapture* (Baltimore and London: Johns Hopkins University Press, 1997); Mordecai Pachter, "Between Acosmism and Theism: R. Ḥayyim of Volozhin's Thought Concept of God" (Hebrew), in Sarah O. Heller Willensky and Moshe Idel (eds.), *Studies in Jewish Thought* (Jerusalem: Magnes Press, 1989), 139–157; Mordechai Pachter, "The Gaon's Kabbalah from the Perspective of Two Traditions" (Hebrew),

in Hallamish et al., 119–136; Shalom Rosenberg, "Kabbalistic Doctrine in the Nefesh Ha-Ḥayyim" (Hebrew), *Analysis and Theory*, 5 (2001): 5–21; Tamar Ross, "Two Interpretations of the Doctrine of *Tsimtsum*: Ḥayyim of Volozhin and Shneur Zalman of Lyadi" (Hebrew), *Jerusalem Studies in Jewish Thought* 2 (1981): 153–169; Raphael Shuchat, "Messianic and Mystical Elements Associated with the Study of Torah According to the Gaon and His Disciples" (Hebrew), in Hallamish et al., 155–172; Shaul Stampfer, *The Lithuanian Yeshiva* (Hebrew) (Jerusalem: Zalman Shazar Center for Jewish History, 1995).

5. R. Ḥayyim is also referred to as "The Volozhiner."

6. The "rabbinic tradition," or "rabbinic literature," refers to Jewish law and traditional exegetical and homiletical literature associated with of the "Oral Law," including the Mishna, Talmud, midrash, and related texts. It connotes the authoritative tradition of biblical interpretation as it evolved during and since the time of the Second Temple, which was destroyed in 70 C.E. Kabbalah refers to the major Jewish esoteric, mystical tradition that began in southern France in the twelfth century and spread throughout North African, European, and Palestinian Jewry in subsequent centuries.

7. Dewey, *Human Nature*, 263.

8. Martha Nussbaum, "Education and Democratic Citizenship: Capabilities and Quality Education," *Journal of Human Development* 7, no. 3 (2006): 394.

9. For examples, see A. Ackerman, "David Hartman's Philosophy of Jewish Education"; R. R. Curren, *Aristotle on the Necessity of Public Education* (Lanham, MD: Rowman and Littlefield), 2000. Michael A. Peters, ed., *Heidegger, Education, and Modernity* (New York: Rowman and Littlefield, 2002). M. Gordon, ed., *Hannah Arendt and Education: Renewing Our Common World* (Boulder, CO: Westview Press, 2001). M. Rosenak and A. Rosenak, "Soloveitchik."

10. In addition to the *Nefesh Ha-Ḥayyim* (NH) and the *Ru'aḥ Ḥayyim* (RH), R. Ḥayyim's other important writings include his response in *She'elot u'teshuvot ḥut ha-meshulash* (HH), an introduction to the Vilna Gaon's Commentary on the section of the Zohar (IS) called *Sifra ditsni'uta*, a public letter to the Lithuanian communities soliciting support for the Volozhin Yeshiva (PL), and his sermon for *Seliḥot* (SS).

11. His *Nefesh Ha-Ḥayyim* has been interpreted as a kabbalistic work, an ethical treatise, a hermeneutic manual, and a defense of his interpretation of *Torah lishmah* ("Torah study for its own sake"). Some have viewed the *Nefesh Ha-Ḥayyim* as demonstrating theosophical consistency between hasidism and mitnagdism (hasidism's opponents), while others have emphasized the polemical aspects of the work in its drawing a clear line between R. Ḥayyim's normative mitnagdic religious framework and that of the hasidic leadership of his day. Recent scholarship has also emphasized salient differences in religious values between R. Ḥayyim and his hasidic contemporaries, and the far-reaching implications of their systems for divergent religious norms. See note 4.

Chapter Three

R. Ḥayyim of Volozhin, John Dewey, and Martha Nussbaum

An Educational Query[1]

It is not difficult to see the challenges of bringing a transcendent, kabbalistic perspective into a meaningful conversation with Dewey's modern American pragmatism. The same may be said for the apparent conceptual stretch necessary to engage kabbalistic discourse with Nussbaum's notions of social, political, and moral responsibilities. So I ask: To what extent, if at all, can modern philosophical discourse converse meaningfully with the Volozhiner's transcendent, spiritual, kabbalistic discourse? Can Dewey's pragmatic notion that the meaning of an act is in its consequences communicate with what I will argue is R. Ḥayyim's spiritually consequentialist educational thought? Can Nussbaum's concept of cultivating capacities across cultural, political, and gender boundaries converse with what the Volozhiner espouses as the fateful role of education in sustaining the spiritual and material worlds? Put differently, how can we avoid simply encoding R. Ḥayyim's kabbalistic discourse with a contemporary mythos of science and rationalism? How can we be sure, using contemporary philosopher Charles Taylor's language, "to encode the other undistortively"?[2]

It is important to recognize that the alternative to bringing very different traditions into meaningful conversation would be that, in articulating contemporary educational theory and purposes, we would be compelled to screen out those aspects of the tradition that are dissonant with modern educators' senses of the world and of their place in it. As Taylor aptly notes: the consequence of such screening would be that "we would find our safest refuge against illogic in saying nothing—playing it safe, with a vengeance."[3]

And contemporary philosopher Calvin Schrag amplifies the efficacy of this kind of interdiscusive engagement in suggesting that recovering "prescientific and prephilosophical thought and praxis" opens the way to a kind of "radical reflection" in which we can move beyond a habituated opposition between transcendental and empirical modes of understanding and inquiry.[4] For our purposes, it would be important, then, to try dismantling some of the seeming incompatibility of R. Ḥayyim's transcendental kabbalism and Dewey's pragmatism in order to reveal their conversational potential.

But how can we avoid subsuming R. Ḥayyim's traditional kabbalistic discourse within a "universal," modern, secular, rational lexicon? Using Schrag's language, I am suggesting that, like all professionals, educators have ranges of "praxial engagements . . . forms of life that lie across each other without coincidence; yet these forms of life do not dissolve into an indeterminate heterogeneity and 'pure' incommensurablity."[5] Now it is important here to note that this study is not a comparison. It is, rather, an approach in which I am taking license to let the language and concepts of one discourse resonate with those of another.

Alan Brill provides a further rationale for this kind of interdiscursivity as he suggests an interpretation of the relationship between *Torah* and *Madda* (secular scientific learning): "Is *Madda* allowed to gaze at *Torah* and view it as an 'other' or does it have to sit politely in its place? What are the irresolvable tensions between the two discourses?"[6] Rather than suggesting a dissolution of distinctions between sacred and secular discourse, I read Brill as implying that contemporary educational theory and practice could be more meaningful to religious sensibilities if we could "find a way to connect the many fragmented parts of our postmodern existence back to spirituality and a sense of the Divine."[7] Doing so may provide a way out of a fragmented professional world by enabling us to see the holy in everyday pragmata and the pragmatic in the holy. Though perhaps considering themselves heirs to the venerable educational thought and efforts of the Volozhiner, modern Jewish educators, more often than not, are situated within a society in which the pragmatism of John Dewey and the inclusive, far-reaching, pluralist humanism of Martha Nussbaum have considerable influence.

PREVIOUS USES OF DEWEY AS A SOURCE FOR JEWISH EDUCATIONAL THEORY

R. Ḥayyim was a vanguard of modern Jewish erudition, rabbinic scholarship, and modern yeshiva education—an archetypal figure of traditional Jewish educational innovation. We can imagine R. Ḥayyim's modern American analogue as John Dewey, whose thought and work has come to be nearly synonymous with American pragmatism, progressivism, and much of American philosophy, and which has become a vital element in the construction of a uniquely American educational ethos. It is also significant that the work of Martha Nussbaum, our third partner in this conversation, represents a unique interdiscursivity of classical, contemporary, pluralist, multicultural, transpolitical, geographically inclusive, feminist philosophy.

However, engaging R. Ḥayyim with Dewey, in particular, presents its own set of challenges. Many religious educators who note their ideational dissonance with Dewey assume a view of his work that caricatures his pragmatism as "a can-do, go-getting, commonsensical disposition that is sometimes fitted out with philosophical trimmings for intellectual occasions . . . instrumentalizing and relativizing truth claims, subjecting every argument or insight to the test of what works."[8] Some go so far as to blame Dewey's pragmatism for "the many social ills that have plagued the nation's landscapes of learning," as he "ardently embraced evolutionary naturalism, challenged classical conceptions of absolute truth and constructed a non-theistic image of God," fostering "ongoing faith in the possibilities of scientific inquiry and democracy that often bypass theological questions."[9]

Despite these reservations from some religious educators, Dewey's educational philosophy is, of course, no stranger to Jewish education, having a long reception history in the field. Since the early twentieth century, theorists of Jewish education have often turned to Dewey, drawing on his pragmatic and progressive educational theory. Dewey's theories of inquiry and educational experience have been well-suited for this purpose. His pragmatism has provided a public space for educators of different traditions and perspectives to make a transition from student-as-object to learner-as-subject, from normative certainty to qualities of uncertainty inherent in a modern world. Offering a theory of deliberation that cuts across denominational differences, Dewey provides a framework wherein educators and students can view themselves as active problem framers and problem solvers who realize, in their educational experiences, external and internal results. The external results are problems' provisional solutions; the internal results are personal and social growth. As Isa Aron notes:

> [A] Deweyan model of curricular decision-making can be particularly useful to Jewish educators, because it assumes neither agreement on goals nor a large body of research on methods. The Deweyan model requires only one thing—a problem, a conflict, a dissatisfaction or a confusion.[10]

For Dewey, an important aim is for the student to become a constructive, active participant in the multiple contexts that constitute his environment and community—religious groups, ethnic traditions, and, most importantly for Dewey, modern democracy. A civilizational perspective on Jewish existence has contributed to this receptive pattern.[11] Jewish values of community, citizenship, and a venerable tradition of interdependence between individual and collective have influenced the readiness of modern North American Jewish leadership's educational platforms as hosts for his philosophy.

But it is important to note that Jewish educational leaders and theorists have invoked Dewey's ideas primarily to promote modern methods, pragmatic sensibilities, social improvement, participation, and effective deliberation. These efforts have been helpful in showing how Dewey's thought can provide modern Jewish education with needed, added value and effectiveness. With notable exceptions, however, Dewey's discourse rarely has been used to interpret, communicate, and apply a better understanding of traditional Jewish conceptions of education.[12] There is often an assumed dissonance between Dewey's conception of religion and the transcendent, spiritual, normative dimensions of religiosity. Consequently, those embracing a more traditional normative conception of education often turn elsewhere to make sense of the transcendent or the spiritual. Thus, emphasis has been placed on incorporating aspects of Dewey's thought that do not encroach on the latter. Before I suggest a broader scope of engagement between Jewish educational theory and Dewey's philosophy, let us first consider some significant recent uses of Dewey in Jewish educational theory.

Michael Rosenak has called for renewed consideration of the theoretical and practical applications of Dewey's thought to Jewish education.[13] Specifically, he has suggested that contemporary Jewish educational theory consider the import of two aspects of Dewey's philosophy. The first is to relate study "to problems, tasks, and actions."[14] The second is to recognize the particular value of the educational process rather than being concerned solely with reaching a particular end-point as a result of the learning experience. Calling for an authentic translation of these problem-oriented and process dimensions of Dewey's thought into Jewish language, Rosenak provides useful examples of congruence between Deweyan deliberation and halakhic problem-solving in relating sacred text to conduct while urging caution to avoid the potential reduction of traditional Jewish principles to contemporary secular norms.[15]

Many traditional religious educators tend to be even more circumspect in utilizing Dewey, assuming a dissonance or irrelevance of much of his thought for normative Jewish religious education. Rosenak is helpful in articulating this ambivalence toward Dewey and in asking questions that may lead to finding a place for a portion of Dewey's thought in such traditional, educational contexts: "What, if anything, can contemporary Jewish educators whose orientation is traditional or even explicitly religious, learn from the iconoclastic Dewey?"[16] He further asks, "Can frameworks be created for the kind of deliberations Dewey saw as essential to intelligent resolution of problems without adopting his polemical opposition to religious truths that claim the right to authoritatively form and inform experience?"[17]

In these examples, Rosenak is employing what I call a supplementary-intersectional approach of relating Dewey to Jewish educational principles, practices, and aspirations. He searches for and finds ways in which beneficial interaction might take place between two seemingly dissonant educational sources: Deweyan deliberative inquiry into problems, on the one hand, and religious truth claims, on the other. Often the former is seen as efficacious only to the extent that it does not encroach on the latter.[18] Fundamentally, the question remains: "Can genuine faith, commitment and commandments live together with authentic deliberation and the ability to deal with perplexity and problems?" Can there be a Jewish education "that takes seriously both the Transcendent and the mundanely experiential, the perennial and the problematic?"[19] Rosenak thus emphasizes the points of consonance—primarily the practical, problem-solving dimensions of Dewey's theory of inquiry—that may complement a more essentialist, normative religious framework.[20]

As I will suggest, Dewey's notion of transcendence is more evocative and elusive than what he calls "the anticipation of future possible consequences."[21] This is, perhaps, what Rosenak alludes to in pointing out Dewey's affinity with "implicit religiosity" and with the social, communal purposes of education.[22] Yet Rosenak tends to emphasize Dewey's potential for helping educators develop the ability "to recognize" and "deal with" the "problems in contemporary Jewish life," in particular those "problems that arise out of immediate experience."[23] Most relevant to Jewish education, then, would be Dewey's emphasis on "problems, tasks and actions" that are responsive to what he calls "anticipations of the possible."[24]

The editors of the landmark work, *Visions for Jewish Education*,[25] also promote Dewey as a vital supplement to help Jewish educators and their students adapt to the unique challenges of modern society and to the new epistemic demands of scientific inquiry[26]:

> Experience in this [Deweyan] light approximates experiment as practiced in modern science . . . Modern science sees practice as the primary source of our general knowledge of nature, for its method is one of experimentation carried out deliberately in the interest of inquiry. The key to Dewey's idea of education is to conceive the school as an active environment for learning, encouraging the connection of the student's intentional acts with their consequences, in such a way as to promote an enhanced understanding of oneself and one's environment . . . "Learning by doing" is thus seen not only to derive from a philosophical vision of meaning, but also to respond to the twin challenges of modern science and the new social forces sweeping America. Far from a mere emphasis on unguided activity, it provides systematic depth and range to an educational practice undergoing challenge by new circumstances.[27]

Again, in this formulation, Dewey's principal value is supplementary, methodological, "systematic," and adaptive, effectively guiding religious educators to face the "challenges" of the particular "new circumstances" of modern society.

To be sure, these applications of Dewey are helpful and provocative, demonstrating some of his potential far-reaching impact on Jewish educational theory and experience. Yet beyond the significant methodological dimensions of Dewey's theories of inquiry, experience-centered education, and democracy, little attention has been given to how his philosophy as a whole can engage more broadly in a conversation with the transcendent, spiritual dimensions of Jewish educational experience.

Nevertheless, there is wide recognition of a "pragmatic turn" in the study of religion and ethics today. Extending and reformulating Dewey's twentieth-century pragmatism, many of today's pragmatists enjoin us to consider important questions of value, obligation, and spirituality. In this study, I am continuing this discourse, suggesting that taking pragmatism seriously implies concern for questions such as: What is to be done in view of my relationships, interdependencies, and obligations toward the other?[28] And how might we "recover our sense of mystery?"[29] I therefore consider the potential of engaging Dewey's discourse more broadly and in relation to that of R. Ḥayyim of Volozhin. Using the terminology of chapter 2, I will show how their interaction serves as a "source" for educational theory, how the relationship becomes what Buchler would call "transordinal," and how it might develop into what Oakeshott would consider a "conversation."[30]

LURIANIC KABBALAH

In order to engage R. Ḥayyim's discourse with modern educational theory, it is first necessary to recall his kabbalistic framework and language, in particular the Kabbalah as it developed in the thought of R. Isaac Luria (1534–1572) and his school in sixteenth-century Safed. R. Ḥayyim provides original interpretations and applications of Kabbalah and the Zohar[31] and, like most of his rabbinic and hasidic contemporaries, these sources' discourses coincide with much of his own.

A fundamental theological and metaphysical question informs the Kabbalah of R. Isaac Luria and his school's conceptions of God, nature, and creation:[32] In kabbalistic terms, God both surrounds and fills the entire material and spiritual cosmos. If this is the case, how can there be distinctions between objects, behaviors, norms, people, even between life and death? Put differently, if there is nothing in existence but God, what room is left for the creation of a world and human life, even if they exist in relation to Him?[33] An answer to this question is expressed in the concept of "*tsimtsum*," which may be translated as a divine "recoiling," "withdrawal," "narrowing," or "contraction." According to Luria's interpretation of the concept of *tsimtsum*, God created the space for creation by withdrawing in order to fill this new void.[34] Creation thus takes place through emanations from the unfathomable, infinite, incomprehensible God (*eyn sof*), who is completely unified (i.e., without any intrinsic distinctions), whose light flows from Him to create the spiritual and material cosmos. And this light is reflexive, as it turns back to God. The world's creation and existence, then, is a sustained process of God's "withdrawing" or "making space" for His emanations and for those emanations' returning again to the infinite, incomprehensible God. Without this sustained cyclical, spiritual organicity, the world and all that it contains would cease to exist.

This relationship between God and nature is based on the understanding that a primordial, spiritual, incorporeal "Adam" was brought into being at the beginning of creation, constituting the entire cosmos. As Scholem notes, this "primal disposition" has enduring implications:

> In his primal disposition, the origin of the elements of his soul, and their relation to specific levels in the structure of the worlds, man was tied to the totality of the universe. There was a certain sympathy between himself and the world rooted in his spiritual makeup, whereby each individual element of his structure reflected back upon the level from whence it came.[35]

Thus, this Adam's soul is inextricably woven into the fabric of the universe. With a series of cosmic ruptures and transformations,[36] five levels of "worlds" emanated from the Godhead. From highest to lowest these are: *adam kadmon* (primordial man), *atsilut* (emanation), *beri'ah* (creation), *yetsirah* (formation), and *asiyah* ("doing"). Each human soul, too, assumed different levels of being, which correspond to these worlds. Often, three levels of the soul are identified in kabbalistic literature: *nefesh*, *ru'aḥ*, and *neshamah.*[37] The *nefesh* corresponds to the lowest world of *asiyah* (doing); *ru'aḥ* corresponds to the world of *yetsirah* (formation); and the *neshamah* corresponds to *beri'ah* (creation) and sometimes even *atsilut* (emanation).[38] At birth, only the portion of the soul called "*nefesh*" is merged with one's body. Depending on the *nefesh*'s eventual merit, it is desirable that it be joined by the supernal *ru'aḥ*, and in certain ways, by the even the most transcendent level of the soul, the *neshamah.*[39] As Scholem explains, with the desired unity of the two higher levels of the soul (*ru'aḥ* and *neshamah*) with the lower level (*nefesh*), one's "entire environment is seen as a cosmic 'energy field' for one's soul."[40] This desired unity recalls the original identity between cosmos and man that forms the basis for an enduring, intimately intertwined relationship of the human soul with the physical and spiritual worlds.

The Meaning of Human Conduct and Perspective

R. Ḥayyim offers a particular interpretation of the Lurianic concept of *tsimtsum*—the primordial divine withdrawal, contraction, and concealment from the world of creation and human experience.[41] Following his teacher, the Vilna Gaon, R. Ḥayyim interprets *tsimtsum* as relating to knowledge and intelligibility rather than to the cosmos's actual metaphysical condition.[42] So to R. Ḥayyim, *tsimtsum* results in a radical distinction between perspectives: "from our perspective" (*mitsidenu*; lit., "from our side") and "from God's perspective" (*mitsido*; lit., "from His side"). It is within the post-*tsimtsum* world, specifically, from "our perspective" (*mitsidenu*), that we carry out deeds (*ma'aseh*), speaking (*dibur*), and thinking (*maḥshavah*).[43] Despite the metaphysical truth of God's completely filling and surrounding the cosmos and the illusory visibility of an actual cosmos (which we cannot understand, since it can only be understood from God's perspective), this very reality, this truth, can dissolve the meaning that human beings make of temporal and spatial divisions, emotions, desirable patterns of conduct, and halakhic life.

Surprisingly, Dewey's language is helpful here, resonating with R. Ḥayyim's warning against emphasizing esoteric inquiries that actually lead one away from halakhah and from Talmudic erudition. Dewey warns against a type of metaphysical inquiry that "identifies knowledge with the beholding or grasp of self-sufficient objects," in that it leads to "the conclusion that Being and knowledge compel 'antinomianism.'"[44] This unnecessary and problematic search for a metaphysical absolute "truth" leads us to the point where "certain problems inevitably force themselves upon us . . . [and] all efforts at solution are hopeless."[45] Indeed, for R. Ḥayyim, struggling to comprehend a self-sufficient acosmic reality is precisely what leads to antinomian tendencies. Though his specific subjects are different from Dewey's, R. Ḥayyim's concern regarding inquiry into the world's self-sufficiency is paramount, as such inquiry could eclipse the essential human role of breathing life into the world through conduct, speech, and thought.[46]

Like other kabbalists, for R. Ḥayyim there are multiple interdependent levels of spiritual worlds (עולמות). He makes a special contribution to this discourse in arguing that one's spiritual and physical being and the worlds' very being are contingent on each individual's deeds (*ma'aseh* מעשה), speech (*dibur* דיבור), and thought (*maḥshavah* מחשבה). Each individual is thus a fatefully integral determinant of the worlds' enduring coming into being, dynamic restoration, and continued existence. Below I will examine R. Ḥayyim's way of expressing this constant responsibility and the need for sustained awareness and vigilance.

Deweyan scholar, Victor Kestenbaum, expresses this contingency in a manner consistent with R. Ḥayyim: "By according as much ontological dignity to possibility and contingency as to actuality and necessity, thinking and vigilance also frustrate any effort to make further thinking and vigilance unnecessary."[47] As we will see below, in Dewey's language, such vigilance comes about through a deliberative process. In such a process, we realize "positive attainment, actual enrichment of meaning and powers."[48] But attainment and enrichment, actually, are not ends. Importantly for Dewey, what we accomplish educationally "opens new vistas and sets new tasks, creates new aims and stimulates new efforts. The facts are not such as to yield unthinking optimism and consolation; for they render it impossible to rest upon attained goods."[49]

In a different context, Nussbaum sees this kind of vigilance as a convergence of thought and action that transcends all boundaries—cultural, political, gender, racial, and religious.[50] Vigilance, then, must have an ever-extending arc of vision that actualizes human capabilities throughout the world. For Nussbaum, such constant attention takes the form of ongoing "self-criticism" toward one's own praxis and tradition and a perennial sense of belonging to "a heterogeneous nation, and world," in all of its diversity. Most important is what she calls "the narrative imagination" that heightens compassionate vigilance by strengthening our "ability to think what it might be like to be in the shoes of a person very different from oneself, indeed a whole range of such persons."[51]

Though operating within a distinct cultural, ontological horizon, seemingly removed from modern and contemporary pragmatic, rational, socio-political assumptions and concerns, R. Ḥayyim has his own notions of human vigilance and influence. These are expressed in his interpretation of Genesis 1:27 and 9:6. In his interpretation, he extends vigilance and influence to a cosmic, metaphysical level. The respective passages read: "God (*Elohim*) created humankind in His image; in the image of God (*Elohim*) did He create it "[52] (וַיִּבְרָא אֱלֹהִים אֶת-הָאָדָם בְּצַלְמוֹ, בְּצֶלֶם אֱלֹהִים בָּרָא אֹתוֹ) and "For in the image of God (*Elohim*) did He create humankind"[53] (כִּי בְּצֶלֶם אֱלֹהִים, עָשָׂה אֶת-הָאָדָם).

Commenting on these scriptural verses, R. Ḥayyim suggests:

> זהו "ויברא אלקים את האדם בצלמו בצלם אלקים וגו'. כי בצלם אלקים עשה וגו'." שכמו שהוא ית' שמו הוא האלקים בעל הכחות הנמצאים בכל העולמות כולם ומסדרם ומנהיגם כל רגע כרצונו. כן השליט רצונו יתברך את האדם שיהא הוא הפותח והסוגר של כמה אלפי רבואות כחות ועולמות. עפ"י כל פרטי סדרי הנהגותיו בכל עניניו בכל עת ורגע ממש. כפי שרשו העליון של מעשיו ודבוריו ומחשבותיו. כאלו הוא ג"כ הבעל כח שלהם כביכול.

> This is the meaning of "God (*Elohim*) created humankind in His image, in the image of God (*Elohim*), did He create it" (Gen. 1:27) [and] "For in the image of God (*Elohim*) did he create humankind" (Gen. 9:6). He, blessed be His name, is God (*Elohim*), the Master of all forces that imbue all the worlds, constantly arranging and guiding them according to His will. He has, thus, empowered the human being to activate constantly the myriad of forces and

worlds through each particular pattern of conduct in all one's affairs, according to the transcendent essence of one's deeds, speech, and thoughts. It is as if one is also the master of these forces, as it were.[54]

R. Ḥayyim here highlights the particular use of the word "*Elohim*," pointing out that this form represents God's (*Elohim*'s) being "the Master of all forces" (בעל הכוחות כולם).[55] To R. Ḥayyim, by stating that human beings are created in the image of "*Elohim*," Scripture emphasizes that each human being is, in an important sense, "the master of all forces." This sense of the extensive, transcendent power in one's deeds, speech, and thoughts provides a basis for sustained vigilance, judiciousness, and thoughtful conduct:

כדי שיתבונן כל אחד לפי שכלו והשגתו עד היכן מגיעים כל פרטי מעשיו ודבוריו ומחשבותיו וכל עניניו בהעולמות והכוחת עליונים ותחתונים, ויתפעל ויתעורר מזה לעשות . . . ועל ידי זה יגרם תקונים יותר גדולים בהעולמות.

When each person, relative to one's intellect and comprehension, becomes cognizant of the extent to which all particular deeds, speech, thoughts, and affairs reach the supernal and lower worlds and powers, one will be motivated and inspired to act . . . Each person, then, will cause restorations of ever increasing magnitudes in the worlds.[56]

Indeed, to R. Ḥayyim, man is the "living soul," "*nefesh ha-ḥayyim*," of the cosmos:

לכן העולמות מתנהגים על ידי מעשי האדם. כי המה כפי נטייתם מעוררים שורש נשמתו העליונה שהיא נפש חיה שלהם.

The worlds, thus, conduct themselves through one's deeds. For each [deed], in its own way, inspires the soul's transcendent essence which is their [the worlds'] living soul.[57]

With this constant influence on the cosmos, no deed, speech, or thought is ever lost; one's reach is unfathomable:

אמנם יבין וידע ויקבע במחשבותיו שכל פרטי מעשיו ודבוריו ומחשבותיו כל עת ורגע לא אתאבידו ח"ו, ומה רבו מעשיו ומאד גדלו ורמו, שכל אחת עולה כפי שרשה לפעל פעולתה בגבהי מרומים בעולמות וצחצחות האורות העליונים.

Indeed, one should come to know, understand, and determine that each and every aspect of one's conduct, speech, and thoughts never perishes, God forbid, and that one's conduct becomes manifold, ascending to very exalted heights.[58]

R. Ḥayyim's articulation of the unlimited consequences of human conduct may be illuminated by Dewey's notion of the "infinite reach of an act."[59] For both, the meaning of an act is in its consequences. First, let's hear Dewey:

> When an event has meaning, its potential consequences become its integral and funded feature. When the potential consequences are important and repeated, they form the very nature and essence of a thing, its defining, identifying, and distinguishing form.[60]

And

> After all, the object of foresight of consequences is not to predict the future. It is to ascertain the meaning of present activities and to secure, so far as possible, a present activity with a unified meaning.[61]

The "funded feature" of an event is its "potential consequences." In an analogous sense, for example, R. Ḥayyim argues that the consequences of Torah study and innovative interpretation are not their predicted termini; rather, the potential consequences bring meaning to the activity.

> חדושין אמיתים דאורייתא המתחדשין ע״י האדם אין ערוך לגודל נוראות נפלאות ענינם ופעולתם למעלה. שכל מלה ומלה פרטית המתחדשת מפי האדם, הקב״ה נשיק לה ומעשר לה. ונבנה ממנה עולם חדש בפני עצמו.

> When one offers authentic innovative interpretations of Torah, their awesome wonders and supernal effects are invaluable. For each and every innovative word from one's mouth is touched by God, enriching it, as an entirely new world is then constructed from it.[62]

To be sure, R. Ḥayyim's notion of consequences is substantially different from that of Dewey. Nevertheless, there are significant structural similarities in the way they relate consequences to meaning. For R. Ḥayyim, the anticipation of being touched by God and constructing an entirely new world brings meaning to the experience of learning and interpretation. As we will see in chapter 5, this parallelism extends to R. Ḥayyim's concepts of educational means, ends, and ideals, and their relationships to deeds, speech, and thought.

The notion of the reach of human conduct is also informed by Nussbaum's concept of leading the mind "forward . . . into ever widening thought and action,"[63] as the educator cultivates a deep, enduring, compassionate sense of belonging to "a heterogeneous nation—and world" that is infinitely extensive.[64] For Nussbaum, the way we need to engage the world's pragmata is by cultivating our potential capabilities and utilizing them to feel, think, and act in a way that reaches beyond the immediately visible, beyond what appear as our limited contiguities to the world. Even the out-of-sight, very remote objects, individuals, and collectives present themselves to us as relevant. This is a central purpose for education. Fostering "the central human capabilities" needs to transcend differences among and within cultures, communities, families, genders, races, and nationalities, thus becoming a universal educational ethos.[65] The arc of action must extend far beyond what we can empirically witness and directly experience, thus ever broadening an educator's "bounds of concern."[66]

In specifying these capabilities, Nussbaum includes those that involve the use of "senses, imagination, and thought":

> Being able to use the senses, to imagine, think, and reason—and to do these things in a "truly human" way, a way informed and cultivated by an adequate education, including, but by no means limited to, literacy and basic mathematical and scientific training. Being able to use imagination and thought in connection with experiencing and producing works and events of one's own choice, religious, literary, musical, and so forth.[67]

Extending these capabilities into the realm of emotions, Nussbaum describes emotional capability as "being able to have attachments to things and people outside ourselves; . . . to love, to grieve, to experience longing, gratitude, and justified anger."[68] The integration of the capabilities of sense, imagination, and thought with emotional attachments, forms the basis for the educational agenda of "implementing rational compassion."[69] Rational compassion allows us to cultivate the habit of "empathy and the judgment of similar possibilities," so that students can develop the "ability to imagine the experiences of others and to participate in their sufferings."[70]

Nussbaum thus can help us understand R. Ḥayyim's view of the earthly and supernal extensiveness of human conduct as an ethos of conscious, proactive pursuit of the ever-widening potential reach of our capabilities. Nussbaum suggests that the concept of "world" is extensive geographically, conceptually, and morally, including what Emmanuel Levinas (in his own interpretation of R. Ḥayyim's notion of "worlds") calls "spiritual collectivities, people, and structures."[71]

For R. Ḥayyim, Dewey, and Nussbaum, the possibilities in the extensive reach of human conduct bring meaning to the educational experience. Though, to be sure, their conceptions of "extensiveness" and "world" are different, there are, nevertheless, powerful structural affinities among them. Equally important, they all give profound importance to potential consequences as a source of meaning, motivation, and inspiration. For R. Ḥayyim, as much as for Dewey and Nussbaum, the "integral and funded feature" of an event—educational or otherwise—is "its potential consequences." For educational experiences, this potentiality of consequence forms their "very nature and essence."[72] In chapter 5, we will return to R. Ḥayyim's and Dewey's notions of potential consequences and their relationship to educational means, ends, and ideals.

Humility

Equally important to R. Ḥayyim is that this sense of being "the master of all forces" with an infinite reach must be tempered with an abiding humility. He develops this notion in his interpretation of *Pirke Avot* 1:4. This mishnaic passage reads:

יהי ביתך בית ועד לחכמים, והוי מתאבק בעפר רגליהם, והוי שותה בצמא את דבריהם.

> May your home be a meeting place for the sages. Cower (or struggle) in the dust at their feet and drink their words with thirst.

Accentuating a meaning of "*mitabek*" (מתאבק) as "struggle," rather than the alternative understanding in this context as "to cower" or "to be covered with dust," R. Ḥayyim interprets the text's assertion that this intellectual struggle should take place at the "dust of the feet" of the teacher:

> וזהו שאמר "יהי ביתך בית ועד לחכמים והוי מתאבק" מלשון "וַיֵּאָבֵק אִישׁ עִמּוֹ" (בראשית ל"ב, כה) שהוא עניין התאבקות מלחמה. כי מלחמת מצוה היא. וכן אנו נגד רבותינו הקדושים אשר בארץ ונשמתם בשמי מרום המחברים המפורסמים, וספריהם אתנו, הנה על ידי הספרים אשר בבתינו, בתינו הוא בית ועד לחכמים אלה, הוזהרנו גם כן וניתן לנו רשות להתאבק וללחום בדבריהם ולתרץ קושייתם ולא לישא פני איש, רק לאהוב האמת. אבל עם כל זה, ייזהר בנפשו מלדבר בגאווה וגודל לבב באשר מצא מקום לחלוק, וידמה כי גדול הוא כרבו או כמחבר הספר אשר הוא משיג עליו, וידע בלבבו כי כמה פעמים לא יבין דבריו וכוונתו, ולכן יהיה אך בענווה יתרה, באמרו "אם איני כדאי, אך תורה היא וללמוד אני צריך." וזהו שאמר "הווי מתאבק," כנ"ל, אך בתנאי: "בעפר רגליהם." רוצה לומר: בענווה והכנעה ולדון לפניהם בקרקע.

> The word "mitabek" is from the verse, "*Vaye'avek ish imo*" (Genesis 32:25), meaning wrestling or struggling in battle, for this is a *milḥemet mitsvah* ("an obligatory war"). Similarly, we struggle with the words of our holy rabbis (who are on earth, though their souls are in the heavens) and with the renowned authors whose books are amongst us. Indeed, through the books being in our houses, our homes are transformed into meeting places for the sages. However, although given license to grapple and battle with their opinions in order to resolve their problematics (since one has been instructed not to favor any person, but to love only the truth), one nonetheless must be circumspect, avoiding speaking with pride and arrogance. For even if having reason to differ, one should imagine that this person is as respected as one's own teacher or as the author of the book from which one is learning, and assume that there could be times when one may misunderstand his interpretations and intentions. Therefore one should be very humble, affirming, "Though I am unworthy, this is the Torah, and I must learn it." This, then, is what is meant above by

> "struggle," (*mitabek*): on the condition that it is "at the dust of their feet," meaning with humility and deference, deliberating on the ground in their presence.[73]

To R. Ḥayyim, then, the intellectual struggle must take place assertively but with the utmost humility. I will consider Dewey's and R. Ḥayyim's notions of educational struggle and effort in chapter 5. It is important here to note how Dewey is helpful in articulating the rationale for humility, illuminating R. Ḥayyim's concept of humble intellectual struggle:

> Humility is more demanded at our moments of triumph than at those of failure. For humility is not a cad-fish self-depreciation. It is the sense of our slight inability even with our best intelligence and effort to command events; a sense of our dependence upon forces that go their way without our wish and plan. Its purport is not to relax effort but to make us prize every opportunity of present growth.[74]

Similarly, Dewey points out the dangers of "spiritual egotism" if students are primarily concerned with the "state of their character" and the "goodness of their souls":

> Some become engrossed in spiritual egotism. They are preoccupied with the state of their character, concerned for the purity of their motives and the goodness of their souls. The exaltation of conceit which sometimes accompanies this absorption can produce a corrosive inhumanity which exceeds the possibilities of any other known form of selfishness.[75]

A humble disposition with regard to one's accomplishing a particular level of spiritual intentionality or motivational purity is remarkably resonant with R. Ḥayyim's (in part, as a subtle polemic against hasidism) exhorting students to avoid arrogance and boastfulness (התנשאות לב).

> אמנם תשמר והזהר מאד שלא תזוח דעתך עליך ותתנשא לבבך מאשר אתה עובד את בוראך בטהרת המחשבה . . . שאף אם לא יתראה ההתנשאות לעיני ב"א רק במחשבת הלב לבד בעיני עצמו היא תועבה ממש לפניו יתב׳.

> Be particularly careful not to become haughty by boasting that you serve your Creator with a purity of thought . . . For even if your arrogance is not apparent to others, even if it is only in your thoughts, it is an actual abomination before God.[76]

While Dewey's language is quite different, one can imagine R. Ḥayyim's concern with *hitnas'ut ba-lev* ("boastfulness," "arrogance") leading to what Dewey calls "spiritual egotism" that results in a "corrosive inhumanity."

ELITIST VS. DEMOCRATIC PRINCIPLES IN R. ḤAYYIM OF VOLOZHIN'S EDUCATIONAL THOUGHT

Notwithstanding this humble disposition toward one's learning, it is important to note that R. Ḥayyim's project was, on one level, for a limited group of elite students and scholars who demonstrated extraordinary abilities and devotion. This apparent elitism presents a challenge to any effort to recognize a commonality with the democratic, pluralist, and universal philosophies of Dewey and Nussbaum; their approaches assume a universally inclusive, democratic educational purpose.

But it is important to realize that, for R. Ḥayyim, concentrating and intensifying study in Volozhin must be seen in the context of this broader, inclusive purpose. In this regard, R. Ḥayyim refers to the prospective distinguished students, teachers, and supporters of the Volozhin Yeshiva with positive attributes of loving Torah and pursuing its insights, thereby contributing to further learning and strengthening Torah in the world: אוהבי התורה, מהם מפישי התורה, דרכיה ועמקיה ומחזיקים בדקיה ומהם תומכיה ומחזיקים לומדיה ("lovers of Torah, who, among them expand its ways and its profundities, strengthening its examination, as well as those who support and maintain its students").[77] For R. Ḥayyim, this ingathering of "lovers of Torah" is part of a strategy to address the sparse condition of Torah study in the world in general. He considers establishing the Volozhin Yeshiva a necessary step in that it would begin to concentrate Torah scholarship and would have a centripetal pull on those for whom the desire and acumen are genuine. This infusion of young scholars would reverse the diffuse condition of what scant Torah knowledge exists:

> כל מבקשי ה' ית"ש נפוצים המה כצאן אשר אין להם רועה' לרעות את עם ד'
> המתאווים ללין בעומקא של הלכה ואמיתה של תורה.

> All those who search for God, blessed be His name, are scattered like sheep who have no shepherd to herd the people of God who long to lodge in the depth of halakha and in the truth of Torah.[78]

Establishing the yeshiva would respond, in part, to the problem of learning's diminution and dissipation; it would awaken the desire for further learning, and would provide an intellectual, spiritual energy.

The interdependence of elite, selective education and inclusive, extensive education is also addressed elsewhere in R. Ḥayyim's writings, albeit obliquely. His *Nefesh Ha-Ḥayyim* displays the dynamics of this dual purpose, in part, through its reference to the import of the deeds of "each Jew" (כל איש ישראל):

> וזאת תורת אדם, כל איש ישראל, אל יאמר בלבו ח"ו, כי מה אני ומה כחי לפעול במעשי השפלים שום ענין בעולם. אמנם יבין וידע ויקבע במחשבות לבו שכל פרטי מעשיו ודבוריו ומחשבותיו כל עת ורגע לא אתאבידו ח"ו ומה רבו מעשיו ומאד גדלו ורמו שכל א' עולה כפי שרשה.
>
> This is the human doctrine. Each Jew should avoid saying to himself, God forbid, "What am I and what power do I have to affect anything in the world through my lowly deeds?" Indeed, one should come to know, understand, and determine that each and every aspect of one's conduct, speech, and thoughts never perishes, God forbid, and that one's conduct becomes manifold, ascending to very exalted heights.[79]

And as he opens the final section of the *Nefesh Ha-Ḥayyim*, R. Ḥayyim reaffirms the universal Jewish obligation of Torah study:

> עוד זאת אמרתי לבא במגלת ספר כתוב, בגודל חיוב של עסק התורה על כל איש ישראל יום ולילה, ולהרחיב מעט הדבור בלשון מדברת גדולת יקר תפארתה ומעלתה של התורה.
>
> As I have said would be forthcoming in this treatise, the magnitude of the obligation for Torah study extends to all Jews—day and night. And they should increase, even slightly, their speaking aloud of the greatness of the precious splendor and virtue of the Torah.[80]

Yet it is also clear that there is a class of students that R. Ḥayyim believes to have special gifts of understanding. This class is delimited even further when considering those for whom esoteric knowledge is appropriate, "whom God has graced and provided with understanding . . . those who are the most understanding among the nation whom God has graced."[81] (שמי אשר חננו ה' וחלק לו בבינה והמבינים בעם אשר חננם הוא ית"ש).

R. Ḥayyim is thus focusing his immediate, direct attention on the most capable students as a step in the longer-term effort to make Torah learning as extensive and authentic as possible. It is for the scholars of each generation to contribute to the enduring, life-giving sustenance of Torah in the world. Each teacher strengthens the world and adds vital power to the cosmos through erudition and teaching—"adding lessons to hermeneutic discussions" (להוסיף לקח בפלפול).[82] Teachers do not simply guide inquiry into reified classics. They provide dynamic, life-giving insights through "the paths of authentic inquiry" (ללמוד דרכי העיון האמת).[83] In chapter 5, I will revisit the relationship between R. Ḥayyim's and Dewey's notions of "authentic inquiry."

CONCLUSION

In this chapter I have considered the methodological bases for interdiscursive engagement, with particular attention to R. Ḥayyim of Volozhin, John Dewey, and Martha Nussbaum. In doing so, I have begun to demonstrate their functioning as sources for interpreting each other and for Jewish educational theory. I have also pointed out some examples of shared traits across distinctive complexes and have begun an interdiscursive conversation in which each discourse is challenged, articulated, interpreted, and augmented for Jewish educational theorizing. In the next two chapters I will examine an important educational dimension in these thinkers' discourses—the relationship between means, ends, and ideals.

NOTES

1. On the concept of "query," see chapter 2.
2. Charles Taylor, "Comparison, History, Truth" in *Philosophical Arguments* (Cambridge: Harvard University Press, 1995), 151.
3. Taylor, "Comparison, History, Truth," 158–159.
4. Calvin O. Schrag, *Radical Reflection and the Origin of the Human Sciences* (West Lafayette, IN: Purdue University Press, 1980), 18.
5. Calvin O. Schrag, *The Resources of Rationality: A Response to the Postmodern Challenge* (Indianapolis: Indiana University Press, 1992), 163.
6. Alan Brill, "Judaism in Culture: Beyond the Bifurcation of Torah and Madda," *The Edah Journal* 4, no. 1 (2004): 21.
7. Brill, "Judaism in Culture," 26.
8. Richard John Neuhaus, "The Public Square: The American Mind," *First Things: A Monthly Journal of Religion and Public Life* 118, no. 1 (2001): 67
9. Alan G. Phillips, Jr., "John Dewey and His Religious Critics," *Religion and Education* 29, no. 1 (2002): 31.
10. Isa Aron, "Deweyan Deliberation as a Model for Decision-Making in Jewish Education," *Studies in Jewish Education* 2 (1984): 136–149.
11. Benjamin M. Jacobs, "Socialization into a Civilization: The Dewey-Kaplan Synthesis in American Jewish Schooling in the Early 20th Century," *Religious Education* 104, no. 2 (2009): 149–165. Jacobs compares "John Dewey's theory of education as socialization and Mordecai Kaplan's theory of Judaism as a civilization" and how they "together served as an ideological base and pedagogical framework for the creation of 'progressive,' 'reconstructed' American Jewish school programs in the early twentieth century (1910s–1930s)," 149.
12. An exception is M. Rosenak's discussion of the intersection between Dewey's theory of deliberation and halakhic problem solving. See Michael Rosenak, "From Strength to Strength: Dewey and Religious Jewish Education," *Courtyard: A Journal of Research and Thought in Jewish Education* 1 (1999–2000): 66–80, and Michael Rosenak, "Zelophehad's Daughters, Religion, and Jewish Religious Education," *Journal of Jewish Education* 71 (2005): 3–21.
13. M. Rosenak, "Dewey and Religious Jewish Education" and "Zelophehad's Daughters."
14. M. Rosenak, "Dewey and Religious Jewish Education," 66–80.
15. M. Rosenak, "Dewey and Religious Jewish Education," 66–80.
16. M. Rosenak, "Dewey and Religious Jewish Education," 68.
17. M. Rosenak, "Dewey and Religious Jewish Education," 75.
18. It is important to note, however, that Rosenak points out how the civilizational approach to Judaism of Mordecai Kaplan has found Dewey to be, not only compatible, but enhancing a type of religious education that Rosenak characterizes as "soft," "implicit," or "deliberative-inductive." M. Rosenak, "Dewey and Religious Jewish Education," 66–80 and M. Rosenak, *Commandments and Concerns*.
19. M. Rosenak, "Dewey and Religious Jewish Education," 75.
20. M. Rosenak, "Dewey and Religious Jewish Education," 71–80.
21. John Dewey, *Democracy and Education*, 136.
22. M. Rosenak, "Zelophehad's Daughters," 5.
23. M. Rosenak, "Dewey and Religious Jewish Education."

24. In this regard, M. Rosenak notes a parallel to Dewey in "the halakhic requirement that all learning of Torah should be for the sake of action." "Dewey and Religious Jewish Education."

25. Seymour Fox, Israel Scheffler, and Daniel Marom, ed. *Visions of Jewish Education.* (New York: Cambridge University Press, 2003), Introduction.

26. On similar previous emphases see Walter Ackerman, "The Americanization of Jewish Education," *Judaism* 24, no. 4 (1974): 420–435; Meir Ben-Horin, "John Dewey and Jewish Education," *Religious Education* 55 (1960): 201–202; Isaac Berkson, "John Dewey's Philosophy of Religion: Its Pragmatist Background," *Judaism* 3, no. 2 (1954): 132–141; Isaac Berkson, "John Dewey's Philosophy: Ethical and Religious Aspects," *Judaism* 3, no. 3 (1954): 209–220; Ronald Kronish, "John Dewey's Influence on Jewish Educators: The Case of Alexander M. Dushkin," *Teachers College Record* 83, no. 3 (1982): 419–33; Kerry Orlitzky, "The Impact of John Dewey on Jewish Education," *Religious Education* 81, no. 1 (1986): 5–18.

27. Fox, *et al.*, *Visions*, 9–10.

28. Ruth Anna Putnam, "Taking Pragmatism Seriously," *Hilary Putnam: Pragmatism and Realism*, ed. James Conant and Urszula M. Zeglen (New York: Routledge, 2002), 7–11.

29. Hilary Putnam, "Pragmatism and Non-scientific Knowledge," *Hilary Putnam: Pragmatism and Realism*, ed. James Conant and Urszula M. Zeglen (New York: Routledge, 2002), 24.

30. See chapter 2.

31. *The Zohar* is a thirteenth-century work of Jewish mysticism and Kabbalah. The work has had a substantial impact on Jewish mysticism.

32. These are questions concerning cosmogony and theosophy. Cosmogony is the theoretical account of the universe's creation. Theosophy is systematic speculation on the relationship between the nature of God and our knowledge of nature.

33. Theologians and philosophers refer to this as the problem of acosmism, "the doctrine that the universe does not exist, or that there is no universe distinct from God." "acosmism, n." OED Online. March 2012. Oxford University Press. http://www.oed.com.ilsprod.lib.neu.edu/viewdictionaryentry/Entry/1673 (accessed May 14, 2012).

34. As Gershom Scholem succinctly explains, in *tsimtsum*, "the existence of the universe is made visible by a process of shrinkage of God." Gershom Scholem, *Major Trends in Jewish Mysticism* (New York: Schocken Books, 1995), 260.

35. Gershom Scholem, *On the Mystical Shape of the Godhead: Basic Concepts in the Kabbalah*, trans. J. Neugroschel (New York: Schocken Books, 1991): 230–231.

36. Scholem, *Mystical Shape*, 229.

37. In many cases, five levels are specified.

38. Eisenman, "Structure and Content."

39. Scholem, *Mystical Shape*, 234; Eisenman, "Structure and Content."

40. Scholem, *Mystical Shape*, 240.

41. In the kabbalistic tradition, *tsimtsum* caused a cosmic shattering of vessels (*shevirat kelim*) that must be restored to wholeness.

42. For R. Ḥayyim, human understanding is thus limited to the results of God's deeds and to manifestations of His will. NH 3:5–6.

43. Much of the third section (*Sha'ar Gimel*) of the *Nefesh Ha-Ḥayyim* makes this critical distinction between perspectives as the meaning of *tsimtsum*.

44. John Dewey, *Experience and Nature* (New York: Dover, 1925/1958), 147.

45. Dewey, *Experience and Nature*, 147.

46. NH 3.

47. Victor Kestenbaum, *The Grace and the Severity of the Ideal: John Dewey and the Transcendent* (Chicago and London: University of Chicago Press, 2002), 90.

48. Dewey, *Human Nature*, 288.

49. Dewey, *Human Nature*, 288.

50. Martha Nussbaum, *Cultivating Humanity: A Classical Defense of Reform in Liberal Education* (Cambridge: Harvard University Press, 1997).

51. Martha Nussbaum, "Political Soul-making and the Imminent Demise of Liberal Education," *Journal of Social Philosophy* 37, no. 2 (2006): 309.

52. Gen. 1:27, Fox, trans.

53. Gen. 9:6.
54. NH 1:4
55. NH 1:2.
56. NH 1:22
57. NH 1:5
58. NH 1:4
59. Dewey, *Human Nature,* 263.
60. Dewey, *Experience and Nature*, 182.
61. Dewey, *Human Nature*, 206.
62. NH 4:12
63. Tagore as translated in Martha Nussbaum, "Education and Democratic Citizenship: Capabilities and Quality Education," *Journal of Human Development* 7, no. 3 (2006): 394.
64. Martha Nussbaum, "Education for Profit, Education for Freedom," *Liberal Education* 95, no. 3 (2009): 11.
65. Martha Nussbaum, *Upheavals of Thought: The Intelligence of Emotions* (Cambridge: Cambridge University Press, 2001), 416.
66. Nussbaum, *Upheavals,* 420.
67. Nussbaum, *Upheavals,* 417.
68. Nussbaum, *Upheavals,* 417.
69. Nussbaum, *Upheavals,* 417.
70. Nussbaum, *Upheavals,* 417.
71. Emmanuel Levinas, "'In the Image of God' According to Rabbi Ḥayyim Volozhiner." In *Beyond the Verse:Talmudic Readings and Lectures*, trans. G. D. Mole (Bloomington and Indianapolis: Indiana University Press, 1994), 161.
72. Dewey, *Experience and Nature*, 182.
73. RH, 4:1.
74. Dewey, *Human Nature*, 289.
75. Dewey, *Human Nature*, 7.
76. NH, Perakim: 1.
77. R. Ḥayyim of Volozhin, Public Letter to Lithuanian Jewish Communities (PL).
78. PL.
79. NH 1:4.
80. NH 4:1.
81. R. Ḥayyim of Volozhin, Introduction to the the GRA's commentary on Sifra di'tsni'vta (IS).
82. IS.
83. PL.

Chapter Four

Ends versus "The End"

Rabbi Ḥayyim of Volozhin's Non-Messianic Vision

The concepts of means, ends, and ideals are ubiquitous in the discourse on educational theory. Intermittently, a notion of messianism informs this constellation of purposes and processes in Jewish education. In those cases, theorists consider means, ends, and ideals in the context of an *ultimate* purposefulness. More often than not, however, messianism is decentered, at most a background concept in Jewish education. This background status is informed by a separation of "historical time" (*divre hayamim*) and "messianic time" (*aḥarit hayamim)* in Jewish tradition—a fundamental boundary between ends and "The End." So before I consider relationships between R. Ḥayyim's and Dewey's conceptions of means, ends, and ideals, in this chapter I evaluate the extent to which messianic aspirations frame R. Ḥayyim's theory and practice.

As mentioned in the previous chapter, R. Ḥayyim was the leading student of R. Elijah, the Gaon of Vilna. The Vilna Gaon was the leader of the rabbinic establishment, a revered Talmudist, kabbalist, and strident opponent of hasidism. In the last few years, studies have characterized R. Elijah and his circle as engaged in an active project to prepare for the messianic redemption.[1] It is not my intention here to question the accuracy of these general analyses of the circle of the GRA's thought.[2] The Gaon's narratives of Jewish learning and his depictions of the spiritual conditions of his times do indeed portray a grim picture of the efficacy of exile—a feature that, for some, is characteristic of acute messianism. Citing additional (though, as I will argue, somewhat dubious) evidence, it has been claimed that this conception of his historical context indicates that the Vilna Gaon was seeking to hasten the arrival of the days of ultimate redemption by attempting to immigrate to the Land of Israel and by expressing his intent to compose a new, resolute, final *Shulhan Arukh* (code of Jewish law).[3] Recently, Shuchat has argued that the GRA's messianic activism extended virtually to his entire school, claiming that its proponents viewed the unprecedented nadir of Torah study as a sign of proto-apocalyptic distress—the "birth pangs" of the messianic era.[4]

Both Shuchat and Morgenstern have argued that the GRA and his disciples responded to the economic, spiritual, and educational crisis of their time by seeking to bring on the ultimate redemption. Morgenstern does not specifically exclude R. Ḥayyim from this group's orientation: "The Gaon's disciples viewed contemporary history in the light of their messianic conception, thus discerning in the events of their day signs of the '*ikveta deMeshiḥa* (footsteps of the Messiah), the last stage of the Exile."[5] Apparently extending this view to the Gaon's full circle, he further claims that "this feeling was shared by his followers who remained in Europe."[6]

Shuchat specifically attempts to show that the *aliyah*[7] of a group of the GRA's students and the establishment of the Volozhin Yeshiva in 1802 by his leading student, R. Ḥayyim, were parallel, perhaps even coordinated, efforts to establish the necessary conditions for the messianic advent. The former was the terrestrial, physical effort to hasten the advent of the messianic era. And by reversing the decline of Torah study, the latter was a parallel effort to create the correct spiritual conditions for the Messiah's arrival.[8]

I will argue that R. Ḥayyim's view represents a significant departure from this messianic conception. Whether or not his position in this regard was distinct from that of the Gaon may be treated separately. Yet, to the extent that the GRA had a messianic agenda, R. Ḥayyim demonstrated his capacity and willingness to divert from it, particularly following the latter's death. His departure from the severity of the Gaon's response to hasidism is well documented.[9] Yet often his departure from his beloved teacher on theoretical matters has been overlooked. Studies on R. Ḥayyim tend to assume a derivative relationship to the Vilna Gaon, explaining the former's more moderate response to hasidism as a function of generous character and realism, rather than an integral aspect of his thought.

I maintain that R. Ḥayyim was concerned with *divre hayamim* rather than *aḥarit hayamim*[10] —with the immediate potential of the world in the context of historical time, rather than with a world to come, in the context of messianic time.[11] Before moving forward with the conversation with R. Ḥayyim and Dewey, I wish to show that R. Ḥayyim's concerns with Torah study and with other types of conduct in his era are informed by what Emmanuel Levinas calls his "remarkable 'materialism' . . . a theory of inspiration that becomes effective . . . through the control it exerts on its bodily life . . . for the worlds (but also by interpreting 'world' broadly, for spiritual collectivities, people and structures)."[12] To Levinas, Rabbi Ḥayyim maintains that our existence "for the worlds" stems from a "connaturality" in which "the life of the human individual sustains and gives life to the cosmos . . . God has subordinated his efficacy—his association with the real and the very presence of the real—to my merit or demerit . . . More important than God's omnipotence is the subordination of that power to man's ethical consent."[13] The existence of the cosmos, the stability of a dynamic, life-giving universe, is fraught with contingency because of the interdependent organic naturality shared by man and world. This contingency is constant, placing human conduct as the central determinant of the world's future.

Though I would maintain that Shuchat and Morgenstern exaggerate the messianic disposition of the GRA, R. Ḥayyim departs from even a modest messianic orientation and, significantly for this study, from the GRA's characterization of the efficacy of Jewish education in exile. R. Ḥayyim's interactions, decisions, and theoretical arguments consistently demonstrate a non-messianic character. As we will see, his theory and practice attest to a concern for the immanent and transcendent aspects of *this* world and for the relationship to its variegated pragmata.[14]

Before turning to his theory, however, I will cite examples of how R. Ḥayyim's conduct, as reported by him and by others, suggests this non-messianic character. Though evidence exists of his financial support for the group of *olim* (those who "ascend" to the Land of Israel) among the GRA's students, R. Ḥayyim distinguishes between the types of individuals who should consider *aliyah.*[15] Extant testimony on this view includes the following anecdote concerning an individual's uncle's query to R. Ḥayyim:

> ויסע דודי לוואלאז'ין לשאול בזה [בשאלת העלייה] עצת הגאון ר' חיים זצוק"ל. והשיב לו הגר"ח ז"ל בזה הלשון: "בשלמא ר' שלמה [מטאלטשין, תלמידו של ר' חיים] הוא נשמה בלוא גוף, לו יאתה לשבת בעיר הקדושה, מה שאין כן אתם ואנחנו כולנו, שנשמת אל חי בנו עם הגוף ביחד, אי אפשר לנו לנסוע שמה בעתים הללו." וחדל דודי ז"ל מלנסוע.

> My uncle traveled to Volozhin to seek advise from the Gaon, R. Ḥayyim, may the memory of the righteous be a blessing, on this [question concerning *aliyah*]. The Gaon, R. Ḥayyim, answered him as follows: "Granted, [in the case of] R. Shlomo, he is a soul without a body. He will [therefore] surely come to settle in the holy city. But this is not the case for you and all of us for whom the soul [breath] of the living God is within us together with the body, and it is thus impossible for us to travel there in these times." So my uncle, may his memory be a blessing, refrained from traveling [there].[16]

According to this anecdote, while R. Ḥayyim implicitly supports the *aliyah* of an individual of extraordinary spiritual character, he considers a broad effort to do so as a misguided encroachment on a messianic threshold.[17] Asserting an inextricable relationship between the soul and the body reflects

R. Ḥayyim's concern with the times in which he lived and his attentiveness to the problems of his day rather than with an active messianism that might be kindled through Torah study or immigration to the Land of Israel.[18]

In addition, R. Ḥayyim's respect for contradictory arguments and for differing interpretations of sacred text suggest a deferring of messianic fervor. There is no expectation of the prophet Elijah's imminent arrival, heralding the messianic era, resolving any remaining difficulties in interpreting sacred text.[19] On the contrary, debate and difference were hallmarks of R. Ḥayyim's pedagogy:

> אסור לו לתלמיד לקבל דברי רבו כשיש לו קושיות עליהם, ולפעמים יהיה האמת עם התלמיד.[20]
>
> It is forbidden for a student to accept his teacher's words when he can challenge them. For sometimes the truth will be with the student.

And

> שאין דעת בני אדם דומה זה לזה ואלו ואלו דברי אלהים חיים, ובלבד שיכויין להוציא הדין לאמיתה של תורה.
>
> Human knowledge is variegated. Yet, the seemingly disparate insights are all the words of the living God, provided that one strives to render judgment based on the Torah's truth.[21]

Such deference to individual intellectual authenticity (to be sure, within scrupulous hermeneutic norms) would not be indicative of messianic stirring that anticipates the revelation of a unitary truth behind the sacred word. By implication, it would not presume the existence, in his time, of a final legal arbiter and resolutive interpreter, even one as revered by R. Ḥayyim as R. Elijah, the Gaon of Vilna.

THE GRA'S NARRATIVE OF TORAH DECLINE

The Vilna Gaon's narratives of his era's place in the history of Jewish life and learning often reflect a grim perspective, characterized by some as indicating an acute messianic orientation. In one of his esoteric works, he narrates a regressive spiritual decline since the time of Moses. He considers the experience of exile in his era to be one of advanced spiritual decay. Referring to the prophet Ezekiel's vision of the dry bones and the prophet Isaiah's promise of redemption, he states: "Thus, we too are in the *galut* (exile), in the dispersion of the dry bones[22] until the 'spirit will pour down upon us from on high' (Isa. 32:15)."[23] Characterizing his own generation as one of advanced decay, he likens it to a generation of the "heel" (*ekev*)—an allusion to the lowly state of being in the "footsteps" of the Messiah (*ikvot mashiḥa*): "[Comprehension of the Torah and its mysteries] has progressively lessened until, in our generations, they do not comprehend but the 'heel' of *asiyah* . . . 'the footsteps of the Messiah' (*BT Sotah*, 49b)."[24] Moreover, speculations and interpretations of Kabbalah have become distorted, "lacking pristine spiritual purity, so they speak through analogies without comprehending anything."[25] Referencing the destruction of the Temple in 586 B.C.E., the Vilna Gaon summarizes the reasons for this decline: "Ever since our House was destroyed, our spirit, the crown of our heads, has gone away. We have, thus, remained only as her body without a soul."[26] Intensifying his characterization of exile, the GRA likens existence "outside the Land [of Israel]" to "being in a grave with a worm surrounding us, there being nothing on our behalf to rescue us. These [worms] are the idolaters who eat our flesh."[27] Though there were times when "there were clusters of great *yeshivot*," eventually "the flesh rotted and the bones were dispersed and scattered repeatedly."[28] These remnants of "bones" are "the Torah scholars of Israel who support the body."[29] But eventually, "the bones rot and only a scoop of decay remains of us. And it becomes the dust that cowers in the dust of our souls. So we now hope for the resurrection of the dead: 'Shake yourself free of the dust, arise!' (Isa. 52). 'And the spirit will pour down on us from on high' (Isa. 32:15)."[30]

Elsewhere, the GRA characterizes the nature of existence in exile as increasingly educationally handicapped, with the Torah's meaning having become progressively obscured:

> וכן הוא בתורה, שעתה אין אנו מקבלים שום דבר חדש בתורה כמו בזמן בהמ"ק אלא מה שאנו מוצאין כתוב בספרי הראשונים ובזמן בהמ"ק היו משקים לתורה . . . ואין לנו אלא ספיחי הראשונים הלואי להבין דבריהם.
>
> This [is the case] with regard to Torah. For now we do not receive any new insights into the Torah compared to the period of the Holy Temple, except what we find written in the books of the early sages and from the time of the Holy Temple in which they would irrigate the Torah . . . and we have only the aftergrowth of the early sages. If only [we could] comprehend their words. [31]

To the Vilna Gaon, then, this ever-thickening veil between the Torah's meaning and one's comprehension is an unavoidable, chronic, degenerative condition of exile. While, for some, this characterization may indicate an acute messianic orientation, this narrative of Torah study in exile is contrary to that of R. Ḥayyim, as we will now see.

R. ḤAYYIM'S NARRATIVE OF TORAH STUDY AND CHARACTERIZATION OF HIS ERA

R. Ḥayyim's theories of the role of human conduct, Jewish learning's historical narrative, and the relationship between educational means and ends represent significantly innovative theories, boldly diverging from the conceptions of the circle of his revered teacher concerning the meaning of these phenomena in exile. A corollary to R. Ḥayyim's theoretical framework is a de-emphasis, even explicit suppression, of messianic activism.

R. Ḥayyim's narrative of his era's historical context foregrounds human decisions and historical circumstances, rather than divine providence, as explanations for the decline of Torah study. The following excerpt from his *Nefesh Ha-Ḥayyim* is a case in point:

> דורות הראשונים היו קבועים כל ימיהם בעסק והגיון תוה"ק (תורתנו הקדושה) . . . ושלהבת אהבת תורתנו הקדושה היה בליבם כאש בוערת באהבת ויראת ה' טהורה, וכל חפצם להגדיל כבודה ולהאדירה, והרחיבו גבולם בתלמידים רבים הגונים למען תמלא הארץ דעה. וכאשר ארכו הימים. . . כמה תלמידים שמו כל קביעתם ועסקם רק בפלפולה של תורה לבד . . . ומילאו את ידם לבוא בתוכחות במוסרים ומידות, וחיברו ספרי יראה להישיר לב העם להיותם עוסקים בתורה הקדושה ובעבודה ביראת ה' טהורה . . . כי לא כוונו בהם להזניח ח"ו העסק בגופי התורה, ולהיות אך עסוק כל הימים בספרי מוסרם, אלא כוונתם רצויה היתה.
>
> והן עתה בדורות הללו בעוונותינו הרבים, נהפוך הוא. הגבוה הושפל. שכמה וכמה שמו כל עיקר קביעת לימודם רוב הימים רק בספרי יראה ומוסר . . . כי המה מלהיבים הלבבות . . . ולהתישר במידות טובות. וכתר תורה מונח בקרן זווית. (נפש החיים, שעד ד פ"א)

> The first generations were consistently occupied with reflection on the holy Torah for all of their days . . . and the flame of love of our holy Torah was in their hearts like a fire burning with love and pure awe of God. Their entire desire was to magnify its honor and glorify it. So they expanded the reach with many suited students so that the earth would be filled with knowledge. Yet as the days went on . . . some students constantly directed their attention and study solely to excessive casuistry on Torah . . . and . . . spent their entire time admonishing through moral principles and composing moralist works in order to straighten out the heart of the nation so that they would become occupied with the holy Torah and awe-filled, pure worship of God . . . They did not intend, through this, to abandon, God forbid, occupation with the essential Torah, becoming occupied constantly with moralistic works. Rather, their intent was proper. . . .
>
> But now, in these times, due to our many sins, the opposite is the case. The lofty has become lowly in that a number of them directed their primary study, most of the time, solely to moralistic and theological works . . . since these inspire one . . . to become righteous through good moral dispositions. But the crown of Torah has become forsaken.[32]

Here R. Ḥayyim foregrounds well intended, though misguided, human conduct as the presenting problem. Moreover, in characterizing earlier exilic generations as having moral and intellectual greatness as well as proper educational aspirations, R. Ḥayyim's portrayal of learning in exile is not uniformly negative. While a "lover of Zion," R. Ḥayyim does not espouse a kind of intrinsic barrenness of exile that would preclude innovation and advancement in Torah study.

After acknowledging the purity of intentions for errant actions, he expands on the educational crisis's gravity:

ועוד מעט בהמשך הזמן יוכלו להיות ח"ו ללא כהן מורה ותורה מה תהא עליה.

> Soon, with the passage of time, they might have no teaching positions, God forbid. What, then, will become of the Torah?[33]

It is important here to note that the consequence most feared by R. Ḥayyim is not the preempting of the messianic era, but the Torah's disappearance. He seeks to prevent the further weakening of what for him is the sustaining force of this world: Torah study. He is concerned with the potential destruction of meaning in this world, rather than with a messianic advent.

In his introduction to the Vilna Gaon's commentary on the section of the Zohar called *Sifra ditsniuta* ("Book of Concealment"), R. Ḥayyim provides another aspect of his narrative of Jewish learning and erudition. Considering his teacher, the Vilna Gaon, as a source of hope for the future of Torah learning, R. Ḥayyim offers his more confident vision: ברוך שומר הבטחתו לישראל . . . כי לא תשכח תורת אמת מפי זרע אמת . . . ועדיין לא זזה אהבתו מאתנו. "Blessed is He who keeps his promise to Israel . . . since the true Torah has not been forgotten from the mouth of the true seed . . . still He has not moved His love away from us."[34] God's promise to Israel here is not a reference to a messianic era; rather, R. Ḥayyim is asserting that his teacher's life and teachings are the best evidence of the eternal promise that the Torah will never be forgotten in Israel.

While attributing to the Vilna Gaon the highest level of learning and teaching, R. Ḥayyim also recognizes the teachings of Torah scholars in the past (including those of exilic eras) as further evidence of God's promise's enduring: הניח לנו ברכה ע"ע שרידים אשר ה' קורא בדורות דור דור וחכמיו. אשר מפיהם אנו חיים. ומימיהם אנו שותים. "To this day, He has left for us the blessing of remnants whom God calls 'each generation's wise ones, from whose mouths we live and from whose waters we drink."[35] These teachers and scholars have provided sustenance and life to the people of Israel from their teachings, "giving merit to the multitudes" (לזכות את הרבים). Even teachers of R. Ḥayyim's own generation (בדור האחרון הזה) function in this merit-giving way.[36]

Yet R. Ḥayyim acknowledges the level of crisis in his own generation:

הצרות תכופות והפרנסות מתמעטות. ועם ה' אלה . . . אשר בכל הגולה שכורים ולא מיין . . . ומה נאמר ונדבר בפנימיות נשמת התוה"ק אשר כל התנאים ואמוראים וכל המקובלים ונאמנים אינם מוסרים אלא ראשי פרקים . . . החכמה מאין תמצא לשכורים ולא מיין?

The troubles are frequent and the sources of making a living are becoming fewer and these people of God . . . throughout the Diaspora are intoxicated, but not from wine . . . And what can be offered or discussed regarding the essential soul of the holy Torah whose mere chapter headings are passed on to us from tannaim, amoraim, kabbalists, and the faithful . . . Where will wisdom be found for those intoxicated, though not from wine?[37]

Noting how poverty and external pressures of his time contribute to the problematic educational condition of his people, R. Ḥayyim characterizes this condition as a kind of spiritual disorientation or drunkenness, invoking the prophet Isaiah's words: וּשְׁכֻרַת, וְלֹא מִיָּיִן ("intoxicated though not from wine").[38] This condition impedes the necessary inquiry since the sacred texts require the very type of wisdom and erudition that this generation lacks.

Nevertheless, R. Ḥayyim's optimistic disposition shines forth in his letter of appeal for public support for the Volozhin Yeshiva at the time of its opening in 1802. Here R. Ḥayyim also diverts from his teacher's characterization of the masses of his generation. Expressing far more empathy, he attributes the difficulties of his generation to problematic, though understandable, human decisions. He acknowledges the degraded state of Torah: התורה שמשתכחת מישראל ואזלא ומדלדלא. "The Torah that is forgotten from Israel and has become increasingly weakened." Yet he maintains that many have the desire for study:

מרבים וכן שלמים, אשר לבם דואג בקרבם ונאנחים ונאנקים על התורה שמשתכחת מישראל ואזלא ומדלדלא. וחלילה לנו לדבר על עם ד' כי באמת לא במרד ולא במעל ח"ו מתרחקים מן התורה. אבל יש שרוצים ללמוד ואין להם מלוא כף קמח. ויש שיש להם ורוצים ללמוד, אבל אין להם רב ללמוד דרכי העיון האמתי, כי זה ימים רבים לישראל שהאנשים הגדולים בתורה במדינתנו זאת, כל אחד בונה לו חדרו לעצמו ואומר לעצמי אני מציל וכונס בדור שאין התורה חביבה על לומדיה.

There are many worthy individuals who worry, sigh, and bemoan the forgotten and weakened Torah. But we should never speak of the people of God [disparagingly], since it has not been with rebellious malice, God forbid, that they have distanced themselves from the Torah. There are indeed those who wish to study but have no financial means. And there are those who have [means] and want to study, but they have no teacher to instruct them in the paths of true inquiry. It has been many days since Israel has had great Torah figures in this, our land. Each person constructs his own *ḥeder* [school house], saying, "I will rescue myself," and so he assembles a generation in which the Torah is not dear to those who study it.[39]

Among the problematic conditions and decisions of the past to which R. Ḥayyim refers are the fragmentation and diffuseness of learning: כל אחד בונה לו חדרו לעצמו ("each one constructs a school house for himself") and an orientation toward self-preservation rather than collective well-being: ואומר לעצמי אני מציל ("saying that I will rescue myself").[40] He further points out that there is a prevalent desire for learning that is impeded by poverty and the shortage of qualified teachers.

The importance of desire for learning is a leitmotif in R. Ḥayyim's thought.[41] Along with the Vilna Gaon's having been the quintessential scholar, his own generation's desire for learning is a profound source of R. Ḥayyim's hope: רעבים גם צמאים נפשם חשקה בתורת ד,' וילך מחיל אל חיל לשמוע דברי ד'. ("They are hungry and thirsty, their soul longs for the Torah of God so they will go from strength to strength to hear the words of God.").[42] R. Ḥayyim addresses potential students, teachers, and supporters with positive attributions of loving Torah and pursuing its insights, thereby contributing to further learning and strengthening of Torah in the world: אוהבי התורה, מהם מפישי התורה, דרכי' ועמקי' ומחזיקים בדקי' ומהם תומכי' ומחזיקים לומדי'. ("Lovers of Torah, among whom are those who expand its ways and its profundities, strengthening inquiry into it, as well as those who support and maintain those who study it.").[43]

But, for R. Ḥayyim, desire is not sufficient; the situation requires a pragmatic strategy to address the sparseness of Torah study. As we saw in the last chapter, he views establishing the Volozhin Yeshiva as a necessary step in that it would begin to concentrate Torah scholarship and would attract those for whom the desire is genuine, "who search for God" and "who hunger to lodge in the depth of *halakha* and the truth of Torah."[44] Establishing the yeshiva would respond to the problem of teaching and learning's diffuseness; it would awaken the desire for further learning, and would provide an eruditional momentum.

Means, Ends, and the Ideal

Theories that attribute a strong messianic orientation to the thought of the Vilna Gaon and his circle point to its invoking Torah study as a means to a redemptive end. As we will see in the next chapter, R. Ḥayyim's educational thought departs from a conception of Torah study simply as a means to an end. But for much of the Gaon's school, it is through Torah study that the learner achieves the necessary level of *teshuvah* (repentance) and *devekut* (spiritual attachment to God), thus leading to *olam haba* ("the world-to-come").[45]

For example, the GRA states: "Torah is eternal life in that it is the way to the world to come." (התורה היא חיי עולם, שהיא דרך לעולם הבא.)[46] R. Abraham, brother of the GRA, considers Torah study as a means to *devekut* (attachment to God): "Through the Torah he is attached (*nidbak*) to the Holy One, Blessed be He."[47] Continuing his discourse on how Torah serves as a means, R. Abraham maintains that the Torah also brings one to *teshuvah* (repentance):

> מפני שמצינו שכל עיקר גדר התשובה והתחלתה הוא התורה שתתעלה, כמאמר חכמינו ז"ל (ע"ז כ ע"ב) תורה מביאה לידי זהירות וזריזות.
>
> For we have found that the entire essence of the definition of *teshuvah* and its origin is the exalted Torah, as our sages, may their memories be blessed, said "Torah brings [one] to caution and diligence"[48] (*BT Avodah Zarah* 20b).

Another member of the Gaon's school, R. Yitzhak (Eizik) Haver, explicitly connects Torah to *devekut* in his writings a generation later:

> ובאמת עקר הדביקות בו יתברך הוא עסק התורה . . . ובזה הוא מגיע לאהבת ה' בהשיגו וטועמו במתק צוף דבש אמריו הטהורות, אשר היא משמחת לו ומעירה את העיניים . . . שעל ידי התורה משיג מידותיו יתברך ופרטי עניני הנהגה בנבראים, וכל המידות שלו יתברך הם שמותיו הקדושים כי כל שם הוא לפי פעולה וההשגחה המושג לנו מאתו יתברך . . . והיאך ידע מדותיו להתדבק בהם אם לא יעסוק בתורה יומם ולילה.
>
> In truth, the essence of *devekut* to Him, may He be blessed, is being occupied with the Torah . . . Through this he attains the love of God through his apprehending and tasting the sweet honey nectar of His pure teachings that gladden him and illuminate his eyes . . . For, by way of the Torah, he grasps His qualities, may He be blessed, and the specific matters of conduct with [God's] creatures. All His qualities, may He be blessed, are His holy names for each name corresponds to activity and vigilance that is grasped by us from Him, may He be blessed . . . So how could one know His qualities and become attached to them, if he is not occupied with Torah day and night?[49]

Again, here the study of Torah leads to a desired end, i.e., attachment to God, in that Torah study allows one to see qualities of God and attach oneself to them. In each of these examples, Torah study is considered a means. It is the vehicle through which one achieves the necessary repentance, apprehension, attachment to God, and the world to come. For some of the Vilna Gaon's circle, the utilization of Torah study for these purposes was of the highest urgency because Jewish learning had reached what was considered to be its nadir.

But though the GRA may have viewed the study of Torah as a means to an end, this does not necessarily indicate an acute messianism.[50] Nor do studies that assert messianic activism in the Vilna Gaon's school consist of more than secondhand suggestions that he was involved in a messianic project. Morgenstern's *argumentum ex silentio*, his pointing to post-Sabbatean[51] repression of messianic writing, his noting the GRA's three extant *haskamot* (written introductory "endorsements" of other scholars' work)—each of which refers to messianic calculation—and his considering *devekut* (attachment to God) a proto-messianic goal are among the unconvincing evidence.[52] Gershom Scholem's own scholarship on messianism and mysticism would also refute these claims. As Scholem states on more than one occasion, interest in a messianic idea in the broader context of one's religious framework does not necessarily connote acute messianic anticipation: "But it is one thing to allot a niche to the ideas of redemption, and quite another to have placed this concept with all it implies in the center of the religious life and thought."[53] In constructing historically authentic mystical and rabbinic biographies, one should consider: "what idea moved them most deeply, motivated them, explained their success."[54] In a later work, Scholem again makes the distinction between messianism in the context of a broader framework of ideas and an innovative, focused, acute messianic agenda: "[T]here is a decisive difference between things they say because they are generally accepted and repeated, and those in which their specific contribution is to be found . . . what constitutes its originality."[55] And with regard to messianic calculation as signifying heightened expectation, Scholem would be equally critical:

> It is a widespread error to interpret Messianic calculation as an indicator of acute Messianism or high Messianic tension . . . It is not more than a common device used by many preachers and moralists to hold out consolation to their contemporaries by establishing a date for redemption within their own lifetime.[56]

Finally, Scholem would challenge the conclusion that concern with *devekut* indicates a substantial preoccupation with the Messiah's advent: "*Devekut* is clearly a contemplative value without Messianic implication and can be realized everywhere and at any time."[57]

A concept that is often associated with the messianic era is "the world to come" (*olam haba*). There are differences in Jewish tradition and among scholars as to the relationship of this concept to the messianic era. For our purposes, I will treat *olam haba* as an associated, albeit distinct notion.[58] Like the coming of the Messiah, for R. Ḥayyim, *olam haba* does not serve as a desired, anticipated end to be pursued. His interpretation of the aphorism: "All Israel have a portion to the world to come" is a case in point. He notes that the use of the preposition "to," rather than "in," indicates an ongoing, unending process:[59]

> וזהו שאמרו רז"ל "כל ישראל יש להם חלק לעולם הבא" ולא אמרו "בעולם הבא" שמשמעו היה שהעולם הבא הוא מוכן מעת הבריאה ענין ודבר לעצמו, ואם יצדק האדם יתנו לו בשכרו חלק ממנו. אבל האמת, שהעולם הבא הוא מעשה ידי האדם עצמו, שהרחיב והוסיף והתקין חלק לעצמו במעשיו. (נה"ח א,יב)

> This is what the Sages meant when stating (in Mishna Avot), "All [the people of] Israel have a portion *to* the world to come," and not stating, "*in* the world to come." [The latter] would mean that the world to come is ready from the moment of creation—a separate, self-contained entity of which a portion would be rewarded to one who acts justly. But the truth is that the world to come is *one's very handiwork itself*, having broadened, expanded, and restored a portion for himself in his deeds.[60]

"The world to come is one's *very* handiwork *itself*." (העולם הבא הוא *הוא* מעשה ידי האדם *עצמו*.) Here is an equation of means and ends. Conduct is a world-to-come; the latter is not a reward waiting to be realized. There is no dualism here between the vehicle (one's conduct) and the outcome ("the world to come"). There is, rather, an identity between them ("one's *very* handiwork itself" (הוא *הוא*).) The world to come is not considered an object or time that may await us. It is a coexistent process of continual human acts. It is neither the incentive that lies at the end, nor is it something that follows the deed; it *is* the deed, "one's handiwork itself." As we will see in the next chapter, this conception of the world to come and its relationship to deeds is an important example of R. Ḥayyim's dissolving the conventional relationship between means and ends, a dualism perhaps more reflective of some of his contemporaries, a dualism lending itself to a utilitarian view of present action serving an ultimate goal. And, as we will see in the next chapter, R. Ḥayyim's notion of *olam haba* has a remarkable resonance with Dewey's characterization of the relationship to the ideal in aesthetic experience: we are "introduced into a world beyond this world which is nevertheless the deeper reality of the world in which we live in our ordinary experiences."[61]

To be sure, R. Ḥayyim's notion of "*olam hama'asi*" or "*asiyah*,"[62] that first level of the kabbalistic concatenating worlds[63] (translated variously as "doing," "action," or "practice"), is not to be equated with Dewey's "world in which we live our ordinary experiences." And it is perhaps an overextension or reduction of "*olam hama'asi*" to translate it as "the practical world." Yet in his interpretation of this first-order world, R. Ḥayyim emphasizes its primacy relative to the "upper worlds" and its direct association with the human body, human conduct, and specific deeds.[64] The effort to connect to the transcendent must take place in the realm of human deeds and the human body, in that most fundamental, most palpable aspect of experience—what in kabbalah is called the first of the four leveled cosmos—the level of *asiyah*.

> ומה שהנר"ן של האדם אין ביכלתם לקשר העולמות עד רידתם למטה בגוף האדם כנ"ל כי לתקן עולם העשיה הוצרכו בהכרח להתלבש בגוף בעולם המעשה.

> The portions of man's soul—*nefesh, ru'aḥ, neshamah*—are unable to interconnect the worlds until they have descended down into the human body, as has been stated above (chapter 1:10) Because in order to repair the world of "doing" (*asiyah*), they absolutely must be embodied in the world of the deed (*ma'aseh*).[65]

It is at the level of human deeds that the soul begins to "repair" the worlds. For R. Ḥayyim, then, the kabbalistic quest to interconnect the aspects of one's soul must start and end in human experience.

CONCLUSION

In this chapter, I have shown how certain aspects of Rabbi Ḥayyim of Volozhin's thought come into sharper relief when we consider his non-messianic theory. In particular, we have seen that he refutes the idea that the world-to-come is an end (or, to use Dewey's language, an "end-in-view") for which he strives. As we will see in the next chapter, he sees the end as inseparable from the learning experience itself. Any sense of an end to be achieved is an intrinsic quality of the struggle to breathe life into the world. In the next chapter, I will argue that this conception of the nature of an end is congruent and convergent with that of Dewey, even as it is not coincident.

R. Ḥayyim is vigilantly attuned to Torah study's diminution in his times. And, acting on this vigilance, he takes practical steps toward reversing this trend. As pragmatic, he does not portray his society as having hit bottom, nor does he consider the decline of Jewish learning to be symptomatic of an imminent messianic advent. His course of action is not directed toward a messianic end; it is directed, rather, by generously and sensitively identifying those inchoate desires and efforts that reflect his vision and belief in the relationship between Torah study, the worlds, and conduct.

Nearly two hundred years later, Richard Rorty, though unlikely to have had knowledge of R. Ḥayyim, serendipitously expresses R. Ḥayyim's somewhat Deweyan stance that the priority of one's educational efforts should be directed by "the finitude of one's time and place . . . and contingent aspects of one's life."[66] Rabbi Ḥayyim's orientations toward the world as it appears to us now and his vigilance regarding contingent possibilities demonstrate a groundedness in earthly human action and its consequences.

As I will elucidate further in the next chapter, for R. Ḥayyim, excessive attentiveness to an absolute ideal like *devekut* preempts efforts to struggle with actual social, educational, and halakhic concerns. It is primarily within the struggles and rhythms of learning in this sensory world that we experience intimations of the transcendent. *Bitul hayesh*, the annulment of the sensory world, is neither an option nor an aspiration in R. Ḥayyim's system,[67] for our world is the primary locus of encounter with the divine in one's deeds, speech, and thoughts.[68] He has confidence in the capacity to change tendencies, to renew learning, and to breathe life into the world that exists in historical time.

NOTES

1. Morgenstern, "The Place of the Ten Tribes"; "Dispersion and the Longing for Zion," *Mysticism and Messianism*; Shuchat, "Messianic and Mystical Elements."

2. "The GRA" is the acronym for the Hebrew title and name of R. Elijah the Gaon of Vilna, the Vilna Gaon (הגאון הרב **א**ליהו: הגר"א)

3. The *Shulhan Arukh* ("the prepared table") is the authoritative code of Jewish law written by Joseph Caro in the sixteenth century. The work, with supplementary glosses by R. Moshe Isserles, came to represent the normative structure of Jewish practice in Europe in subsequent centuries.

4. Shuchat, 217–225.

5. Morgenstern, "Messianic Concepts," 144.

6. Morgenstern, "Messianic Concepts," 148. In his footnote to this assertion, Morgenstern notes that R. Ḥayyim of Volozhin was the head of the *Rozne Vilna*, the support organization for the messianic-oriented group of "*perushim*" who had immigrated to the Holy Land. I am not disputing the historicity of R. Ḥayyim's holding this post. I will demonstrate, however, that his support should not lead one to conclude that R. Ḥayyim shared the messianic fervor of these contemporaries.

7. *Aliyah* means "ascent." Religiously, it connotes the spiritual and physical ascent to the Land of Israel and Jerusalem. It is also used in conjunction with the mystical practice of "ascent of the soul" (*aliyat ha-neshamah)*.

8. Shuchat, "Messianic and Mystical Elements."

9. Lamm, *Torah Lishmah*, 12; Etkes, "R. Ḥayyim of Volozhin's Response," 152.

10. See Ravitzky, *Jewish Religious Radicalism*, "The Land of Israel: Longing and Trembling," and "Messianic Agitation."

11. In his arguing for considering R. Ḥayyim's kabbalism as antimystical, Magid seems to concur with the non-messianic perspective, summarizing R. Ḥayyim's view as claiming that "we must only live within 'our perspective' (*mitsidenu*) where God is eclipsed and, as such, beyond the realm of human experience." Magid, "Deconstructing the Mystical."

12. Levinas, "'In the Image of God'," 161.

13. Levinas, "Judaism and Kenosis," 126.

14. In his characterization of pragmatism, Charles Taylor felicitously explains the concept of pragmata as: "Things appear for us from the very beginning with their relevances, as 'pragmata,' to use the Greek term that Heidegger invokes. 'Pragmatism' would then be the view that we primordially, and in a sense always, are dealing with pragmata, and not just neutral objects. This might be the core meaning." Taylor, "What Is Pragmatism," 74. While I am not suggesting a kind of affinity between R Ḥayyim's thought and modern pragmatism, I believe that R. Ḥayyim's thought contains some elements in common (albeit unrelated) with this modern philosophical movement.

R. Ḥayyim's *sha'ar gimel* ("Gate 3") in his *Nefesh Ha-Ḥayyim* includes an extensive exposition of the distinction between our ontological perspective (מצידנו) and God's perspective (מצידו). Directing the reader's attention to the former, R. Ḥayyim claims that the intrinsic nature of the latter (God's perspective) is not the proper subject of inquiry. Contrary to this, messianic activism would have placed much greater emphasis on the providential aspects of "God's perspective" (מצידו) driving human conduct and history.

15. See note 7.

16. S. Asaf, "The Altshul Family Tree," as quoted in Ravitzky, "The Land of Israel," 39 (my translation). On the relationship between soul and body, see Alfred L. Ivry, "Body and Soul," *Encyclopaedia Judaica*, ed. Michael Berenbaum and Fred Skolnik. 2nd ed. Vol. 4. (Detroit: Macmillan Reference USA, 2007), 30–31. *Gale Virtual Reference Library*. Web. 21 Aug. 2012.

17. On this norm, see, Ravitzky, *Messianism, Zionism*, "The Land of Israel," and "Messianic Agitation."

18. Rabbi Ḥayyim is following the traditional rabbinic prohibition against messianic activism (against "hastening the End"). *BT Kebubot* 111a and *Song of Songs Rabba* II, 7. On the "three oaths" found in *Song of Songs* 2:7, 3:5, 5:8 and Rashi's gloss, see Ravitzky, "Impact of the Three Oaths in Jewish History," in *Messianism, Zionism,* 211–234. In reviewing R. Ḥayyim's application of Lurianic Kabbalah, Etkes points out: "It should be emphasized that even though Rabbi Ḥayyim was influenced by the Kabbalah of the ARI [Isaac Luria], and he sometimes relied on it as a source, its messianic element does not play a role in his doctrine." Etkes, *Gaon of Vilna*, 56.

19. On the prophet Elijah's proto-messianic role in arbitrating disputes and settling legal difficulties, see for example, *BT Baba Metsi'a* 3a, 29b, 37a, *BT Sanhedrin* 48a, and *BT Pesahim* 15a.

20. R. Ḥayyim of Volozhin, *Ru'aḥ Ḥayyim,* 17.

21. R. Ḥayyim of Volozhin, *Hut Hamishulash,* 1:8. See *Tosefta*, *Berakhot* 6:5; *JT Berakhot* 63b, 9:1; *BT Berakhot* 58a, 58b (my translation).

22. See Eze, 37.

23. וכן אנחנו בגלות ובפיזור עצמות היבשות (יחזקאל לז) עד יערה רוח כו' (ישעיהו לב,טו.)

24. On *"asiyah"* see chapter 3. והולך ומתמעת עד דבדורותינו אין משיגים אלא בעקב עשיה . . . בעקבות משיחא כו" (סוף סוטה.)

25. אלא שהן אחורים דאחורים ואינן מצחצחים. לכן מדברים דרך משל ואינן מבינין כלל.

26. כי מעת שחרב הבית יצאה רוחנו עטרת ראשנו ונשארנו רק אנחנו הוא גוף שלה בלא נפש.

27. ויציאה לח"ל הוא הקבר (ו)רימה סובבת עלינו ואין בעדינו להציל הן העובדי כוכבים ואוכלים בשרינו.

28. ומ"מ היו חבורות וישיבות גדולות עד שנרקב הבשר והעצמות נפזרו פיזור אחר פיזור.

29. ומ"מ היו עדיין העצמות קיימות שהן הת"ח שבישראל מעמידי הגוף.

30. עד שנרקבו העצמות ולא נשאר אלא תרווד רקב מאתנו ונעשה עפר שחה לעפר נפשינו. ואנחנו מקוין עתה לתחית המתים התנערי מעפר קומי כו' (ישעיה נ"ב) ויערה רוח ממרום עלינו (ישעיהו לב,טו.)
R. Elijah Gaon of Vilna, "Introduction to the Secret of *Tsimtsum*."

31. R. Elijah Gaon of Vilna, "Introduction to *Tikkune Zohar* with the GRA's Commentary."

32. *Nefesh Ha-Ḥayyim* 4:1. It is difficult to fully understand these kinds of passages from R. Ḥayyim's works without recognizing the polemical challenge to Hasidism behind much of his depictions of "misguided motivations." Nevertheless, the particularity of R. Ḥayyim's disposition toward the world's pragmata has a positive, proactive, prospective dimension even as it is informed, in part, by a response to hasidic thought.

33. *Nefesh Ha-Ḥayyim* 4:1

34. Ḥayyim of Volozhin, "Introduction to the Vilna Gaon's commentary on *Sifra ditsni'uta*."

35. Ḥayyim of Volozhin, "Introduction to Vilna Gaon's commentary on *Sifra dits'ni'uta*"

36. Ḥayyim of Volozhin, "Introduction to Vilna Gaon's commentary on *Sifra dits'ni'uta.*" Beyond the Gaon as an example of the efficacy of *talmud torah* in his day, R. Ḥayyim attests that each generation's scholars contribute to the enduring life-giving sustenance of Torah in the world. Each teacher strengthens the world and adds sustaining power to the cosmos through erudition and teaching—"adding hermeneutic lessons" (להוסיף לקח הפלפול). So while R. Ḥayyim's view of the *galut* is certainly not celebratory, neither is it as grim as that which characterizes much of his teacher's school, whether or not we consider that school to be messianic in orientation. Torah scholars, *talmide ḥakhamim*, play a compensatory role for the difficulties of *galut* through their writings and teachings:

> ועיניהם ראו שמכובד הגלות . . . לזאת התעוררו לחבר חיבורים מהלכות מרובות. להורות אחב"י את הדרך ילכו בה ואת המעשה אשר יעשון.

> Their eyes saw the weight of the exile . . . so they awoke to compose works from many laws in order to teach our brethren, the children of Israel, the [proper] path on which to walk and the deed they should do.

Toward the conclusion of his introduction to the Gaon's commentary on *Sifra diẓniuta*, R. Ḥayyim suggests that the Gaon served as an example of focusing on *this* world, rather than on the world to come:

> והעיקר מה שהאדם משיג בזה העולם ע"י עמל ויגיעה כאשר הוא בוחר בטוב ומפנה עצמו לד"ת בזה עושה נ"ר ליוצרו ית"ש.

> The essential aspect of what one grasps in this world through toil and exertion [is that] when he chooses the good and directs himself to matters of Torah, he pleases his Creator, blessed be His name.

37. "Introduction, Commentary on *Sifra ditsni'uta.*"
38. Isa. 51:21.
39. Letter to Lithuanian communities soliciting support for the Volozhin Yeshiva (1802).
40. Letter to communities.
41. See chapter 5.
42. Letter to communities.
43. Letter to communities.
44. Letter to communities.
45. The concept of *olam haba* ("the world-to-come") is to be contrasted with *olam hazeh*, "this world." The former term designates the hereafter and, more technically, the period following the messianic advent.
46. The Vilna Gaon's commentary on Proverbs 13:12.
47. *Ma'alot Ha-Torah*, 102, as quoted in Lamm, *Torah Lishmah*, 342 n. 62.
48. *Ma'alot Ha-Torah*, as quoted in Shuchat, 156.
49. *Or Ha-Torah* on *Ma'alot Ha-Torah*, 33–34, as quoted in Shuchat, 168.
50. This is the case whether we consider that messianism to be apocalyptic, rationalistic, restorative, or utopian, to use Scholem's typologies. Scholem, *The Messianic Idea in Judaism,* 28, 32, 342. For a distinction between rationalist and apocalyptic messianic tendencies see Maimonides, *Mishna Torah*, "Laws of Kings" and his Introduction to *Mishna Sanhedrin* 10.
51. Shabbetai Tsvi.
52. Morgenstern, "The Place of the Ten Tribes," "Dispersion and the Longing for Zion, 1240–1840," *Mysticism and Messianism.* Morgenstern's *argumentum ex silentio*, pointing to post-Sabbatean repression of messianic writing, his pointing to the GRA's three extant *haskamot* (written introductory "endorsements" of other scholars' works), each of which refers to messianic calculation, and his considering *devekut* (attachment to God) a proto-messianic goal are among the unconvincing evidence. His conclusion that the Vilna Gaon was considered in his time as "*posek ha'aḥaron*," the final legal judge or resolutive legislative interpreter, is equally dubious, especially when we consider R. Ḥayyim's own conceptions of his beloved teacher and of the efficacy of exilic talmudic learning, as we will continue to see below.
53. Scholem, *Major Trends in Jewish Mysticism*, 329.
54. Scholem, *Messianic Idea* 180.
55. Scholem, *Messianic Idea* 181.
56. Scholem, *Messianic Idea*, 184.
57. Scholem, *Messianic Idea*, 185. Though Idel and Tishby, compellingly, have suggested flaws in Scholem's view of "messianic neutralization" in early Hasidism, neither would argue against Scholem's claims regarding the limited significance of messianic calculations and the implications of aspiring for *devekut*. Idel, *Hasidism: Between Ecstasy and Magic*; Tishby, "The Messianic Idea and Messianic Trends in the Growth of Hasidism."
58. See note 44. Rosenblatt, "*Olam Ha-Ba.*"

59. R. Ḥayyim's view on *olam haba* appears in his *Ru'aḥ Ḥayyim* and *Nefesh Ha-Ḥayyim* 1:12.

60. NH 1:12.

61. Dewey, *Art as Experience*, 195. It is important to point out that the world of human experience is emphasized by the Vilna Gaon as well as by R. Ḥayyim. As R. Ḥayyim relates:

> שמעתי כמה פעמים מפי קדשו של רבנו הגאון החסיד מו"ה אלי' מוילנא ז"ל נ"ע מה העולם הבא חשוב, ואין ערך ודוגמא כלל נגד שעה אחת בעה"ז בעסק התורה והמצוה, מאחר שבעוה"ב אי אפשר לעבד ה' (דרשת מוהר"ח)
>
> I heard several times from the mouth of his holiness, our rabbi the righteous Gaon, our teacher, Rabbi Elijah of Vilna, may his memory be a blessing and his soul in paradise, that the importance of the world to come is not in any way comparable in value even to one hour in this world being occupied *with Torah* and *mitsvot*, in that in the world to come it is impossible to serve God.

62. The adjective, "*ma'asi,*" is from the same verbal root as the gerund, "*asiyah,*" which might be translated as "doing," "acting," "practicing." In the phrase "*olam hama'asi,*" R. Ḥayyim is referring to this lowest world of "*asiyah.*"

63. The concept of four worlds in medieval Kabbalah is based on interpretations of the biblical verse "Everything called by my name—for my glory I have created it, have formed it, yea I have made it" (Isaiah 43:7). This verse is thought to allude to three "worlds": *beri'ah* (creation), *yetsirah* (formation), and *asiyah* (making, doing, or acting). Later the fourth and "highest" world, *atsilut* (emanation), was added to this constellation. By the fourteenth century, the doctrine became clearer that God created these four worlds, each corresponding to a letter of his name. Each world is considered a certain level of being, corresponding to a sequence of divine activity and to a particular balance of spiritual and material qualities.

64. *Nefesh Ha-Ḥayyim* 1:10, וגם הג' בחינות נר"ן של האדם עצמו, לא ניתן להם זו הכח ההעלאה וההתקשרות של העולמות ושל עצמם, עד רידתם לזה העולם המעשי בגוף האדם.
The three aspects of man's own soul—*nefesh*, *ru'aḥ*, and *neshamah*—are not empowered to cause the ascending and interconnecting of the worlds and of themselves until their descent to this practical (*ma'asi*) world in the body of man.

65. *Nefesh Ha-Ḥayyim* 1:12.

66. Richard Rorty, *Consequences of Pragmatism,* xix.

67. The concept of *bitul hayesh* had a significant place in certain Hasidic circles, including the Ḥabad movement of R. Shneur Zalman of Lyadi.

68. Noting this aspect of R. Ḥayyim's thought, Tamar Ross points out: "Only the existence of the external deed, as commanded in the Torah and halakha, establishes this connection [between God and man], since every other contact with God is impossible in the world of *asiyah* . . . The halakhic way of life is based not on the hidden metaphysical truth of the total divine reality . . . R. Ḥayyim wants to fight the antinomian danger of the breaching of the borders between the holy and the commonplace that he says is a demand in Habad's annulment of 'that which is' (*bitul hayesh*)." Characterizing R. Ḥayyim's epistemology, she further notes that "the absolute character of the divine reality is concealed, and the world appears as a variegated reality, defined and full of distinctions." Ross, "Two Interpretations" (my translation), 160–161.

Chapter Five

Walking and Talking Together

John Dewey and R. Ḥayyim on Means, Ends, and the Ideal

We saw in the previous chapter that a number of individuals in the Vilna Gaon's circle considered Torah study a means to an end. For some, the desired end was to achieve the conditions considered necessary for the advent of the messianic era and for release from the shackles of exile. Yet R. Ḥayyim's conceptions of means, ends, and the ideal are quite different from this view. His distinctive notions inform what, in the last chapter, I have suggested is his non-messianic theory of the relationship between the present and the future, as well as his more reconciled conception toward the efficacy of Torah study in diaspora. In this chapter, I continue the conversation begun in chapter 3 between R. Ḥayyim and John Dewey, considering their conceptions of educational means, ends, and ideals. In doing so, I continue to illustrate the value of interdiscursivity in educational deliberation.

There is, of course, more divergence and dissonance than similarity and consonance between John Dewey's twentieth-century American pragmatism and R. Ḥayyim's early-nineteenth-century, Eastern European, kabbalistic discourse. It is not my purpose here to demonstrate these differences, such as those between Dewey's theory of deliberation and R. Ḥayyim's ontology. To be sure, differences are plentiful. It is my purpose, rather, to demonstrate the value of a conversation between the two, how aspects of one's discourse place the other's in sharper relief, and how their understandings of the dynamics of means, ends, and the ideal show a remarkable parallelism (if not coincidence) that can inform our educational thinking and conduct.

JOHN DEWEY, JEWISH EDUCATION, AND THE IDEAL

As explained in Chapter Two, our inquiry considers how Dewey's philosophy can be more than an experimental, practical instrument with which to recognize and solve the problems of being a Jew in today's society. Are there dimensions of traditional Jewish educational theory, particularly in the thought and work of R. Ḥayyim of Volozhin, for which a Deweyan hermeneutic may be illuminating?

In recent years, Deweyan scholars have noted significant gestures toward the transcendent in his writing, reframing the way he is interpreted.[1] These qualities of Dewey's thought are often eclipsed when emphasizing the instrumental, experimental, and process features of his pragmatism. But consistent with a recent pragmatic turn in religious studies, Dewey's relationship to the transcendent is receiving a renewed hearing.[2] It is this dimension of his work that is particularly resonant with R. Ḥayyim's discourse, inviting inquiry that Buchler (see chapter 2) would call "transordinal" or "coordinative."[3] As we will now see, there is much shared between the structures of Dewey's and R. Ḥayyim's notions of the ideal and its place in education.

For Dewey, the ideal provokes a "quickening and extension" of thought "to contemplate the continuities of existence, and restore the connection of the isolated desire to the companionship of its fellows."[4] To be sure, this sense of extensive connections of desire requires the palpable or empirical, but is not limited to these. For in striving for betterment, there are intimations of what Dewey calls "the ideal":

> Every end that man holds up, every project he entertains is ideal. It marks something wanted, rather than something existing. It is wanted because existence as it now is does not furnish it. It carries with itself, then, a sense of contrast to the achieved, to the existent. It outruns the seen and touched. It is the work of faith and hope even when it is the plan of the most hard-headed "practical" man.[5]

What "outruns the seen and touched," however, is not a clear, envisioned end. The ideal is not "a goal of final exhaustive, comprehensive perfection which can be defined only by complete contrast with the actual."[6] It is not "a far away perfect world."[7] In order to "recover the genuine import of ideals and idealism," we need to recognize that any intended consequence of our deliberation and conduct "is set in an indefinite context of other consequences just as real as it is, and many of them much more certain in fact. The 'ends' that are foreseen and utilized mark out a little island in an infinite sea."[8] Aims are thus always selected from "an indefinite context of consequences."[9] This elusive context is "sensed," intimated, in "the present meaning of activity." There is, then, an indefinite, even transcendent, "field" from which the end is selected and imagined, "the figured pattern at the center of the field through which runs the axis of conduct."[10] Intelligence senses, but cannot fully know, the infinite context in which it operates:

> About this central figuration [of ends] extends infinitely a supporting background in a vague whole, undefined and undiscriminated. At most intelligence but throws a spotlight on that little part of the whole which marks out the axis of movement. Even if the light is flickering and the illuminated portion stands forth only dimly from the shadowy background, it suffices if we are shown the way to move. To the rest of the consequences, collateral and remote, corresponds a background of feeling, of diffused emotion. This forms the stuff of the ideal.[11]

Though this deep background can never be fully comprehended, it gives our acts and decisions "infinite import"[12] because our conduct "is continuous with the rest of the world." The ideal is the "consciousness of this encompassing infinity of connections."[13] Profoundly resonating with R. Ḥayyim, Dewey writes of the transcendent ideal's relationship to conduct: "When a sense of the infinite reach of an act physically occurring in a small point of space and occupying a petty instant of time comes home to us, the meaning of a present act is seen to be vast, immeasurable, unthinkable."[14]

For Dewey, these notions of "infinite reach" and "encompassing infinity of connections" have a remarkably religious (and aesthetic) quality. Indeed Dewey says as much: "It is the office of art and religion to evoke such appreciations and intimations; to enhance and steady them till they are wrought into the texture of our lives."[15] And for Dewey, no less than for R. Ḥayyim, evoking these intimations of transcendence occurs, not as a *result* of our learning and conduct, but *within* our experience of "striving," within "the midst of effort":

> The religious experience is a reality in so far as in the midst of effort to foresee and regulate future objects we are sustained and expanded in feebleness and failure by the sense of an enveloping whole. Peace in action not after it is the contribution of the ideal to conduct.[16]

As we will see, this notion of religious experience is particularly illuminating when placed in conversation with R. Ḥayyim's concept of *Torah lishmah* ("Torah for its own sake")[17] as a context or background that sustains learning and conduct.

Practices draw ideals into experience. Ideals function to bring meaning to experience, as moral, educational, theological, or aesthetic contexts for conduct. In professional experience and professional learning, we can become more aware of "the capacity of immediate sensuous experience to absorb into itself meanings and values that in and of themselves—that is in the abstract—would be designated 'ideal' and 'spiritual.'"[18] There is, then, much in experience that Dewey argues far "outruns the seen and touched"[19] of the specific constituent elements of a problematic situation. Though he often speaks of sequential, calculative reflection on distinctly framed problems, these notions, taken in isolation, belie Dewey's holistic theory of a broader experiential life-world:[20]

> [E]xperience is something quite other than "consciousness," that is, that which appears qualitatively and focally at a particular moment . . . It is important for a theory of experience to know that under certain circumstances men prize the distinct and clearly evident. But it is no more important than it is to know that under other circumstances twilight, the vague, dark and mysterious flourish . . . What is not explicitly present makes up a vastly greater part of experience than does the conscious field to which thinkers have so devoted themselves.[21]

Thus, contrary to the way he is frequently invoked, Dewey does not assume the constancy of problematic instability and the sustained need to problematize experience. Discovering what ignites a students' love of reading, responding to a distraught parent, or preparing for an observation are not necessarily problem-framing and problem-solving experiences. They may be opportunities to sense intimations of ideals in professional experience when virtues like sensitivity, conscientiousness, and collegiality are expressed in action and cultivated in professional learning.

Kestenbaum compellingly articulates this particularity of Dewey's negotiation of the transcendent ideal and practical conduct:

> Dewey's pragmatism, I propose, is not a philosophical or cultural substitution of tangible goals for intangible ideals. His pragmatism is an attempt to respect the authority of the "tangible and the real" at the same time that it does justice to meanings which transcend the verified and the evident and which, in their most perfect expressions, are intimations of the ideal. Dewey's pragmatism does not simply, or only, "naturalize" ideals by bringing them "down to earth." His pragmatism is far more complicated than the instrumentalist and naturalistic interpretations which render ideals as "tools" to be used in the natural world. Ideals for Dewey are situated at the intersection of the tangible and the intangible, the natural and the transcendent. Ideals were the best evidence he had that in the realm of meaning, but not of fact, something simultaneously can be and not be.[22]

Let us, then, consider how this conception of the ideal, at the "intersection of the tangible and the intangible, the natural and the transcendent," can inform our understanding of R. Ḥayyim's educational thought. In terms of our discussion in chapter 2, I here seek to articulate how Dewey becomes a source for Jewish educational theory when placed in conversation with R. Ḥayyim, and how the discursive "complexes" of these two very different educational thinkers intersect.

TORAH LISHMAH ("TORAH STUDY FOR ITS OWN SAKE") AS EDUCATIONAL IDEAL

The intrinsic value of Torah study—"Torah study for its own sake" (*Torah lishmah*)—is an enduring educational ideal in rabbinic tradition.[23] Study for extrinsic motives (*Torah shelo lishmah*, "Torah study *not* for its own sake") has been valued in as much as it leads to a more intrinsic motivation.[24] In R. Ḥayyim's time, the value of *Torah lishmah* was paramount in the intellectual centers of Lithuania and Poland.

With the rise and expansion of the hasidic movement in eighteenth- and early-nineteenth-century Eastern Europe, that movement came to espouse *Torah lishmah* as an ideal for intense devotion in study, with the goal of reaching a state of *devekut*—"closeness" or "attachment" to God.[25] And there were times when hasidic leaders would chastise the rabbinic establishment for studying Torah for extrinsic motives (*Torah shelo lishmah*) such as monetary gain, reputation, recognition of intellectual achievement, or simply as an obligatory, perfunctory act. Thus, the ideal of *Torah lishmah* was a point of contention between R Ḥayyim and his hasidic contemporaries. The latter regarded *Torah lishmah* as a precondition and standard for Torah study. Contrary to this view, R. Ḥayyim maintained that *Torah lishmah* is not an external standard; it is a source and context of meaning in the learning experience itself, rather than a criterion for evaluating the level or quality of one's Torah study.

In a Deweyan sense, I suggest that, for R. Ḥayyim, educational ideals like *Torah lishmah* function as background meanings and contexts, not foregrounded perfections to reach. For example, the ideal of acquiring knowledge of "all the mysteries of the world and its fullness"[26] (כל סתרי העולם ומלואה) may lend meaning to the process of Torah study. Attaining this ideal, however, is neither the end goal, nor does its imagined attainment drive the learning process, since this ideal concerns the Torah's infinite meaning that is always beyond full comprehension.

In his innovative interpretation of *Torah lishmah*, R. Ḥayyim presents it as a reflexive ideal—an ideal that serves as its own means: "The truth is that the concept of *lishmah* means for the sake of Torah [itself]."[27] *Talmud Torah* ("the study of Torah"), as an activity, includes qualities of the ideal of *Torah lishmah*. To use Dewey's language, the ideal is drawn into experience and functions to bring meaning to that experience. R. Ḥayyim thus maintains, "Adding teaching and deliberation"[28] (להוסיף לקח ופילפול) to Torah allows the flow of divine energy to infuse the worlds. Indeed, a major theme of the *Nefesh Ha-Ḥayyim* is that without this constant study and interpretation of Torah, the cosmos would revert to a primordial chaos. No less than Dewey, R. Ḥayyim would maintain that the ideal is "a significance to felt," "intimations" of meaning in the present act of learning.[29] Ideals serve as the moral, educational, and theological contexts for study and conduct.

Moreover, in a certain Deweyan sense, R. Ḥayyim cautions against becoming preoccupied with ideals and conflating them with aims, as I noted in the last chapter. He thus argues that such conflation actually impedes successful conduct to the point that it neglects the opportune or required times for that conduct. Referring to keeping appointed times for fulfilling the commandments and for prayer, R. Ḥayyim discourages excessive efforts to reach an ideal state of spiritual devotion prior to proceeding with a commandment, learning experience, or prayer:

> [You would then] have to prepare your heart and elevate the soaring of your thinking to reach the purest thought of all prior to doing any mitsvah or prayer. Your thinking, then, would be so preoccupied with preparing for the mitsvah that the appointed time for the mitsvah or the prayer will have passed.[30]

Thus, excessive focus on the ideal, rather than on immediate experience, causes the ideal to fall from its intended position, leading to an ironic reversal: "The lofty has become lowly."[31] When we seek the ideal condition, paths are taken that unwittingly lead to "the crown of Torah" being "neglected."[32]

Aims and the Ideal

There is also a remarkable structural parallelism between Dewey's and R. Ḥayyim's notions of ends or aims. For both thinkers, aims are determined in action and effort, not prior to these. They are inevitably emerging in the student's and teacher's refusing "to rest upon attained goods." Both Dewey and R. Ḥayyim value humility in any learning experience in that all achievement is limited, never absolute; its value is its opening up new windows so the student can adjust, redirect, and go further.[33]

For Dewey, transcendence is intimated through the "action of deliberation" as we select ends that will function, paradoxically, as means to present action, even as we become increasingly aware of the unfathomable, infinite, ideal context from which any end is chosen. The selected end is a "foreseen consequence" that serves "as a stimulus to present action."[34]

Dewey here articulates his theory of the interplay of means, ends, and ideals and the intimations of the transcendent in deliberation:

> The action of deliberation, as we have seen, consists in selecting some foreseen consequence to serve as a stimulus to present action. It brings future possibilities into the present scene and thereby frees and expands present tendencies. But the selected consequence is set in an indefinite context of other consequences just as real as it is, and many of them much more certain in fact.[35]

As Kestenbaum notes, Dewey here is "asking us to do two things at once."[36] The first is an intellectual act of selecting, clarifying, illuminating an end-in-view to guide us. The second is to sense something transcendent, infinite in experience, from which the end is selected. And as we have seen, this transcendent dimension is what Dewey calls the ideal.

The end is formed in thought. It is a "foreseen consequence," "a stimulus," "future possibilities," "freeing and expanding, present tendencies." The end is that "little island," the "central figuration," "that little part of the whole which marks out the axis of movement," "the illuminated portion" showing "the way to move." It identifies "that small effort which we can put forth," "physically occurring in a small point of space and occupying a petty instant of time." The end, though influential, is modest in light of the incomprehensible scope and depth of ideal possibilities.

Unlike the end, which is intellectually selected, the ideal is felt, sensed. It is that "indefinite context of other consequences," "the infinite sea," "the expansive field," a "supporting background in a vague whole," an "undefined background of feeling," and "indefinite context of consequences," "an infinity of events that sustain and support," "the consciousness of this encompassing infinity of connections," the "sense of the infinite reach of an act," "the meaning of a present act," "a significance to be felt, appreciated."[37]

Interweaving while distinguishing his concepts of the end and the ideal, Dewey articulates how the indeterminate and uncertain—the ideal—interacts with the known and stable—the selected, realizable end. As we will see below, this interaction takes place through struggle and effort, fostering growth. For Dewey, the dynamic interaction of wish and thought, ideal and end, emotion and intellect, desire and intelligence is the ground pattern of educational and religious experience, "fostering those impulses and habits which experience has shown to make us sensitive, generous, imaginative, impartial in perceiving the tendency of our inchoate dawning activities."[38] With sensitivity, generosity, and imagination, the student can perceive possibilities while becoming aware that these possibilities exist within a context of elusive, but intimated, ideal meanings. For Dewey, this interplay of perception and awareness is the form of good educational habit.

Inquiry and Desire *(iyyun and ḥafitsah)* "in the midst of effort"

As we will now see, both R. Ḥayyim and Dewey express profound regard for the value of effort and struggle in learning. Dewey explicitly relates struggle to his concept of the ideal. While here he is speaking of moral experience, when we consider the moral responsibility of teaching, this applies to pedagogy and learning as well:

> Morality thus assumes the form of a struggle. The past satisfaction speaks for itself; it has been verified in experience, it has conveyed its worth to our very senses. We have tried and tasted it, and know that it is good. If morality lay in the repetition of similar satisfactions, it would not be a struggle. We should know experimentally beforehand that the chosen end would bring us satisfaction, and should be at rest in that knowledge.[39]

The passive possession of acquired knowledge, then, is not a sufficient outcome of educational experience even if that knowledge prescribes virtuous conduct. There is an uncertainty in moral and pedagogical decision-making that demands effort and intimates an ideal context. This effort involves springing forth into uncharted terrain beyond what has been a verified, secure good:

> But when morality lies in striving for satisfactions which have not verified themselves to our sense, it always requires an effort. We have to surrender the enjoyed good, and stake ourselves upon that of which we cannot say: We know it is good. To surrender the actual experienced good for a possible ideal good is the struggle.[40]

This surrender of the security of the verified and known, of the "tried and tasted," is propulsive even as it is a risk, an act of faith in the efficacy of moral, intellectual, aesthetic, and social efforts to reach something as yet unattained:[41]

> From this point of view morality is a life of aspiration, and of faith; there is required constant willingness to give up past goods as the good, and to press on to new ends; not because past achievements are bad, but because, being good, they have created a situation which demands larger and more intricately related achievements. This willingness is aspiration and it implies faith. Only the old good is of sight, has verified itself to sense. The new ideal, the end which meets the situation, is felt as good.[42]

The new good beckons for our pursuit, requiring "the staking of self upon activity as against passive possession."[43]

Let us now consider how the Deweyan notions of struggle and effort may inform analogous notions of R. Ḥayyim. R. Ḥayyim develops his own theory of desire, effort, struggle in his interpretation of the tanna[44] R. Meir's statement, “All who engage in the study of Torah for its own sake, merit many things”[45] (כל העוסק בתורה לשמה, זוכה לדברים הרבה). In his interpretation, R. Ḥayyim emphasizes that inquiry, effort, and desire are integral to the learning process and that, within that process, the ideal of *Torah lishmah* (“Torah for its own sake”) is intimated. Analogous to Dewey, he situates struggle and effort at the center of the learning experience, viewing the educational “good” as one of action rather than attainment. Dewey’s discourse, again, is helpful as he articulates how religious reward and educational attainment are not simply results of effort; they occur primarily “in the midst of effort,”[46] kindling desire for further inquiry. So too, for R. Ḥayyim, ideals such as *devekut* or *kirvat elohim* (“attachment” or “closeness to God”) are experienced in the intellectual effort, intimated in the flux of struggle.[47]

In his articulation of this theory, R. Ḥayyim maintains that *lishmah* means essentially “for the sake of love of the Torah, to labor to understand its essential foundation” (ענין הלשמה, עקרה לשם אהבת התורה, ליגע ולעמוד על שרשה). It is important here to note that R. Ḥayyim is suggesting three different dimensions—behavioral, affective, and cognitive—in articulating how *Torah lishmah* is part of the learning experience itself. The behavioral dimension expressed in the verb “to labor” (*l’ega,* “hard effort”); the affective is suggested by *ahavah* (“love”); and the cognitive is *amidah al sharshah* (“understanding its essential foundation”—literally, “standing on its very root”).

He then begins to contrast his definition of *lishmah* with what he considers to be that of his hasidic contemporaries:

> אבל אם יחשוב אדם כי לשמה הכוונה לדבקות, אם כן לדעתו ודמיונו יחשוב שיעסק בשירות ותשבחות . . . המעוררים אהבת ה’ וקרבתו וזה די לו ובזה יחיה חיים ערבים. אבל לא כן הוא.
> (RH 6:1)
>
> But if one considers *lishmah*’s intended meaning as attachment to God (*devekut*), one would have to imagine that, to lead a satisfying life, it would be sufficient to engage in hymns of praise . . . that arouse the love of God and His closeness. But this is not the case.

To R. Ḥayyim, then, *devekut*, is not the true meaning of *lishmah*; and longing for “closeness to God” (קרבת אלהים) is not a meditative prior condition for study; it is awakened in the midst of intense intellectual effort.

He supports this refutation, returning to the cognitive, behavioral, and affective dimensions of *Torah lishmah*. First, he explains the concept of cognition, emphasizing “*l’hasig*” (“to comprehend”) and “*lada’at*” (“to know,” “to understand”) as intentionally extending and deepening one’s knowledge,

> לפי שעיקר הלימוד לא לעסק רק בדבקות, כי אם להשיג על ידי התורה המצוות והדינים ולידע כל דבר על בוריו, כלליו ופרטיו, ולהשיג גם כן סתרי פלאי מעשיו וחקר כבודו.

> For the essence of learning is not to engage exclusively in cleaving (or "attaching") to God (*devekut*), but rather, through the Torah, mitsvot, and laws, understanding every matter to its core—both its broad and specific principles, comprehending the hidden wonders of His deeds and the mysteries of His glory.

He then turns to the behavioral dimension of learning implied by *lishmah*, again emphasizing "intense labor" or "intense effort":

> ולזה צריך ללמד ביגיעה עצומה, להשיג אמיתת כוונות התורה לפי השגתו.

> One must therefore study with intense effort in order to comprehend the truth of the Torah's intentions, according to one's [individual] comprehension.

Torah lishmah ("Torah for its own sake") requires the intense effort of inquiry into the Torah's truth. Aiming toward the "the truth of the Torah's intentions," however, is not a terminal end, nor is it what Dewey would call a uniform end-in-view. Hence he adds the qualifier, "according to his [individual] comprehension."

Finally, regarding the affective dimension of learning, R. Ḥayyim emphasizes the awakening of desire in learning:

> וכל אשר יוסיף ללמוד, כן יוסיף לחפוץ ללמוד עוד ובאהבת התורה ישגה ויחשב והלואי שיוכל לא לישן ולא לאכל, רק כל הימים וכל הלילות ליגע ולעין ולשתות בצמא את דבריה. (RH 6:1)

> With increased learning comes increased desire for further learning, so that one will then exult in the love of Torah, thinking "If only I could forego sleeping and eating in order to quench my thirst by toiling and studying its lessons."

As Dewey maintains, learning is not purely an experience of knowing; it is also an emotional experience evoked and driven by desire, propelling the learner forward with an increasing desire for deeper inquiry. For R. Ḥayyim, too, *Torah lishmah* is an enduring spiral of strenuous intellectual inquiry awakening desire for further insight and understanding.

R. Ḥayyim's educational theory of this interplay between desire and intellectual effort is further developed through his analogy of entering a king's concentrically chambered palace:

> כדמיון הנכנס לחדר המלך, בבית גנזיו המלך אור יקרות, ומשם רואה דלת לחדר פנימי עוד, וחפץ לכנוס לתוכו, ומשם רואה עוד חדרים פנימיים, וכל הקרוב יותר לחדר המלך עצמו, יותר יקר, ומהודר, עד אין חקר, מהחדר החיצון. ואם לא נכנס מתחילה, בחדר הראשון, לא היה יודע מאומה, אם יש חדרים פנימיים זה לפנים מזה. וכן לענין התורה, כי על ידי אור שמשיג מתחילה, רואה כי יש עוד אור גדול מזה וכן להלאה. ועל ידי זה יתאווה תאווה. להבין ולהשיג עוד עד כי

ישיג כל סתרי העולם ומלואה. כרבן יוחנן בן זכאי אשר אמרו עליו (סוכה כ"ח) שלא הניח כו', עד דבר גדול וקטן כו', לקיים מה שנאמר "להנחיל אוהבי יש וגו." וזהו "זוכה הדברים הרבה" שאמור במשנה. (RH 6:1)

This may be compared to one who enters the king's [outer] chamber, his treasure house full of precious light. From there one sees a door to a more interior room and desires to enter it; and from there one sees rooms even further in, seeing that the nearer a room is to the king's room itself, the more precious and adorned it is beyond comprehension compared to that outer room. And if one had not initially entered the first room, one would not have known a single thing about the existence of increasingly interior rooms, each more interior than the one before it.

And this is the case in the matter of Torah. For on account of the light that one first apprehends, one sees that there is even greater light, and so on. On account of this he will have an appetite to understand and grasp more until he comprehends all of the secrets of the world and the fullness thereof . . . This, then, is [what is meant by] "merits many things," as said in the Mishna.

Elsewhere, in his introduction to the Vilna Gaon's commentary on the esoteric Zoharic work, *Sifra ditsniuta*, R. Ḥayyim more explicitly, though still with due ambiguity, refers to these *devarim*, these "many things," that one merits during and through *Torah lishmah*:

הלא מסורת בידינו מהתנא ר"מ שזוכה לדברים הרבה. סתם ולא פי' מה המה אלה הדברים ואא"ל (אי אפשר לומר) שהם הדברים שפרט אח"ז (אחרי זה) שהרי אמר אח"ז ולא עוד כו' הרי שהם מילתא באפי נפשא. אמנם רמז לדברים נפלאים הגילויים עליונים נוראים שאינם דבר המושג לאומרו ולבארו.

Has it not been passed down to us from the tanna Rabbi Meir that "one merits many things"? He refrained from explaining just what these things are. It is impossible to claim that they refer to the things that he specified after this, since, following this statement, he states "and the entire world is worthwhile for him." So indeed these *devarim* ["things," "matters," "concepts," "lessons"] are a *sui generis* matter. Nevertheless, he hinted at wondrous things that are awesome, supernal revelations that are not something that can be comprehended, stated, and clarified.[48]

Here R. Ḥayyim suggests that these anticipated outcomes of *Torah lishmah,* these *devarim*, i.e,. "things," "matters," "concepts," "lessons" are *sui generis* (literally, "a thing in itself," מילתא באפי נפשא). They are qualities of an infinite horizon. They clearly are not an end-in-view; they are too elusive. They also do not serve to guide conduct; they are too ambiguous to serve as a guide. They serve as an enveloping context and meaning of the learning experience. Using Dewey's language with that of R. Ḥayyim, we can say that these *devarim* "vibrate" in the "midst of effort" as we come to appreciate their intimations in our experience of *Torah lishmah.*[49]

In the following allegory, R. Ḥayyim suggests a pedagogical phenomenology in which ideals, means, and ends interact dynamically in a quite Deweyan sense. He adds to his interpretation of R. Meir's above mentioned aphorism, "All who engage (*osek*) in the study of Torah for its own sake (*Torah lishmah*) merit many things (*devarim*)," (כל העוסק בתורה לשמה זוכה לדברים הרבה), making an analogy between the learning experience and navigating a river raft:

> ויתבאר עוד ענין לשמה לשם התורה עד"ם כענין הדוברות העושים בים דרך אשר האדם יושב עליהם ומנהיגם למחוז החפץ אשר שם יעשה מהם קורות בנין או כלים. וכאשר האדם יושב עליהם ומנהיגם למחוז החפץ הנה הוא מציל את נפשו מן הנהר וגם העצים יבואו לתכליתם. אבל אם יבדל מהם אל הים שוב אין לו חיים וטובע וגם להם אין מי שיובילם ויאבדו ואין להם תיקון לצאת מגולמי עצים לצורך בנין או כלי. אבל אם יוליכם למקומם הוא חי' יחי' עליהם וגם השכר רב יהיה לו על הולכתם והם יבואו לשלמותם. כן עסק התורה אם ח"ו אנחנו פורשים ממנה אין לנו חיים וגם לה כדי בזיון. (RH 6:1)

> The matter of *lishmah* being for the sake of Torah will become clear through an analogy of a raft's logs making their way on the water. A person is situated on them and guides them to the desired destination at which he will make lumber or tools from them. When one sits on them [the logs] and guides them to the desired destination, one [also] rescues himself from the river, and the logs, too, achieve their purpose. But if one becomes separated from them [and falls] into the water, one would then not live and would drown; and they [the logs], too, would have no one to transport them and will become lost, irreversibly unable to emerge from their crude state to serve the needs of a building or a tool. But if one directs them to their place, one will surely live by them and will have great reward on account of having guided them. And so they will reach their fulfillment. This is [analogous to] being engaged with Torah (*esek hatorah*). If, God forbid, we separate from it, we will have no life and it [the Torah] too will be disgraced.

In this passage, we note a number of candidates for desired outcomes or ends: reaching the desired place (מחוז החפץ), constructing walls of buildings and tools (אשר שם יעשה מהם קורות בנין או כלים), preserving one's life (מציל את נפשו), keeping oneself together with the logs of the raft (אם יבדל מהם), and obtaining unspecified reward (שכר רב יהיה לו). Each of these are desired ends from the perspective of one steering the raft. One should also note that the raft and its logs have a kind of organic existence in relation to the one who steers the raft. R. Ḥayyim thus also specifies desired ends from the perspective of the raft and its logs: the logs' surviving, the raft's having a guide to hold the logs together and steer them, avoiding irreparable damage or loss, and the logs' fulfilling their purpose as building material or tools.

Parallel to Dewey and central to the Volozhiner's thought, the objects in one's environment (and the environment as a whole) have a purposeful existence in interaction with and dependent on one's conduct. The raft is effected directly by what one does, even as that conduct also affects one's own well-being. With remarkable resonance with Dewey, R. Ḥayyim here expresses his sensitivity to ends serving equally as means. To be at an end is to arrive safely, intact. And even the arrival is an immediate redirection of activity from navigation to construction. The attentiveness to each end becomes the means for further achievements, provided that these ends (which, of course, are also means) are part of the effort, the process, the experience. This allegory also illustrates how R. Ḥayyim conceives of *Torah lishmah* as a background ideal intimated within the activity itself. Each aspect of this activity, each "pivot point" (to use Dewey's language), is an end. In his analogy, overlooking the importance of each part of the activity would cause self-destruction and the destruction of the raft itself. Each end in this cycle is equally a means to propel and sustain the activity in the context of its holistic sense of purposefulness.

We may get a greater appreciation of R. Ḥayyim's analogy by considering the way Dewey dissolves the means-ends dualism:

> The "end" is merely a series of acts viewed at a remote stage; and a means is merely the series viewed at an earlier one. The distinction of means and end arises in surveying the course of a proposed line of action, a connected series in time. The "end" is the last act thought of; the means are the acts to be performed prior to it in time. *To reach an end we must take our mind off from it* and attend to the act which is next to be performed. We must make that the end.[50]

Keeping the raft's logs connected, maintaining navigational balance and good direction are "acts" that for R. Ḥayyim must be the focus. These ends are ultimate and fateful, even as they also function as means. The raft will fall apart on its journey if one is not at least as attentive to keeping the logs together as one is to the destination. Here a detached idealism—analogous to a misreading of *Torah lishmah* as a kind of perfected state of mind—would be fatal. In this interpretation, then, R. Ḥayyim emphasizes *Torah lishmah* as intimated in the activity itself rather than a condition that must be attained prior to the learning experience.

Nor does R. Ḥayyim view *Torah shelo lishmah* ("Torah not for its own sake") as a means to the goal of *Torah lishmah*. He asserts the positive value of *Torah shelo lishmah* in that, without it, we will never experience *Torah lishmah*. Yet he does not claim simply that *Torah lishmah* is the goal toward which to strive through the vehicle of having an extrinsic objective (*shelo lishmah*). The cosmically intrinsic value of the Torah study (*lishmah* or *shelo lishmah*) is immeasurable; it is the activity of learning itself that is desirable, not as a medium toward a detached goal.[51]

It is thus important to note that R. Ḥayyim concludes his magnum opus, *Nefesh Ha-Ḥayyim*, without mentioning *Torah lishmah*:

ובשעת העסק והעיון בתורה ודאי שאין צריך אז לענין הדבקות כלל, כנ"ל. שבהעסק ועיון לבד הוא דבוק ברצונו ודבורו יתברך והוא יתברך ורצונו ודבורו חד. (NH 4:10)

> While engaged (*b'sh'at ha'esek*) with Torah inquiry, one should not be concerned with the issue of *devekut* at all, as stated above. In the very act of engaged inquiry (*esek v'iyyun*), one is attached (*davuk*) to His will and His word, blessed be He. He (blessed be He), His will, and His word are one.

He thus concludes his argument, focusing simply on "*esek hatorah*" ("being engaged with Torah study"). Preserving the integrity of the learning engagement and of inquiry itself (*mishmeret ha'esek*) are his preeminent concerns.

CONCLUSION

To use contemporary terminology, R. Ḥayyim was a theoretician, practitioner, community activist, influential public intellectual, and an innovative educational leader who heralded a new era for Torah learning. When we view R. Ḥayyim's activities and thought in conjunction with Dewey, we more readily discern the former's cultural criticism, the way in which he took issue with many of his era's prevalent assumptions and articulated their problematic consequences. In Dewey's idiom, R. Ḥayyim is concerned with dissolving illusory dualisms, maintaining integral, non-dualistic connections between conduct and character, means and ends, actions and ideals. R. Ḥayyim sees the educational good as growth pursued in a thoughtful, deliberate pursuit of a passionately desired, dynamic end, while holding the fixed, terminal, and *a priori* in abeyance.

For R. Ḥayyim, the importance of ideals is derived from what Whitehead calls "the immanence of the infinite in the finite,"[52] though their imagined referents may be quite different. His educational purpose is grounded in the assumption that our fates and the fate of the world rest on ongoing vigilance and the cultivation of habits (סדרי הנהגה, הרגל) in our deeds, speech, and thought, as they influence our environment with an extensive, even transcendent reach. Learning and growth do not come easily, however, and there is an ineluctable "intense struggle" (יגיעה עצומה) in the learning process that continuously fosters desire (חפיצה) and impetus for further inquiry.

R. Ḥayyim's discourse provides important language for a theory and practice of Jewish education today. For he sought to change his society's educational tendencies by changing habits of thought and conduct—in particular, with regard to Torah study—demonstrating the differences that thought (מחשבה), speech (דיבור), and deed (מעשה) make in human experience and in the world's physical and spiritual condition. Educators whose work is informed by R. Ḥayyim can consider the infinite reach of their own professional conduct as they influence their students' understandings of contingencies in their lives and their worlds: "Indeed, one should come to know, understand, and determine that each and every aspect of one's conduct, speech, and thoughts never perishes, God forbid, and that one's conduct becomes manifold, ascending to very exalted heights."[53] (אמנם יבין וידע ויקבע במחשבותיו שכל פרטי מעשיו ודבוריו ומחשבותיו כל עת ורגע לא אתאבידו ח"ו, ומה רבו מעשיו ומאד גדלו ורמו).

The empowerment and responsibility that come with recognition of the import of action, word, and thought can indeed be a driving force in recognizing the purposes of the education profession. At the same time, resisting the tendency to overly operationalize and engineer learning, we can help students recognize, feel, and experience the intimations of ideal meanings in their efforts and accomplishments. We can acquire a renewed, redefined sense of self as we contemplate and respond to our intimate, integral relationship to the social, natural, spiritual, and professional worlds we inhabit. Equally important, we can recognize how motivation stems from the learning experience itself and how pedagogical excellence creates the precious desire (חפיצה) for further learning.

We educators could be well served by considering R. Ḥayyim's interpretation of the complex interplay of means, ends, and ideals in planning, conducting, and evaluating learning experiences. For R. Ḥayyim, meaningful Torah teaching is an end in itself, even as it influences a wide range of future conditions and capacities. The act of good teaching is intrinsically sacred when we consider what is at stake in the dynamic relationships that connect students, teachers, and the world to one another. Teaching is nothing less than a sustained renewal of the cosmos by the conduct of teachers and students. In a Deweyan sense, R. Ḥayyim's ongoing restoration of Torah study is directed by generously and sensitively identifying those inchoate desires and efforts that reflect and enhance the relationship between Torah study, mitsvot, the worlds, and human experience. Deconstructing the means-ends dualism of his contemporaries, R. Ḥayyim, like Dewey, would maintain that every learning experience ends with the affirmation: "Concluded but incomplete" (*tam velo nishlam*).[54]

NOTES

1. This recent Deweyan scholarship challenges a conception of Dewey's work that divides it into an early "Hegelian" idealist phase and a later empiricist, naturalist pragmatism. See Kestenbaum, *John Dewey and the Transcendent*; Garrison, *Dewey and Eros: Wisdom and Desire in the Art of Teaching*; Saito, *The Gleam of Light: Moral Perfectionism and Education in Dewey and Emerson.*

2. In addition to his early writings on the ideal, in particular in *Outlines of a Critical Theory of Ethics*, renewed attention is being given to Dewey's *Theory of the Moral Life*, *Human Nature and Conduct*, *Experience and Nature*, and *Art as Experience.*

3. See chapter 2.

4. Dewey, *Human Nature and Conduct*, 259.

5. Dewey, *Human Nature and Conduct,* 259.
6. Dewey, *Human Nature and Conduct*, 260.
7. Dewey, *Human Nature and Conduct,* 261.
8. Dewey, *Human Nature and Conduct,* 261.
9. Dewey, *Human Nature and Conduct,* 261.
10. Dewey, *Human Nature and Conduct,* 262.
11. Dewey, *Human Nature and Conduct,* 263.
12. Dewey, *Human Nature and Conduct,* 263.
13. Dewey, *Human Nature and Conduct,* 263.
14. Dewey, *Human Nature and Conduct,* 263.
15. Dewey, *Human Nature and Conduct,* 263.
16. Dewey, *Human Nature and Conduct*, 264.
17. The rabbinic concept of "*Torah lishmah*" ("Torah study for its own sake") expresses the value of studying Torah (and related rabbinic literature) without an extrinsic purpose or incentive.
18. Dewey, *Art as Experience*, 29.
19. Dewey, *Human Nature and Conduct* , 259.
20. See Kestenbaum, *The Phenomenological Sense of John Dewey.*
21. Dewey, *Experience and Nature*, 7
22. Kestenbaum, *Dewey and the Transcendent*, 1
23. The "rabbinic tradition," or "rabbinic literature," refers to Jewish law and traditional exegetical and homiletical literature associated with of the "Oral Law," including the Mishna, Talmud, midrash, and Scriptural exegesis. It connotes the authoritative tradition of interpretation of Scripture as it evolved during and since the time of the Second Temple, which was destroyed in 70 C.E.
24. "מתוך שלא לשמה בא לשמה" BT Sanhedrin 105b.
25. Often, the preferential way to achieve *devekut,* in early hasidism, however, was devotional prayer.
26. RH 6:1.
27. NH 4:3.
28. NH 4:3.
29. Dewey, *Human Nature,* 263.
30. NH pre-4:4.
31. NH 4:1.
32. NH 4:1.
33. See chapter 3 on Dewey's and R. Ḥayyim's concepts of humility.
34. Dewey, *Human Nature and Conduct*, 261. See Kestenbaum, *Dewey and the Transcendent*, 49.
35. Dewey, *Human Nature and Conduct*, 261.
36. Kestenbaum, *Dewey and the Transcendent*, 47.
37. Dewey, *Human Nature and Conduct*, 263.
38. Dewey, *Human Nature and Conduct*, 207.
39. Dewey, *Critical Theory of Ethics*, 212.
40. Dewey, *Critical Theory of Ethics*, 212.
41. On moral experience, see Dewey, *Theory of the Moral Life*. On intellectual experience, see his *Quest for Certainty* and his *Logic: The Theory of Inquiry*. On aesthetic experience, see his *Art as Experience.* On social experience and learning experience, see his *Human Nature and Conduct* and *Democracy and Education.*
42. Dewey, *Critical Theory of Ethics*, 212–213.
43. Dewey, *Critical Theory of Ethics*, 213. Dewey develops this theme of acquisition and aspiration, or the consummatory and the critical, more extensively in his middle and later works, *Human Nature and Conduct*, *Art as Experience*, and *Experience and Nature*. We will return to his conception of the place of effort and struggle in educational experience below.
44. A *tanna* is a scholar-teacher of period of the mishna (the end of the first century B.C.E to the second century C.E.).
45. *Pirke Avot* 6:1.

46. Dewey, *Human Nature*, 264.
47. NH 4:1; RH 6:1.
48. R. Ḥayyim's introduction to the GRA's commentary on *Sifra Ditsni'uta*.
49. On the "midst of effort" and "vibration." See Dewey, *Human Nature and Conduct,* 264: "The religious experience is a reality in so far as in the midst of effort to foresee and regulate future objects we are sustained and expanded in feebleness and failure by the sense of an enveloping whole," and Dewey, *Experience and Nature* (Chicago and London: Open Court, 1926), 8: "When disease or religion or love, or knowledge itself is experienced, forces and potential consequences are implicated that are neither directly present nor logically implied. They are 'in' experience quite as truly as are present discomforts and exaltations . . . Experience is no stream, even though the stream of feelings and ideas that flows upon its surface is the part which philosophers love to traverse. Experience includes the enduring banks of natural constitution and acquired habit as well as the stream. The flying moment is sustained by an atmosphere that does not fly, even when it most vibrates."
50. Dewey, *Human Nature and Conduct,* 34 (my italics).
51. R. Ḥayyim devotes an entire section of the *Nefesh Ha-Ḥayyim*, the *"perakim,"* to this theme. Included in this section is the following statement:

> וגם אם נראה שכל ימי חייו מנעוריו ועד זקנה ושיבה היה עסקו בה שלא לשמה גם כן אתה חיב לנהג בו כבוד, וכל שכן שלא לבזותו ח"ו, שכיון שעסק בתורת ה' בתמידות, בלתי ספק שהיה כונתו פעמים רבות גם לשמה, כמו שהבטיחו רז"ל (פסחים נ). שמתוך שלא לשמה בא לשמה, כי אין הפרוש דוקא שיבא מזה ללשמה, עד שאחר כך יעסק בה תמיד כל ימיו רק לשמה. אלא הינו, שבכל פעם שהוא לומד בקביעות זמן כמה שעות רצופים, אף שדרך כלל היתה כונתו שלא לשמה, עם כל זה, בלתי אפשר כלל שלא יכנס בלבו באמצע הלמוד על כל פנים זמן מעט כונה רצויה לשמה, ומעתה כל מה שלמד עד הנה שלא לשמה, נתקדש ונטהר על ידי אותו העת קטן שכון בו לשמה.

> Even if we see that for one's entire life, from youth to old age, one's involvement with [Torah] has been *shelo lishmah* ["not for its own sake"], you must extend honor to him, and especially not denigrate him, God forbid. Since he was constantly involved with the Torah of God, undoubtedly his level of devotion was *lishmah* many times. As the Sages (*Pesaḥim* 50) promised, "Out of study *lo lishmah* he arrives at *lishmah.*" But the meaning is not just that he will arrive *from* this [*lo lishmah*] to *lishmah* so that following this he will consistently be at [the level of] *lishmah* for his entire lifetime. Rather, it means that each time that he regularly studies a few consecutive hours, even though usually his devotion was *shelo lishmah*, despite this, it would be impossible that, for a few times, the desired devotion of *lishmah* would not enter his heart. From that moment, everything that he has learned up until that point with [devotion at the level of] *shelo lishmah*, would be sanctified and purified on account of that short time that he devoted himself to it *lishmah.*

The study of Torah *shelo lishmah* is therefore not a vehicle intended to bring one to *lishmah.* The level of *lishmah* is a natural condition that is intrinsic to sustained Torah study. Furthermore, *lishmah* has a retroactive effect on all previous study, even if that earlier learning experience had been driven by extrinsic concerns (*shelo lishmah*). The entire learning experience—past and present—is transformed to a level of holiness and purity. In a sense, what would normally be considered the end—*lishmah*—by way of its retroactive transforming power, becomes the means.
52. Whitehead. "Understanding," 75.
53. NH 1:4.
54. "Concluded but not completed." The phrase *Tam venishlam,* "Concluded and completed," is used to indicate the completion of reading a sacred text as a celebratory "signature," most often in completing the study of a chapter of Talmud. Here I add the negative, "*lo*," to indicate that the study is never complete—something always remains as the elusive object of intellectual desire.

Part 3

Agnon's Narratives: An Ethics of Alterity in Reading and Teaching

Increasingly, teaching has come to be recognized as a narrative act. In this sense, teachers have a dual role of guiding inquiry into idiosyncratic stories and contextualizing those stories, situating them within a broader cultural narrative and disciplinary framework. In Chapters Six and Seven, I hold a conversation between modern literary theory and educational theory as I address the tension between narrative containment and exclusion as a common issue in modern Hebrew literature, Jewish studies pedagogy, and Jewish education in general. In the discourse of literary theory, then, I consider the tensions in this dual role when teachers respond to multiple, at times conflicting, sources of responsibility—students, texts, disciplines, and traditions. In providing different types and degrees of context, the teacher, like the narrator, decides what to reveal and what to conceal. It would be a rich area of inquiry to consider how these kinds of hermeneutic trade-offs are recurring motifs in making curricular and pedagogical decision-making. Such an inquiry could reveal the stratified, tensional nature of teaching modern and traditional narrative texts.

Shortly after the Volozhin Yeshivah's closing in 1892 and over 700 kilometers away, Buczacz was about to begin achieving its own prominent place in Jewish memory and imagination through the literary artistry of that town's native son, Hebrew writer and 1966 Nobel Prize Laureate S. Y. Agnon (1888–1970, b. Shmuel Yosef Halevi Czaczkes). Perhaps the most significant figure in modern Hebrew literature, the ironies and tensions in Agnon's unique narrative artistry are reflected in the very titles of well-known works of literary scholarship on his oeuvre: *Nostalgia and Nightmare*, *The Revolutionary Traditionalist*, *From Exile and Return*, and *Cunning Innocence*.[1] These titles' dual, tensional qualities suggest how Agnon's readers encounter ambivalent recollections of Jewish life in Eastern Europe and prestate Palestine. Reading Agnon's fiction is, of course, far from equivalent to reading historical accounts. Yet despite this difference, as Gershon Shaked explains, Agnon's fiction is his "very personal interpretation of historical reality" through which "his world view" influences "our own interpretation of the extraliterary world" since "so well made and persuasive is it in its comprehensiveness, so convincing in its fidelity." His prose engenders a kind of readerly "trust" as if it "mirrors nonfictional reality."[2]

Like R. Ḥayyim of Volozhin, S. Y. Agnon recalls the waxing and waning of Jewish learning and Torah study in Eastern Europe. Though in very different genres and more than a century apart, both depict ironies and tensions in the theory and practice of Torah study. Both allude to a time "when Torah was dear to Israel"[3] and both lament the periods of Torah study's decline.

As we saw in Part One, R. Ḥayyim recalls such episodes in Jewish educational history:

> The first generations were consistently occupied with reflection on the holy Torah for all of their days . . . and the flame of love of our holy Torah was in their hearts like a fire burning with love and pure awe of God. Their entire desire was to magnify its honor and glorify it. So they expanded its reach with many suited students so that the land would be filled with knowledge.[4]

In Agnon's story, "Two Scholars Who Were in Our Town" (the subject of chapter 6), the narrator offers his own idealized account of a previous era's reverence for Torah study:

> Three or four generations ago, when Torah was dear to Israel and learning it constituted a man's dignity . . . everyone would make the Torah their priority, knowing that the joy of the Lord is our strength.

And each writer provides empathic accounts of how Torah study declined. As we saw in part 1, R. Ḥayyim explains:

> For there are many worthy individuals whose hearts worry within them, sighing and bemoaning the forgotten and weakened Torah . . . Each person constructs his own *heder* (school house), saying, "I will rescue myself," and so he assembles a generation in which the Torah is not dear to those who study it.[5]

Agnon's narrator, too, presents his account of the decline, a point to which I will return in chapter 6:

> Three to four generations ago, nothing was dearer than Torah; but beginning two to three generations ago, Torah study increasingly declined . . . Those who were studying did so for their own selfish benefit so that they could be called "Rabbi" and be seated as a head . . . Anyone who could use his fingers would write new interpretations and publish them . . . but . . . [most of these were] baskets full of hollow gourds.[6]

For our purposes, these brief excerpts attest to common concerns with regard to the purposes, hopes, and practices of Jewish education. They reveal the surface beneath which I now seek to delve as I consider the conversations, possible relationships, and deliberative engagements that could meaningfully take place between the study of Agnon's remarkable literary works and contemporary educational discourse.

As we will now see, pedagogical and narrative tensions are prevalent in Agnon's "Two Scholars Who Were in Our Town" (*Shnei talmdei ḥakhamim shehayu b'ireinu*, שני תלמידי חכמים שהיו בעירנו) and "The Outcast" (*Hanidaḥ*, הנדח). As I will suggest, the range of narrative styles in these two stories suggests alternative dispositions toward an "other": in the first story (Chapter Six), the enigmatic other of the storyteller; in the second story (Chapter Seven), the objectified other as reflected in a narrator's speech. In the first story, the core enigmatic tale is too transgressive for the narrator as it seemingly dismantles an idealized reconstructed memory. In the second story, the narrative's limiting effect on the "other" overwhelms a student's effort to be released from narrative objectification.

Since Jewish studies teachers traverse historical reasoning, factual depiction, folkloric tales, mythic stories, and other literary forms in their pedagogy, the narrative dynamics in Agnon's stories suggest a number of educational implications. For example, Jewish studies teachers might consider the qualities and effects of their representations of narrative boundaries. Furthermore, like narrating and interpreting narratives, teaching involves overcoming the interdicts of presupposed emplotments and recognizing modes of negotiating the need for closure with an enduring need for deferring and problematizing closure. In both texts, the narrators' efforts to conceal the multiple and the transgressive are most evident in awkward attempts at closure, an abiding issue for Agnon, and, as I suggest, for teachers as well.

If we consider the modern need to make sense of tradition through honest engagement with ironies and contradictions embedded within it, secular Jewish fiction should be squarely within the scope or paideia of contemporary Jewish education. Students (and teachers) need a sense of continuity with those who have preceded them as well as sensitivity to the ironies and discontinuities. Such recognition can allow the student to recognize the human, individual stories within a multivocal narrative tradition and see her reflection in this inheritance of cultural achievements.[7]

Modern Jewish literature calls out for interpretation, no less than do timeless, sacred texts. I therefore suggest that educators should no longer consider modern Jewish literature too new in Jewish life to be an integral dimension of efforts to engage and teach.[8] Interpreting this "new tradition,"[9] this "modern Jewish canon,"[10] can be fruitful for curriculum inquiry and for investigation into the ways teachers mediate interpretation and how students uncover cultural meanings.

Beyond the argument that cultural continuity and adaptation are at stake, I suggest that there is also value in considering the ethical dimensions of modern Jewish literature.[11] Fictional texts and their implied authors, whose "company we choose to keep,"[12] provide an imaginative landscape in which to consider ethical issues that surround and engage students and teachers every day. As I suggest below in my analysis of the narrative voices in Agnon fiction, considering the "ethics of fiction," to use Wayne C. Booth's felicitous term, need not diminish the intrinsic, artistic value of a work. Indeed, as I hope to demonstrate, even the artistry and interplay of voices in these stories reveal their ethical dimensions, including the need to recognize multivocality, multiple meanings, and pluralist dispositions toward different modes of telling and retelling.

One way in which Jewish teaching, traditionally, has expressed values is, as Abraham J. Heschel reminds us, through maxims and sayings stating ultimate or allegorical normative claims (such as "Better to throw yourself into a burning furnace than to embarrass a human being in public."[13]). But another way is through teachers' transporting themselves and their students into an empathic experience of reading and listening to narratives—including modern fiction, with all its inconsistencies, contradictions, and implicit critiques—and confronting them honestly and directly.[14] We need, then, to consider how the normative and the narrative are both important dimensions in teaching values.

Inquiry into education might consider how teaching modern fiction can provide ways to graciously accept what Booth calls narrative "gifts" that transcend any one set of maxims, allowing students to form relationships with new "lasting friends."[15] This stance demands an active role for students. Modern authors can serve as models in that they are both readers of prior texts and writers constructing new texts that respond to or rebel against "sayings of the fathers."[16] The research challenge, then, is to consider how teaching modern Jewish fiction might engender narrative formation as well as narrative interpretation.

So I here offer three agendas for educational inquiry: 1) the educational functions of revealing narrative mediation and multivocality in modern fiction and how these narrative voices provide a language for considering analogies between teacher and narrator; 2) the value-added in finding an essential place for this new tradition in contemporary curricula and; 3) the nuanced way in which modern stories can provide a landscape for ethical inquiry that goes beyond illustrating expository, normative principles, that engages the learner with ethical questions and struggles of the implied authors and how these authors' stories and our own—to use Dewey's words—may be "wrought into the texture of our lives."[17]

Chapters 6 and 7 each begin with a literary analysis of one of Agnon's stories and its critical reception. I then consider how a Jewish studies field—modern Hebrew literature—has the potential for being a conversation partner and source for educational theory.

NOTES

1. Arnold Band, *Nostalgia and Nightmare: A Study in the Fiction of S. Y. Agnon* (Los Angeles, University of California Press, 1968); Esther Fuchs, *Cunning Innocence: On S. Y Agnon's Irony* (Hebrew) (*'Omanut ha-hitamemut: 'al ha-ironiah shel Agnon*) (Tel Aviv: Tel Aviv University Press, 1985); Anne Golomb Hoffman, *Between Exile and Return: S. Y. Agnon and the Drama of Writing* (Albany: State University of New York Press, 1991); Gershon Shaked, *Shmuel Yosef Agnon: A Revolutionary Traditionalist*. Jeff M. Green, trans. (New York: New York University Press, 1989).

2. Gershon Shaked, "By a Miracle: Agnon's Literary Representation of Social Dramas," in Gershon Shaked, ed.,*The Shadows Within: Essays on Modern Jewish Writers* (Philadelphia, New York, Jerusalem: The Jewish Publication Society, 1987), 143.

3. See *Babylonian Talmud* , Tractate Berakhot 63a and 63b.

4. R. Ḥayyim of Volozhin, *Nefesh Ha-Ḥayyim* 4:1.

5. R. Ḥayyim of Volozhin, "Letter to Lithuanian Communities" soliciting support for the Volozhin Yeshiva (1802) in *Ha-Peles* Vol. 3 (1912), 140–43 (my translation).

6. Agnon, "Two Scholars Who Were in Our Town," 31 (my translation). "ועתה נשא קינה על בגידת הזמן. לפני שלושה ארבעה דורות לא היה דבר חביב מן התורה, לפני שנים שלושה דורות התחילה התורה יורדת והולכת."

7. On being "born into an inheritance of human achievements," see Oakeshott, "Learning and Teaching."

8. Cynthia Ozick once made a similar claim in broadening the notion of Jewish cultural texts: "Jewish mainstream culture was once confined to the content of the traditional religious texts, hundreds of classics that were oceanic enough even without novels and secular poetry, and which of course preceded the existence of such forms, and, when they arose, never dreamed of admitting them. The old definition didn't include imaginative literature as we know it now, or what we might term, if the term were still useful, belles-lettres . . . But since the rise of *Haskalah*, the Jewish Enlightenment, which arrived in Eastern Europe a century later than in the West, the idea of what Jewish culture is about has been radically altered. We seem not to know exactly what to do with this difference in perception of the nature of textual culture; it is simply too new in Jewish life." Cynthia Ozick. "Interview," 358.

9. Shaked, *The New Tradition*.

10. Wisse, *The Modern Jewish Canon*.

11. Booth, *Ethics of Fiction*; Miller, *Ethics of Reading*.

12. Booth, *Rhetoric of Fiction* and *Ethics of Fiction*. In his seminal work on fictional narrative and authorship, Booth argues that the narrator "is only one of the elements created by the implied author who may be separated from him by large ironies." Booth, *Rhetoric of Fiction*, 73; Fludernik refers to the implied author as "the entire novel's frame of values," "the frame of the text's values as a whole," "non-attributable features of discourse," "an abbreviation for the narrative's overall meaning structure," "the world view that the reader constructs for the text as a whole." Fludernik, "Towards a 'Natural' Narratology," 183, 203, 218, 381, 395. Chatman refers to the implied author as "the source of the narrative text's whole structure

of meaning—not only of its assertion and denotation but also of its implication, connotation, and ideological nexus." Chatman, "Defense of the Implied Author" as quoted in Darby, "Form and Context," 845.

13. Heschel, "The Values of Jewish Education."

14. On this role of narrative in education and educational research, see Shapiro, Ph.D. Dissertation, "Cultivating a Viable Relationship Between North American Jews and Israel."

15. Booth, *Ethics of Fiction.*

16. Students who draw upon these models are aptly characterized in Geoffrey Hartman's notion of the work of reading: "Refusing the subterfuge of a passive or restrictive role, he becomes at once reader and writer—or takes it fully into consciousness that he is both an interpreter of texts and a self-interpreting producer of further texts." G. Hartman, "The Work of Reading."

17. Dewey, *Human Nature and Conduct,* 263.

Chapter Six

Multivocal Narrative and the Teacher as Narrator

Agnon's "Two Scholars Who Were in Our Town." *("*Shnei talmidei ḥakhamim she-hayu be-'ireinu*")*

> When two scholars are comfortable with each other's legal opinions, the Holy One Blessed Be He attends to them. (BT *Shabbat* 63a)

> Regarding two scholars living in the same town who are unsettled by each other's legal opinions, Scripture says "I have given them laws with which they will not flourish." (BT *Megilah* 32a)

> When two scholars go for a walk together without exchanging Torah insights, they might as well be consumed by fire. (BT *Sotah* 49a)

As "narrators," educators assume responsibility for both the ambiguous indeterminate aspects of unmediated tales as well as their contextualization within a normative framework. They thus engage students with the less apparent, idiosyncratic meanings of the storyteller's art along with instructing them in the more encompassing meanings of broader cultural metanarratives. S. Y. Agnon's story, "Two Scholars Who Were in Our Town," provides a particular kind of multivocal narrative that can inform how teachers navigate these two responsibilities—to engage as well as to instruct.[1] I suggest that the relationship between distinctive, agonistic narrative voices within this story reflects how teachers may overly mediate narratives that were once more directly connected to the folk and therefore had less of a global, meta-intent. The tendency to expansively frame a traditional tale can lead a teacher into an undesirable role analogous to that of an over-totalizing narrator.

As reflected in Agnon's "Two Scholars," the tension between teacher-as-storyteller and teacher-as-modern-narrator suggests the need for educators to be circumspect in their judgments and selections of these narrative "voices." There are times when we frame stories within the broader values and ideals of a tradition, as does our narrator here when he idealizes an era of valuing Torah study and of elevating the status of Torah scholars to the highest level. And there are other times when there is value in focusing on the tale itself—its uncertainties, tensions, and problems that transgress the broader, mythic story of a people. Sometimes a story's context is best considered simply to be "our town," rather than an expansive cultural tradition and collective.

The plot itself also provides rich sources for ethical inquiry: the vicissitudes of the two scholars' relationship, their missteps, the value of family traditions, the dissonance between societal ideals and actual conduct, the values and risks of friendship, forgiveness, empathy, controlling inclinations, avoiding embarrassing a human being in public, recognizing what would be considered society's "betrayals of the times" in which we live, and sensing the infinite import of seemingly incidental acts.

One familiar with the Talmudic aphorisms of this chapter's epigrams cannot help but wonder if the title of Agnon's story, "Two Scholars Who Were in Our Town," portends success or doom. Fraught with an abiding dynamic tension between both, the story's narration waffles stylistically and substantively. I wish to explore this story's particular narrative tension as it expresses multivocal, even contradictory, characterizations of the past. I will show that the story's shifts in narrative tone and its apparent internal contradictions may be understood by considering how it is structured around more than one narrative voice. Distinguishing the story's different narrative voices—the first, that of a traditional storyteller, the second, a modern narrator—allows us to read against the grain of efforts to present a coherent image of the past. This reading will help explain the tensions between that rendering of the past, on the one hand, and traditional dynamics of storytelling, on the other.[2]

First, a few words about the story's central relationship will provide a context. The relationship between the two young scholars in Agnon's story is marked by stark contrasts in family background, socioeconomic position, marital status, deportment, and disposition. Rabbi Moshe Pinḥas is a downtrodden, unfortunate, introverted, socially coarse rural villager, whose father died when he was young. In contrast to R. Pinḥas, Rabbi Shlomo is a charismatic, pleasant, engaging young man from the wealthy, venerable rabbinic Horowitz family line.

Though close study companions for a short time, the scholars' relationship deteriorates precipitously, beginning with an unfortunate public encounter as R. Moshe Pinḥas shouts out a legal opinion concerning the synagogue's repair:

> Leaping up, Moshe Pinḥas declared, "It is forbidden to alter the interior space of a synagogue by reducing it even by one finger's length, as this would violate a prohibition of the Lord your God!"[3]

Uncharacteristically and impulsively, R. Shlomo responds to Moshe Pinḥas's sudden, unseemly pronouncement. Though R. Shlomo wishes to "politely silence" (לשתקו בנעימה) and reassure him, he instead shakes his finger at Moshe Pinḥas dismissively, while mockingly scolding, "An [unmarried] boy should just make kiddush on kasha grains!"[4] The narrator explains that this Yiddish saying is a common insult "used to tease unmarried men who presume to act as equals with their [married] superiors."[5] Publicly embarrassed, "Moshe Pinḥas . . . recoiled . . . From that point on, he did not speak to R. Shlomo."[6]

Despite his deep contrition and repeated valiant efforts to ask forgiveness, R. Shlomo is unable to change R. Moshe Pinḥas's unrelentingly hostile disposition toward him. Much later, just before leaving to accept the rabbinical post in another town, he tries again to make peace, only to be spurned yet again by Moshe Pinḥas: "There is no peace between us, neither in this world nor in the world to come."[7]

Toward the story's conclusion, following a brief description of Moshe Pinḥas's death at a relatively young age (as he completes studying the remaining chapters of the Talmud), the narrator describes how R. Shlomo, now very ill, still struggles to offer something redeeming, albeit posthumously, for Moshe Pinḥas. Near death and too weak to reach the memorial ceremony where he was to give the eulogy marking the first anniversary of Moshe Pinḥas's death, R. Shlomo requests to be buried next to him.

Like all previous efforts, this attempt at a postmortem reconciliation is also undermined. Though the gravedigger had supposedly buried R. Shlomo next to Moshe Pinḥas in the snow-covered cemetery, with the spring thaw it was revealed that R. Shlomo's grave and its marker had "moved" away from that of Moshe Pinḥas and next to that of a wealthy ancestor who had predicted that one hundred years after the latter's own death, a descendent (i.e., R. Shlomo) would be buried next to him. As Moshe Pinḥas had previously insisted, no restitution or reconciliation was possible even in "the world to come."

NARRATIVE TENSIONS

> Let's relate a bit of what our town elders always tell about two great scholars who were in the town. (ונספר מקצת משהו שזקני עירנו רגילים לספר על שני תלמידי חכמים גדולים שהיו בעירנו.)[8]

Here, modestly and casually, a narrator introduces his tale. But this casual, folk-like relating "a bit" (מקצת משהו) of a local tale is framed in a formal, expansive, even mythic mode:

> Three or four generations ago, when Torah was dear to Israel and learning it constituted a man's dignity, our town won the highest status in the land on account of its scholars whose Torah study would bring divine tenderness and consideration to it . . . The schools would expand wisdom as one was built after another.[9]

Here the temporal lens is suddenly pulled back from a present habitual, "always tell," to a deeply rooted past, "three or four generations ago." This narrator now invokes classical rabbinic and scriptural phrases (such as "when Torah was dear to Israel"[10]) as the provincial "our town" is expanded to the whole collective of Israel. What began as a simple human local tale now alludes to divine "tenderness and consideration"[11] as the "expansion of wisdom"[12] itself reflects the expansive nature of this paragraph.

In addition to recurring, frictional shifts of this kind between casual folktale and more formal, mythic, even epic style, the narrative has temporal inconsistencies. Even though only a few years pass, by the middle of the story, the narrator, reverting to his formal style in the form of a "lamentation on the era," moves up the story's temporal placement:

> Now let us offer a lamentation for this era's betrayal. *Three to four generations ago*, nothing was dearer than Torah; but beginning *two to three generations* ago the Torah increasingly declined.[13]

While at the beginning of the story, the narrator sets the timeframe at "three to four generations ago," he seemingly moves up the temporal setting by the middle of the story to "*two to three* generations ago." Yet the plot's relatively short duration does not warrant this kind of temporal reframing as the narrator purportedly had begun his story in the period of "*three to four* generations ago."

The narrative's temporal shift is further confirmed in the coda or colophon at the end of the story declaring that even only *two to three* generations ago, the ideal of Torah learning was a defining feature of the age:

> I have related the tale of two scholars who were in our town two or three generations ago when Torah dignified Israel and all Israel would follow it. It is the joy of the Lord, our Stronghold until the coming of the redeemer and beyond, at which time we will be able to hear God's Torah directly from our righteous messiah as he sits and learns Torah with all Israel who will have been studying it lovingly.[14]

No break in Torah learning is narrated in this concluding paragraph. Rather, the Torah held its status "two to three generations ago" and it is expected to retain its strength even into the messianic era.

Beyond the stylistic and temporal shifts, there is a third noteworthy type of friction in the narrative as it offers divergent attributions of its socio-religious and educational context. The story's plot, characters, and episodes seem to refute the assertion that Torah was the guiding priority of that era. At first, with subtle hints and textual allusions,[15] a counterplot develops, comprised of a causal sequence of interpersonal and social decline due to socio-economic divisions, corruption of communal authority, and impulsive callousness (the immediate catalyst for the central unraveling conflict). In an apt poetic characterization near the story's midpoint, the narrator captures these narrative tensions in two sentences, beginning with the rabbinic aphorism, "עולם כמנהגו נוהג" "The world conducts itself as it is accustomed,"[16] followed by an ironic disavowal: "ובאמת העולם לא היה עולם והמנהג לא היה מנהג" "But the truth is that the world was not a world and what was accustomed was not the custom."[17]

Critical Reception: Explaining the Contradictions

The transitions between casual localized storytelling and formal, epic-like narration, the temporal reframings, and the inconsistent characterizations of the setting may be explained, in part, by Agnon's unique integration of romanticism, on the one hand, and his modernist, realist critique, on the other. But this type of broad explanation has not been satisfactory to critics and scholars since this story's first publication in 1946, as they pose questions regarding its apparent narrative contradictions: Why does the narrator frame a tragic story that exposes the community's moral and spiritual decline within the context of an idealized era? Why the temporal shifts? How can the stylistic contrasts be understood? Explanations have converged on the character of the story's narrator and the extent of his reliability, an issue on which scholars differ. I will summarize the range of interpretations of the narrator's motives in order to contrast them from my own argument below.

For some, the narrator is a credible storyteller who relates to his reader as a complicit Talmudist,[18] a dramatic guide,[19] an allegorizing religious moralist,[20] or a nostalgic but realistic storyteller.[21] In this view of the narrator as reliable, the narrative tensions merely create an ironic impression, as the discerning reader will see through the story's apparent contradictions. Others, however, consider him decidedly unreliable—either unwittingly or coyly. From this perspective, the frictions testify to the narrator's unreliability—his simplicity, ignorance, or skittish, cunning denial of the significance of what he has related. The nature of a narrator's unreliability has been an enduring theme in Agnon scholarship. While each interpretation adds important dimensions to understanding Agnon's relationship with his narrator, they each overlook what I will argue are agonistic narrative "voices" in an artistically stratified redaction.

Most recently, Michal Arbel has offered a compelling argument for considering this narrator unreliable and calculating.[22] Offering an insightful, helpful analysis of the work's internal formal and structural properties, particularly with regard to its symmetry and strategies for closure, Arbel argues that the narrator is proud, reluctant, apologetic, and intentionally undermines narrative closure. Describing the narrator's efforts to preempt "any possibility of interpretation" by the reader, Arbel argues that the fragmentary nature of the narration and its awkward, contradictory conclusion reflect both the outer world as described and the story's own "breaking up, its own fragmentation."[23] Recognizing the awkwardness of the story's contradictions, the narrator realizes that he should not have even ventured to tell this tale. As I will argue below, what Arbel calls fragmentation is a function of dissonant narrative voices.

Sharing the conception of the narrator as unreliable, Leah Goldberg and Esther Fuchs see this storyteller as a coy, naïve, sentimentally endearing, pious simpleton. Somewhat ahead of her time, Goldberg was the first to argue for distinguishing Agnon from his narrator in the story: "The writer, S. Y. Agnon, does not identify completely with the narrator of the story, and surely does not identify with its concluder."[24] She argues that the narrator, in fact, is a character in the story, Agnon's "hidden hero" whose contradictions result in "blurring of [the narrator's own] image," unwittingly creating an "elusive identity, that misdirects us." To Goldberg, Agnon uses this narrative technique "to enrich the work's content, to transfer it from one realm to another, to show the image from different points of view, to reveal the multiple meanings in the event, to open different possibilities hidden in any one situation, to bridge contradictions, and to present reality in all its nakedness."[25]

Echoing Goldberg, Fuchs agrees that Agnon is fabricating his unreliable narrator as an important character in the story.[26] In her aptly titled work, *'Omanut ha-hitamemut* ("Cunning Innocence"), Fuchs maintains that much of the confusion around the story (and with Agnon scholarship in general) is that critics have identified the narrator with Agnon himself.[27] This misidentification causes misreadings, blurring the critical distinction between "reality and literature, existence and art."[28] As she demonstrates, often there is inconsistency between the narrator's omission of facts or sound explanations and our own (and Agnon's) sense of actual historical conditions and experience, while we, as readers, know full well the kind of predicaments and struggles of the characters in historical context.[29]

But in our story, there is not merely oversight or omission by a narrator who is ironically distant from the author's (and often from our own) perspective. Rather, this is an act of commission by a narrator who seeks to dominate the narrative, to overwhelm another narrative voice that is very present. So in our story there is more than distance and ironic incongruity between what Fuchs calls "auctoral and figural points of view," and there is less reliance on what she calls the reader's assumed "referential context" that contradicts the narrator's depictions. Rather, here the incongruity stems from a multivocal narration. And the contradictions and oversights described by Goldberg are perhaps a function of our experienced tension in the relationship between narrative voices competing for our attention.[30]

These narrative issues have also been explained, in part, by theories of Agnon's unique style and concerns. This story may, then, reflect what Daniel Miron calls the "unnatural" relationship between Agnon and modern fiction (the novel, in particular), as the author attempts to blend that genre with traditional forms such as Yiddish folk literature, exempla and romances, and communal record books.[31] Thus, Miron might explain this story's narrative tensions as functions of Agnon's broader struggle to adopt the novel as a modern form for his writing.[32] What appears particular in this story, however, is Agnon's expressing this discomfort or awkwardness in a struggle between two voices. And, as I will suggest, this agonistic relationship is actually part of the story's structure and is displayed implicitly and explicitly throughout.

Gershon Shaked has also offered a helpful explanation for these kinds of tensions, maintaining that many of Agnon's narrators often need to invoke a superimposed, miraculous intervention that saves the plot from its "proper advancement."[33] But in this story, the "saving" of the plot is the function of one narrator's frictional relationship with another. What Shaked elsewhere suggests is Agnon's "Jewish-Western dialectic" here unravels before any synthesis can take place.[34]

Competing Narrative Voices

So what does the implied author in this story demand of his readers beyond what has been previously suggested?[35] I suggest that even those who see the narrator as unreliable are overlooking how this story is a uniquely layered set of narratives. Efforts to resolve the story's discordance in terms of a single narrator's persona have not fully explained the narration's dissonant appraisals of the story's characters, setting, and period. How is a reader to reconcile positive characterizations such as: "Standing by the well, even menial laborers would fill their hearts with Torah interpretations"[36] with portrayals of duplicitous business practices like: "But the carpenter was not diligent, as is common with artisans who constantly pursue work and then, upon securing a project, neglect it and just continue to look around for other work"?[37] Or veneration of the times such as: "in those very days when everyone would make the Torah their priority,"[38] with indictments for overemphasizing family lineage as a basis for scholarly respect: "like most of those in our land who have family connections . . . who come [to be ordained] because of their respected lineage."[39] Or generalizations like "nothing was dearer than Torah" (לא היה דבר חביב מן התורה)[40] with the "lamentation on the era's betrayal,"[41] (קינה על בגידת הזמן) bemoaning the decline of Torah values.

These differences in appraisal exist alongside stylistic differences in the narrative's shifting between formal, temporally expansive declarations and casual, localized storytelling by a more transparent, human narrator. Examples of the former are: "One bet midrash after another would be built, encouraging further study. Even in our town's markets and lanes, the scriptural proverb would be confirmed: 'Wisdom resounds in the streets' (Proverbs 1:2)"[42] and "Our town's eminence is due to its being one of the venerable communities. Even before the year 5408 [1648] it was highly regarded."[43] In contrast, a typical example of the local storyteller is: "*I do not know* where this saying comes from, but it was used in our town to tease unmarried men who would presume to act like equals with their [married] superiors."[44]

While shifting in and out of a formal, expansive, epic mode is not unusual in Agnon's fiction, the stylistic divergence, along with contrasting appraisals, and the temporal-frame inconsistencies suggest that previous assessments of the narrative's internal oppositions may be insufficient. Like R. Yudel's ironic, absurd vicissitudes in Agnon's *Bridal Canopy*, our story is set against a backdrop of a traditional society's efforts to hold its shape when being buffeted by modern economic, political, and cultural forces, and their accompanying inevitable human missteps that compromise values and increase societal tensions.[45] But a distinguishing feature of our story is that its depictions of tensions, conflicts, and losses are contextualized by a narrator who seemingly wishes to smooth over their rough edges or, at the very least, to suggest that they are not representative of the epoch in which they occurred.

I suggest, then, that the previous explanations do not fully explain the stratified nature of this particular story. The story, rather, may be viewed as having more than one narrator. Removing the opening and closing of the story (and intermittent glosses) reveals that its core is presented primarily as a traditional tale, handed down orally from previous generations.

As mentioned, following a formal introductory opening, the story makes a transition in its narrative style: "Let's relate a bit of what our town's *elders* tell."[46] This opening of what I consider the casual, personal, or folkloric part of the story, not only introduces us to the subject, but more importantly, makes clear that this is a tradition not fabricated by the narrator and surely not related firsthand. It is something that was told a number of times by the town's elders. And even the elders do not have firsthand knowledge of the events or characters, but rely on the testimony of the bet midrash's (the house of study's) beadle who, in turn, has related it to the collective first-person voice in the narrative, the "we":

> If the beadle was not being a sensationalist, *we* have to believe that he [the poor scholar, Moshe Pinḥas] would drink the cholent lukewarm and that it appeared that he never even rested his head on the pillow that had been given him.[47]

And much of the information in the story comes from a tradition passed down from the collective of "mothers" and "men." Like the elders of the town, the women did not come upon their information and impressions first-hand, but received them from the men:

> *Our mothers*, who heard from the *men* who knew him [i.e., Moshe Pinḥas], tell of his average height, broad shoulders, square face, and how the separate strands of hair sprouting from his jaw would not quite form a beard.[48]

Throughout the story, the narrator makes it clear that this is a community's inherited tale that he has heard from others. A few further examples will suffice:

> *They* relate further that, throughout his life, he never appeared to laugh.[49]
>
> Moshe Pinḥas had not yet found his mate. *Some say* this was because he gravitated so much to his studies leaving no time for marriage arrangements. And *some say* that his mother deterred him.[50]
>
> There are *those who say* that R. Shlomo [the wealthy, distinguished scholar] would drop hints that this scholar [Moshe Pinḥas] was well qualified and that they should seek out his teaching.[51]
>
> *They tell* of a butcher who shouted excitedly, "I hereby stand ready to stick out my neck for slaughter for the sake of our new rabbi [R. Shlomo]!"[52]
>
> *They even say* that when he delivered his sermon, they saw tears in the eyes of the venerable Gaon, R. Shlomo's father, and, as R. Shlomo nodded his head toward him, his father would gesture toward the holy ark. *Some speculate* that nodding his head toward his father was as if to say, "Father, this is all from your [Torah]," and that his father's gesturing toward the holy ark was as if to say, "Your Torah, my son, comes from there."[53]
>
> The bet midrash's *elders would say* that if you have not seen a man who was to die while studying Torah, take a look at R. Moshe Pinḥas."[54]

These recurring references to collective voices that express the community's tradition are not surprising when we recognize that the story, to use Vladimir Propp's language, bears many classic folktale "functions"[55]: a disquietude leading to a hero's disappearance, often a kind of return to seek a solution or redemption (Moshe Pinḥas's return to the primitive, superstitious world of his mother and his return to seek the counsel of his childhood rabbi); a hero's departure on a quest for resolution or fulfillment, often following a parent's death (R. Shlomo's departure from his town, leaving his rabbinic post in order to assume his late father's rabbinic post in another town, while urging his former town's leadership to accept R. Moshe Pinḥas as their rabbi to succeed him); the veneration of ancestors (the seemingly supernatural or magical fulfillment of R. Shlomo's great-great-grandfather's prophecy that one of his progeny would be buried next to him one hundred years in the future and the reverence for the rabbinic Horowitz family lineage); the public foibles of stereotypical characters who, in dramatic episodes, are presented as foolish or as subversively discrediting established authority (Moshe Pinḥas's misguided, naïve attempt to publicly embarrass and discredit R. Shlomo during the latter's inaugural sermon); a mocking of those who transgress communal norms (R. Shlomo's public insult of R. Moshe, the bachelor, when the latter acts as if he had the status of married scholars); the use of cultural archetypes (the poor Talmud student; the privileged, charismatic scholar; the superstitious mother, the gullible commonfolk, the venerated ancestor). In addition, the brief references to the "lamentation on the era's betrayal" and to the messianic era resonate with the classic folk experience of chanting laments on the physical, moral, and even eschatological descent of characters or communities.[56]

The archetypal characters' flaws appear as our storyteller narrates ineluctable perturbations in their encounters with each other while modernity's economic and social realities encroach.[57] The implied author invokes, often ironically, these classic folkloric functions, as he displays the broader story's narrator's attempt to marginalize or trivialize the characters' distressing circumstances.

The story, then, may be interpreted as a narrator's reframing of a traditional tale. The narrator's efforts to distance the reader from the tale (and from its storyteller) become transparent as he, literally and figuratively (and somewhat artificially), reframes it as his new redaction. Agnon, as implied author, positions the narrator between the core folktale and the reader.

TWO PEDAGOGIES: TRADITIONAL STORYTELLING AND MODERN FICTION

In reading this story, we experience how traditional stories and storytellers have grown distant from us and from modern educational practice. Ten years before the publication of Agnon's story, Walter Benjamin wrote his famous essay, "The Storyteller: Reflections on the Works of Nikolai Leskov" (1936). The essay laments the loss of the traditional story—its personal, idiosyncratic qualities, and its sharing of experience. Though not simply romanticizing the storyteller, Benjamin demonstrates how modern fiction and historiography have eclipsed the valued but fading narratives of the storyteller and have supplanted the experience of their tellings and re-tellings. For Benjamin, the storyteller is a receding form of life: "Familiar though his name may be to us, the storyteller in his living immediacy is by no means a present force. He has already become something remote from us and something that is getting even more distant."[58] This form of narration placed a high value on sharing experience with vocal resonance and bodily gesture. No synthetic explanation is required; no grand theory is needed to appreciate and value the story; no information or discrete data must be conveyed. Rather, storytelling is an act of companionship.

But to Benjamin, while the storyteller does not totalize the narrative, he does provide counsel—though not resolute answers or definitive interpretations. His counsel is an invitation into the story's world and an offering of its reception into our own:

> After all, counsel is less an answer to a question than a proposal concerning the continuation of a story which is just unfolding. To seek this counsel one would first have to be able to tell the story . . . Counsel woven into the fabric of real life is wisdom. The art of storytelling is reaching its end because the epic side of truth, wisdom, is dying out.[59]

The storyteller, thus, tries to offer a kind of wisdom that is not to be confused with providing explanation. As Benjamin suggests, "Actually, it is half the art of storytelling to keep a story free from explanation as one reproduces it."[60] The wisdom of storytelling lets contradictions speak for themselves, resisting a modern tendency to universalize narratives that render a "meaning of life" over and above the "simple or profound meanings in a story."[61]

Related to this distinction is the significant difference in disposition toward closure. The novel's form requires a kind of closure not befitting the traditional story.[62] The reader's or listener's response to a story always can elicit the legitimate query: "And then what happened?" Benjamin argues that the unresolved question is an essential storytelling feature: "Actually there is no story for which the question as to how it continued would not be legitimate." Not so, for the novelist. For Benjamin, "the novelist . . . cannot hope to take the smallest step beyond that limit at which he invites the reader to a divinatory realization of the meaning of life by writing 'Finis.'"

It is thus significant that, at the ending of "Two Scholars Who Were In Our Town," we hear two contrapuntal voices, as if the modern narrator concludes with "I have related the tale of two scholars who were in our town two or three generations ago when Torah dignified Israel and all Israel would follow it."[63] Then the storyteller responds, using a traditional signature trope, "*tam v'lo nishlam*" ("Concluded, but incomplete").[64]

Parallel to modern fiction's relationship to storytelling, historiography, too, has transplanted an older art, that of the chronicle. How one narrates history is of concern to Benjamin. Like the storyteller, the stock and trade of the chronicler is telling and relating, whereas that of the historian is explanation. So to Benjamin, history and fiction are quintessentially modern narrative forms that distance themselves from the chronicle and the story.[65]

It appears, then, that the storyteller of the core narrative in "Two Scholars" is made somewhat obscure. What Benjamin would call his "living immediacy," his "present force," is made "something remote," "more distant," by narrative reframing. That narrator achieves this by doing just what the storyteller does not: offering explanatory glosses, presenting a totalizing narrative, and providing a rationale for it.[66] Agnon may have sought to reveal, ironically, a narrative eclipse of the storyteller, a certain kind of teacher. This chapter has only begun the process of considering this kind of wisdom in teaching—a wisdom that is less didactic, less pedantic, and ultimately, less reductive. At the same time, it has begun to unveil some the pedagogical compromises made when this kind of wisdom is eclipsed in an education that is more concerned with a specific framing of the past and with precise targeting of objectives than with cultivating relationships to one another and to the range of narratives we inherit.

The storyteller's footprints appear as we read the core of this tale. But their contours are framed by a narrator—another teacher—who simplifies, generalizes, abbreviates, and at times, contradicts the real. The outline of the storyteller becomes visible, however, "from a certain distance," to use Benjamin's language:

> Viewed from a certain distance, the great, simple outlines which define the storyteller stand out in him, or rather, they become visible in him, just as in a rock a human head or an animal's body may appear to an observer at the proper distance and angle of vision.[67]

Reading Agnon requires these variegated vantage points from which to read. This type of reading involves a careful, imaginative recovery of the past in a context of a present that wittingly or unwittingly, cunningly or innocently, recasts it. The storyteller in "Two Scholars" calls out to share experience even as the narrator awkwardly but deliberately seeks to muffle his voice, trying to provide a kind of guide for the perplexed reader. The core enigmatic tale is apparently too transgressive for the narrator as it seemingly dismantles an idealized reconstructed memory.

Agnon is perhaps enjoining us here not to settle for forced contextualization of the past, even as we may hold dear its ideals and romanticize what might have been lost. A balance between text and context may provide a clearer vision that will help us recover aspects of that authentic beloved past, even as we come to recognize its human fallibilities, societal instabilities, and moral uncertainties. This implied author wants us to put a check on the subjectively recast story; he demands our overcoming the somewhat forced narrative contextualization.[68]

Perhaps the narrator who reframes this story is partially correct. Perhaps we should recognize the value placed on Torah learning and embrace the ideal of societal wholeness in our memory. Maybe we should try to feel that world's "preeminence" and simply "salute it from afar," to use Matthew Arnold's characterization of literary criticism's relationship to great literary epochs of the past.[69] Agnon, however, does not settle for simply saluting a distant lost world. His distinction is that he carries us to that world, to "our town," with its textures, imperfections, tensions, and ideals, as if to recapture its paradoxical web of meanings and even to somehow reconstruct a world view that is both authentically his and uniquely our own.

NOTES

1. S. Y. Agnon, "Two Scholars Who Were In Our Town" (Hebrew) (*Shnei talmidei ḥakhamim she-hayu be-'irenu*). Hereafter designated as "Two Scholars." To the best of my knowledge there are no English translations of this story to date. All translations of the story and of its critical reception are my own unless otherwise indicated.

2. This is a differentiation distinct from that of "the narrator" and Agnon (as "implied author").

3. "Two Scholars," 11. "קפץ משה פנחס ואמר, אסור לשנות חלל בית הכנסת ולמעטו אפילו כדי אצבע אחת, שיש בזה משום לא תעשון כן לה ' אלקיכם."

4. "Two Scholars," 11. "ניענע לו בידו דרך ביטול ואמר לו בלשון של הלצה, א בחור מאכ"ט קידוש אוי פ א גרוי"פ.

5. "לקנטר בו את בחורים שדחקו עצמם לעמוד במקום גדולים."

6. "Two Scholars," 11. "נרתע לאחוריו . . . מכאן ואילך לא דיבר עם ר ' שלמה."

7. "Two Scholars," 16. "אין שלום בינינו לא בעולם הזה ולא לעולם הבא."

8. "Two Scholars," 5.

9. "Two Scholars," 5.

> לפני שלושה ארבעה דורות שהיתה התורה חביבה על ישראל וכל תפארתו של אדם היא התורה, זכתה עירנו להמנות עם הערים המצויינות שבמדינה על ידי תלמידי חכמים שבה, שמשכו עליה חוט של חסד על ידי תורה שלמדו . . . בתי מדרשיות שנבנו זה אחר זה הגדילו תושיה.

10. "שהיתה התורה חביבה על ישראל." See for example, *Yalkut Shim'oni* on Psalms 119, 126. "When you see that the Torah is dear to Israel . . . " "ילקוט שמעוני, תהלים קיט, קכו. בשעה שאתה רואה שהתורה חביבה על ישראל והכל שמחים בה."
And Jerusalem Talmud, Tractate *B'rakhot*, Chapter 9." "If you have seen that the Torah is dear to Israel . . . "
ירושלמי- מסכת ברכות פרק ט. וכן היה הלל אומר אם ראית את התורה שהיא חביבה על ישראל והכל שמחין בה.

11. See, for example, Babylonian Talmud, Tractate *Tamid*, chapter 1, citing Proverbs 28, "pull over him a thread of lovingkindness (tenderness and consideration) . . . " "חבירו לשם שמים זוכה לחלקו של הקדוש ברוך הוא שנאמר (משלי כח) מוכיח אדם אחרי ולא עוד אלא שמושכין עליו חוט של חסד שנאמר (משלי כח) חן ימצא ממחליק לשון . . . "

12. See Isaiah 28. "הפליא עצה הגדיל תושיה."

13. "Two Scholars," 31 (emphasis mine). "ועתה נשא קינה על בגידת הזמן. לפני שלושה ארבעה דורות לא היה דבר חביב מן התורה, לפני שנים שלושה דורות התחילה התורה יורדת והולכת."

14. "Two Scholars," 53.

> סיפרתי מעשיהם של שני תלמידי חכמים שהיו בעירנו לפני שנים שלושה דורות בזמן שהיתה התורה תפארתם של ישראל וכל ישראל היו הולכים בדרכי התורה, שהיא חדות ה' מעוזנו עד ביאת הגואל ועד בכלל, לכשנזכה לשמוע תורת ה' מפי משיח צדקנו כשישב וילמוד תורה עם כל ישראל שלמדו תורה מאהבה.

15. See Auerbach, "Two Scholars Who Were in Our Town: Sources and Commentary."
16. *Babylonian Talmud*, *Avodah Zarah* 54b.
17. "Two Scholars," 31–32.
18. Auerbach, "Sources and Comentary."
19. Tsimerman, "On 'Two Scholars Who Were In Our Town.'"
20. Weiss, *Commentary on Five Stories of S. Y. Agnon.*
21. Band, *Nostalgia and Nightmare*, 402–05.
22. Arbel, "Societal and Strategic Closure Dilemmas."
23. Arbel, "Societal and Strategic Closure Dilemmas."
24. Goldberg, "S. Y. Agnon: The Author and His Hero."
25. Goldberg, "S. Y. Agnon: The Author and His Hero."
26. Fuchs, *Cunning Innocence*, 39–40.
27. Fuchs, "Ironic Characterization."
28. Fuchs, "Ironic Characterization."
29. Fuchs, "Ironic Characterization," 105.
30. Fuchs, "Ironic Characterization," 110.
31. Miron, "Domesticating a Foreign Genre," 6.
32. Miron, "Domesticating a Foreign Genre," 4–8. Miron points out how, in his novels, Agnon tried to "connect the particular with the general, personal lives with history, the individual soul with collective culture," as the author sought to "break out of its impasse," as he "stood against a narrative perfection based on a finished past." I see this struggle for interconnection portrayed in the two narrative voices of "Two Scholars." Most illuminating, for our purposes, is Miron's insight that "[i]n Agnon's oeuvre then two long narrative patterns serve side by side, competing yet integrated one with the other: that of the *pinkas* or *midrash* or *geste* preceded the novelistic one and served as an alternative to it. When Agnon finally took up the novel, it is as if he submerged the first kind of narration into the depths of his work."
33. Shaked, "By a Miracle," 136. "Agnon believes that this doomed society, in its parlous state, can be saved only in the imagination, not in the proper advancement of the plot."
34. Shaked, "Jewish Tradition and Western Impact in Hebrew Literature," 92–93.
35. See note 6. As he further developed his theory of "unreliable narrator" and "implied author," Booth, citing Jean-Paul Sartre, suggests "that I as reader have the right to make demands on the author—particularly the right to demand that he demand more of me." Booth, *Ethics of Fiction*, 127; Sartre, "What is Literature?" 40.
36. "Two Scholars," 5. "ואפילו שאבי מים שאצל הבאר היו ממלאים לבם דברי תורה."
37. "Two Scholars," 10–11. "אבל האומן לא נזדרז, כדרך האומנים שרצים כל ימיהם אחר עבודה, כיון שבאה עבודה לידיהם אינם פונים לעשותה, ומחזרים אחר עבודה אחרת."

38. “Two Scholars,” 5. "באותם הימים שהכל היו עושין את התורה עיקר."
39. “Two Scholars,” 8–9. "כרוב הייחסנים שבמדינתנו שבאים בזכות אבותיהם."
40. “Two Scholars,” 5.
41. “Two Scholars,” 31.
42. “Two Scholars,” 5.
43. “Two Scholars,” 33. "הרי מעולה היא עירנו, שהיא מן הקהילות הישנות, וכבר קודם לשנת ת"ח היתה מפרסמת לשבח."
44. (Emphasis mine.) A Yiddish expression: "א בחור מאכ"ט קידוש אוי"ף א גרויפ." "פתגם זה איני יודע מניין הוא, אבל מקובל היה בעירנו לקנטר בו את בחורים שדחקו עצמם לעמוד במקום גדולים."
45. Shaked, “By a Miracle,” 133–144.
46. “Two Scholars,” 5.
47. “Two Scholars,” 7. "אם אין השמש מן המגזימים, צריכים אנו להאמין לו, שחמין שהיה מביא לו היה שותה פושרין והכר שנתן לו לא ניכר בו שהניח ראשו עליו."
48. “Two Scholars,” 7. "אמותינו ששמעו מאנשים שהכירו אותו רגילות לספר, קומתו בינונית היתה וכתפיו רחבות ופניו מרובעות וקמצים קמצים של שער שלא נתחברו כדי זקן היו מבצבצים מלסתותיו."
49. “Two Scholars,” 8 (all emphases are mine). "עוד זאת מספרים, שמימיו לא נראה שחוק על פניו."
50. “Two Scholars,” 10. "<משה פנחס עדיין לא מצא זיווגו. יש אומרים שמתוך שנמשך אחר תלמודו לבו לא היה פנוי לעסקי שידוכין, ויש אומרים יד אמו היתה לעכבו."
51. "יש אומרים, רמז רמז ר' שלמה, שראוי תלמיד חכם זה שיבקשו תורה מפיו."
52. “Two Scholars,” 17. "מספרים שקצב אחד צעק מרוב התפעלות, הריני מוכן ומזומן לפשוט את צוארי לשחיטה בשביל רבינו חדש."
53. “Two Scholars,” 17–18.

> אף הם מספרים שבשעת דרשתו ראו דמעות בעיני הגאון הישיש אביו של ר' שלמה וראו שפעמים היה ר' שלמה מנענע ראשו כלפי אביו, ואביו הראה בידו כנגד ארון הקודש. דורשי רמזים אמרו, הבן ניענע ראשו כלפי אביו לומר אבא הכל משלך הוא, ואביו הראה בידו כנגד ארון הקודש לומר, תורתך בני היא מכאן.

54. “Two Scholars,” 24. "זקני בית המדרש היו אומרים, אם לא ראיתם אדם כי ימות באוהל, ראו את רבי משה פנחס."
55. Maintaining that “functions” appear with “surprising regularity” in folktales, Propp defines “function” as “the action of the character from the point of view of its significance for the progress of the narrative.” Vladimir J. Propp, *Theory and History of Folklore* (Minneapolis, MN: University of Minnesota Press, 1984), 73–74. Also see Propp’s classic work, *Morphology of the Folktale*, trans. Laurence Scott. Second revised edition, (Austin, Texas and London: University of Texas Press, 1968).
56. Faith Wigzell, “Folklore and Russian literature,” in *Routledge Companion to Russian Literature*, ed. Neil Cornwell (London: Routledge, 2001), 44.
57. Wigzell, 37–42.
58. Walter Benjamin, “The Storyteller: Reflections on the Works of Nikolai Leskov” in *Walter Benjamin, Illuminations: Essays and Reflections*, trans. Harry Zohn, ed. Hannah Arendt (New York: Schocken Books, 1968), 83–109.
59. Benjamin, “Storyteller,” Section VI, XIV. 20. Also see Miron, “Agnon’s Transactions,” “What bothered him especially was the simplistic optimism of these ideas and their faith in the power of human and national will – in short, their positivist self-assurance that disregarded the subtle complex of difficulties, mistakes, blindnesses, and just plain foolishness that abound in all realms of life.” Also see Dan Miron, “The Literary Image of the Shtetl.”
60. Benjamin, “Storyteller,” Section VI, XIV. 20.
61. Benjamin, “Storyteller,” Section XIV.

It would be overly simplistic to conclude that Benjamin is idealizing the premodern world. For him, forms of art, including narrative, are functions of the economic and social dialectic of his historical materialism. As Allison Schachter has recently pointed out: “In the essay, Benjamin then examines the effects of cultural modernization on literary form, looking at the dialectical relationship between the experience of lost traditional worlds and the emergence of new modern cultural forms.” Allison Schachter, “The Shtetl and the City, 76. Schachter illustrates Benjamin’s dialectic and considers how his “reflection on the relationship between historical transformations and literary form," illuminates how a "new Jewish nostalgia for a lost traditional world accompanies the creation of a modern Jewish literature." Specifically, Schachter utilizes Benjamin to suggest how S. Y. Abramovitsh (Mendele Moykher Sforim) struggled to maintain a sense of the traditional storyteller in his works (86.)

62. Miron, 9. As Miron points out, there are times when Agnon's narrator is sensitive to the modern novel's demand for a kind of closure not befitting the traditional tale. So we have cases of forced, or seemingly artificial endings, such as the "apologetic inscription" ending of *A Simple Story*: "Hirshl and Mina's story is over, but Blume's is not." Also see Arbel, "Societal and Strategic Closure Dilemmas."

63. "Two Scholars," 53.

> סיפרתי מעשיהם של שני תלמידי חכמים שהיו בעירנו לפני שנים שלושה דורות בזמן שהיתה התורה תפארתם של ישראל וכל ישראל היו הולכים בדרכי התורה, שהיא חדות ה' מעוזנו עד ביאת הגואל ועד בכלל, לכשנזכה לשמוע תורת ה' מפי משיח צדקנו כשישב וילמוד תורה עם כל ישראל שלמדו תורה מאהבה.

64. See conclusion of chapter 4.

65. Benjamin, "Storyteller," Section XII.

66. Benjamin, "Storyteller," Section IV.

67. Benjamin, "Storyteller."

68. Geoffrey Hartman has warned that, "In the matter of art we cannot draw up a Guide for the Perplexed. We can only urge that readers, inspired by hermeneutic tradition, take back some of their authority and become both creative and thoughtful, as in days of old." But Hartman, echoing Benjamin, would enjoin us to avoid simplistically interpreting past events and memories as discrete happenings, separate from one another with no coherent story linking them. This would be an offense of, "a trivialized theory of reference," a subversion of our critical mandate to interpret, to tell, to re-tell, "to discharge our powers." Hartman, "The Work of Reading," 161.

69. Arnold, "The Function of Criticism at the Present Time," 61. "In an epoch like those is, no doubt, the true life of literature; there is the promised land, towards which criticism can only beckon. That promised land it will not be ours to enter, and we shall die in the wilderness: but to have desired to enter it, to have saluted it from afar, is already, perhaps, the best distinction among contemporaries; it will certainly be the best title to esteem with posterity."

Chapter Seven

The Student as Outcast

Double-Voice in S. Y. Agnon's "Hanidaḥ"

In the previous chapter, we saw how multivocal narrative can be a source for ethical and educational inquiry when a reader or teacher exposes a prevailing multiplicity despite an apparent narrative unity. Vigilant, responsive teachers hear and recognize this kind of narrative tension within texts and among their students. In the case of Agnon's "Two Scholars Who Were in Our Town," the two central narrative voices were a modern narrator and a traditional storyteller. While both of these kinds of narration may be necessary aspects of teaching, we saw how teacher-as-storyteller and the teacher-as-explanatory-narrator often struggle against each other as each responds to competing pedagogical demands.

I now extend this concept of multivocal narrative to an ethics and pedagogy of alterity as I consider an Agnon story in which a text's multiple narrative voices have an intersubjective quality, responding to each other. In his story, "*Hanidaḥ*" ("The Outcast"), Agnon creates an interactive narrative tension in which an ubiquitous "other" influences a narrator's speech and how diverse discourses in the text interact or bypass each other. In the final section of this chapter, I will suggest how careful attentiveness to this intersubjective, dialogic quality of narrative discourse evokes significant ethical and pedagogical questions concerning teachers' and students' perceptions, interactions, expectations, responses, and discursive practices.

Significantly, no educational issues are posed explicitly by the author, narrator, or other figures in the story. But, in the sustained prevalence of intersubjective dialogue, in the rhythm of contrapuntal responses to an other, ethical and pedagogical issues emerge. Though it is problematic to apply contemporary pedagogical standards to the story's nineteenth-century Eastern European setting, Agnon here is not simply writing a piece of historical fiction. He is, rather, composing a modern story with characteristic irony and socioreligious, educational critique.

As noted in the previous chapter, literary criticism has come to consider how interpretation can inform ethical dispositions, decisions, and conduct. For some, the ethics of reading and teaching literature is found in a work's particular plot and themes; for others, ethical understanding can be achieved by interpreting the poetics of the narrative, discovering the implicit responsibility that its structure and discursive styles place on the reader,[1] and revealing an embedded stance of the implied author.[2] A significant artistic style of modern fiction involves a narrator whose "insights do not entirely add up" to a plausible stance by the implied author.[3] There is thus a distance created between implied author and the narrator. Rather than simply reflecting the text's actual author, the concept of implied author helps us render a full complex of values, principles, perspectives, and understandings in the text. As I will suggest in the final section of this chapter, aspects of the role of teacher are akin to that of an implied author. Thus, the notion of implied authorship has the potential to reveal an oft-overlooked, variegated, conflicted, dialogic quality in teaching.

Continuing this book's emphasis on a discourse's particularity *and* conversability, I will first consider this story in the context of modern Hebrew literature and literary theory—conversation partner one. I then suggest what happens when we engage this discourse in conversation with that of educational theory—conversation partnership two. No synthesis is suggested or sought. Rather, I wish to let one discourse converse with another while respecting discursive distinctiveness. Thus, the first portion of this chapter is a literary analysis, after which I introduce educational discourse as a partner in this interdiscursive conversation. I seek to make transparent how this interdiscursive approach maintains fidelity to both discursive particularity and conversability, in contrast to an approach that would integrate or blend two fields.

CONVERSATION PARTNER 1: MODERN HEBREW LITERATURE AND LITERARY THEORY

It is widely acknowledged that S. Y. Agnon's story, "*Hanidaḥ*" ("The Outcast"), represents a landmark in the author's oeuvre.[4] Agnon, too, considered it to be so, expressing enthusiasm for the work and repeatedly revising it over decades.[5] Characterizing the story as transitional or inaugural, Agnon scholars tend to emphasize its themes and structure: its commencing a dialectical historical narrative of European Jewry's phase of "inner collapse"[6] or in its intensifying a "dialectic play" between spiritual and material worlds and between epic and realistic points of view.[7] Others expand these assessments, noting that the story achieves what Arnold Band calls an unprecedented "sustained integration of theme and mood"[8] or that it inaugurates what Dan Miron characterizes as the author's first "stirring of intention" toward the novel in its being "the only time in his early work" that Agnon incorporates, albeit in a limited way, the novelistic theme of "the individual who breaks with family and community to follow his own heart."[9]

Beyond the noteworthy transitional and inaugural aspects of the story's themes and structure, I wish to consider how the discursive style itself constitutes a significant development in Agnon's literary work and how this style provides a rich narrative landscape for considering an ethics of pedagogy. While a systematic examination of Agnon's language is far beyond the scope of this study, I will argue that particular qualities in the story's narrative discourse, significantly more so than in his earlier work, anticipate Agnon's later literary achievements, including his novels and many of his novellas and short stories.[10] Drawing on Mikhail Bakhtin's theory of discourse in the novel, I will also seek to demonstrate how the story's dialogic, double-voiced ("polyphonic") qualities not only anticipate these later works, but suggest some new avenues to reading Agnon in the context of an ethics of alterity. For Bakthin, in the development of modern fiction (the novel in particular), there is a "deepening of dialogic essence" that increasingly resists unified "rock bottom truths."[11] In attending to this quality, I consider how polyphonic, multivoiced discourse, in contrast to monophonic, unitary speech, insinuates itself on all levels.[12]

Before examining the story's polyphonic dialogue, which I will also refer to as "double-voiced" discourse, a summary of its plot and narrative context is in order. The story is set against the background of the raging social, religious, and political battle between adherents of hasidism (the *ḥasidim*) and the rabbinic, communal establishment (the *mitnagdim*, i.e., "opponents") in nineteenth-century Galicia: "The *mitnagdim* would battle the *ḥasidim*, banishing hasidic men from their in-laws' homes along with their wives, even breaking their windows, befouling their *tsitsit*, and lending destruction to their houses of prayer." Having no recourse, the *ḥasidim* were left "embittered" (בנפש מרה) (50).[13]

At the beginning of the story, before this intracommunal conflagration, the town of Shibush is anticipating a momentous (or ominous) visit from the iconoclastic hasidic spiritual leader, the "*tsadik*," Rebbe Uriel.[14] This pending dramatic event causes a stir among R. Uriel's small number of hasidic followers in the town, as well as among the *mitnagdim* and the curious townsfolk. As the hasidic followers joyously greet their rebbe with ecstatic street celebrations, the town's cantankerous arch-*mitnagdic* leader, the Parnas R. Avigdor, who has been at his dying daughter's bedside, "stormed out with a vengeful wrath to the authorities" (11). His appeal succeeds as R.

Uriel is abruptly banished from the town by the local officials. Leaving the town with his followers, R. Uriel utters a curse on R. Avigdor that the latter "will have an outcast banished from his midst" (כי ידח ממנו נדח).[15]

After the death of R. Avigdor's daughter, Eidele, the story focuses on her son, Gershom, who has been away studying at a yeshivah. A sorrowful, forlorn, seemingly lost young man, Gershom has been mourning his mother as he returns home from his yeshivah.[16] When he arrives, Gershom is consumed by feelings of emptiness and spiritual yearning, drawing him to the anathematized hasidic sect and to its tsadik, R. Uriel. Fearing that he will suffer banishment from the community, Gershom struggles with his feelings, trying to conceal them from his grandfather and the town's leaders, as he is overcome with emotional, spiritual longings and neglects his Talmud study.

The story culminates with the arrival to town of R. Uriel's hasidic disciple, referred to as the "*Ḥozer*."[17] Surreptitiously, even clandestinely, the *Ḥozer* endears himself to R. Avigdor and becomes Gershom's teacher and spiritual mentor. Hiding his hasidism, the *Ḥozer* channels Gershom's spiritual desires through ecstatic mystical experiences. The story ends with Gershom's "ascending" in a fatal ecstatic fervor while reciting the Song of Songs, dying as he recites the verse, "the King leads me to his chambers" (הביאני המלך חדריו).[18]

Though he arrives in the last portion of the story, the story's ethics of pedagogy center around the actions of the *Ḥozer* and this teacher's curious conduct: "[H]e concealed his deeds and hid his comings and goings, suppressing his Torah in his gut, answering whatever he answered" (53). ("סתם את מעשיו והצניע את הליכותיו וכבש את תורתו בתוך מעיו והשיב מה שהשיב.") An emissary of the hasidic *tsadik* Rebbe Uriel, this teacher's mission is to travel, identifying potential new *ḥasidim* who will find their spiritual fulfillment in what the rabbinic establishment and R. Avigdor (the *mitnagdim*, "opponents") considered a banned sect.

Double-Voiced Discourse: "Polyphony" in *"Hanidaḥ"*

In considering this story from the perspective of a theory of dialogue in modern fiction, it is important to note that Bakthin differentiates three different, yet intersecting, types of "polyphonic" discourse. In shorthand terms, I will label them as follows: (1) interlocutory discourse, (2) "microdialogue," and (3) "heteroglossia" (literally, "multi-speechedness").[19] Though there is limited polyphonic, dialogic discourse in Agnon's earlier works (a point I will return to below), all of these types are prevalent in Agnon's writing beginning with *"Hanidaḥ."* This story thus represents a significant transition in the scope and depth of these multivoiced discursive styles.

Interlocutors in Discourse

The first type of double-voiced discourse, what I am referring to as "interlocutory," is most significant. This type of discourse is informed by an actual or implicit "continual sideways glance at another person," toward an imagined or real interlocutor whose anticipated responses influence one's thought and speech.[20] There is a sense here of "dialogic inter-orientation"[21] in which two voices interpenetrate within one. This interpenetration takes place in "the crossing and intersection, in every element of consciousness and discourse, of two consciousnesses, two points of view, two evaluations—two voices interrupting one another intraatomically," often expressing "an inner reservation" or responding to an implicit "interruption."[22]

The effect of these internal dialogues is enhanced as they are set against a more dominant discursive style in which individual characters, as well as their group associations, are effaced, and groups are referred to in a way that asserts their superficial typicality more than their particularity, their group affiliation over their individual concerns and aspirations.[23] An individual's delight is referred to as a "layman's joy" (שמחה של הדיות); simple archetypes prevail over individual personalities: "a simple man with a wonderful simple faith" (איש פשוט ומופלא באמנותו הפשוטה); "a Jew who knew to how to celebrate on Simḥat Torah and how to cry on Tishah b'av" (יהודי שהיה יודע לשמוח בשמחת תורה ולבכות בתשעה באב). The hasidic followers of the *tsadik* R. Uriel are referred to as "members of the group" (בני החבורה), "the devotees," (הנלבבים). When the narrative refocalizes the point of view on the discourse of the established rabbinic authorities ("opponents" "*mitnagdim*"), the *ḥasidim* are referred to as "members of the sect" (אנשי הכת) and "empty and reckless people" (אנשים ריקים ופוחזים).

But within monologues, polyphonic internal voices mark strong contrasts to the often seemingly overwhelming voices that reduce characters to types. Though the story's interactive, interpersonal discourse is decidedly monophonic as it asserts characters' archetypal qualities over their particularities, repeatedly, the story's primary characters and narrator reveal a double-voiced, polyphonic interiority. Just as snow and black earth, light and darkness, heaven and earth, ascent and descent[24] give way to each other at the story's beginning, so too seemingly unified voices and sentiments give way to critical moments of internal polyphonic atonality. In other words, based on a group's or an individual's utterances and responses, the reader can infer agonistic, dissonant norms, values, and linguistic usages. Unpacking individual voices to reveal plurality within singularity suggests stratified qualities and relationships that have not been fully addressed in previous scholarship on "*Hanidaḥ*."

Repeatedly, the story's characters think and act as if interlocutors are giving them pause and reason to reconsider their own conduct and inclinations. Within monologues, double-voices mark strong contrasts to the often seemingly overwhelming voices that reduce characters to types. At such times, an individual character's or the narrator's halting, self-conscious discourse indicates something other than unified, objectified internal consciousness. The windows into these internal figural pluralities reveal characters' subjective, human qualities as well as an intersubjectivity.[25] In competition with the narrator's and other figures' efforts to unify, objectify, and totalize these internal differences and relationships, the story's double-voiced discourse functions, in part, to allow characters to overcome the distancing of historical and social typicality.

Let us first consider the voices of the antagonists, R. Avigdor and R. Uriel. Angered by the loud celebrations welcoming the hasidic *tsadik* R. Uriel to Shibush, the town's leader, the Parnas R. Avigdor, prepares to have him expelled. At this early point in the story, he has just been at Eidele's bedside as she lays dying. R. Avigdor exhibits an internal double voice when he considers how to respond to the noisy festivities: "Hearing the hasids' sounds as they were joyfully escorting their rebbe, he became agitated—'How long will I have to assume responsibility for this transgression?'" (שמע קולותיהם של החסידים שמוליכים את רבם בשמחה. נזדעזע ואמר, עד מתי יהא עוון זה טמון בידי?) (11).[26] This quoted monologue is followed directly by the narrator's empathic paraphrasing of Avigdor's conflicting emotions: "Looking at Eidele's two little children, R. Avigdor felt like holding them, hugging them, consoling and comforting them" (נסתכל רבי אביגדור בשני בני איידילי הקטנים וביקש לגפפם ולחבקם ולומר להם דברי ריצוי ותנחומין).

But this expression of desire to act compassionately toward his grandchildren is abruptly interrupted in a discursive shift describing his sorrowful agitation, intense anger, and desire for vengeance: "But being so disconcerted he did not approach them, instead storming out with a vengeful wrath to the authorities" (11) (אך מחמת טרדת הלב לא נתקרב אליהם ויצא בחמת נקם לחצר השררה). The narrator then characterizes the nature and import of this latter fateful act: "This devilish deed [literally, "the devil's deed," מעשה שטן] succeeded in appealing to the prince who sent an officer to expel R. Uriel from the town on account of R. Avigdor's having defamed him" (11) (הצליח מעשה שטן ונתרצה השר ושגר סרדיוט אחד לגרש את רבי אוריאל מן העיר, כי הביא עליו רבי אביגדור דבתו רעה). Though "devil's deed" is a common Hebrew idiom, in a Bakhtinian sense (if only figuratively), the "devil's deed" suggests a dialogic interlocutor with whom Avigdor has conversed. The narration suggests overlays of contradictory emotions, social priorities, intentions, and thoughts as R. Avigdor moves instantly from feeling "like holding them, hugging them, consoling and comforting them," to being "disconcerted," to having a "vengeful wrath."

Deeply offended by his forced expulsion, R. Uriel considers how to respond. Following a spontaneous, emotional protest by the rebbe's followers, the *tsadik* conducts an internal monologue as he pauses, second-guessing his reasons for feeling offended and questioning how he is inclined to respond: "His holiness's heart was aroused as he thought, 'Uriel, Uriel. Are you indeed taking offence for God's sake? Perhaps it is just for your own sake that you are offended. And on what basis would you be able to discern the truth?'" (12) (נתעורר לבב קדשו ואמר, אוריאל אוריאל, כלום באמת על כבוד שמו יתברך אתה חס, או שמא על כבוד עצמך אתה חס, ובמה תדע להבחין את האמת?) But R. Uriel's double-voice here is trumped by the "voice" of his "natural inclination": "Nevertheless, his natural inclination made him curse the Parnas, releasing a vigorous curse from his mouth: 'Let an outcast be banished from him'" (12) (אף על פי כן נתגברה מטבעיות וקלל נמרצת נתעקרה מפיו, כי ידח ממו נדח).

This is a halting monologue, interrupted by several seemingly false starts, as the contradictory yet coexistent voices suggest the dialogic engagement of an "other" who challenges and fragments R. Uriel's thoughts and discourse. "Natural inclination's" dialogic role as "other" thus parallels that of the Avignor's "devil." R. Uriel implicates a dialogic "other," rather than simply ruminating rhetorically. The narrative style and language suggest a kind of conversation of which we are only hearing one side. Yet the "double-voiced" discourse invites us to infer plausible responses to each of the three questions: "for God's sake?" "for your own sake?" and "on what basis?"[27] Each of these narrative examples implicates dialogic voices appealing to broader norms within a single consciousness. R. Avigdor appeals to the "authorities"; R. Uriel appeals to religious, moral norms—"for God's sake?" In the case of R. Avigdor, the broader norm dominates; in the case of R. Uriel, the religious norm is overcome by "natural inclination." Each of the antagonists' discourses reflect something other than a unified, objectified disposition. Both seem to make sense of their actions through an intersubjective conversation with an other.

Foreshadowing the story's ending, R. Uriel's double-voice reveals his reticence for complete spiritual ascent, holding himself in check and reversing course:

> As he rose, R. Uriel peered into the core of the world . . . until he became frightened of losing complete contact with any reality. So he rested his forehead on the window pane to cool off his wondrous divine bonding, maintaining his soul within his body. (23)

> קם רבי אוריאל ונסתכל בגופו של עולם ונתלהב התלהבות נוראה מהשתלשלות העולמות ומן העולמות המצוחצחים, עד שנתיירא שלא יתבטל מן המציאות. הניח מצחו על זכוכית של חלון כדי לצנן דביקותו הנפלאה ויוכל להחזיק את נפשו בגופו.

This narrative of his perception and experience reveals shifting needs and competing aspirations—to ascend *and* to descend. The verbal shifts from being "entranced," to being "frightened," to "maintaining" reveal these narrative dynamics, as do the transitions from "he rose" to "he rested." These shifts can be considered not only as a temporal progression of perspectives and responses, but also as a synchronic display of a complex multiplicity of concerns and aspirations within a single experience and consciousness—what Wayne Booth calls "a vertical structure, rather than a given temporal structure and its technical transformations."[28] As we will see, this particular polyphonic monologue serves as a marked contrast to Gershom's fatal ascent at the story's conclusion, suggesting the latter's inability to let competing voices modulate his ecstatic mystical fervor.

This pattern of narrating an internal dialogue between an inclination and a normative action is also evident in the narrated monologues of R. Uriel's disciple, the "*Ḥozer,*" Gershom's teacher. The *Ḥozer*'s discourse suggests repeatedly that his sentiments and dispositions are dialogic, intersubjective, double-voiced. For example, having become Gershom's teacher and spiritual mentor, the *Ḥozer*'s monologue reveals a back-and-forth, internal, contrapuntal dialogue:

> He said to himself, "As long as I will be staying with them, I will direct my attention to enlightening their souls with vitality and divine joy—especially the soul of Gershom whose importance is equivalent to a whole group of Jews. There is, of course, no difference between one Jew and another as the entire Jewish people is part of divinity, as it is written, 'for His people are apportioned from God'[29] as a portion is separated from something. But there is, however a difference between souls, since there are different types, levels, and aspects of Jewish souls. There are souls whose source is taken from the 'head' and there are souls whose only source of sustenance is from the 'heel.' But Gershom's soul is great because it is [corresponding to] the aspect of the heart, warming the entire body. Happy is one who gets a hold of him and ignites his passion so that this warmth, for which all people on earth yearn, will be scattered throughout the world. (53)

> אמר אל לבו, הואיל ואדור במקומם אכוון דעתי להאיר נפשם ולהמשיך בהם חיות ושמחה אלהית. ובפרט בנפש גרשום שהיא שקולה כנגד כמה מישראל, באמת אין חילוק בין ישראל לישראל שכל האומה הישראלית היא חלק אלוה ממעל, כמו שכתוב, כי חלק ה' עמו, כחלק שנחלק מאיזה דבר, אלא יש הבדל בין נשמה לנשמה, שיש בנשמות ישראל כמה מיני מדריגות ובחינות. יש נשמות שמקור מחצבתן מן הראש ויש נשמות ששורש יניקתן אינו אלא מן העקב. אבל נשמתו של גרשום גדולה היא והיא מבחינת הלב שהוא מחמם כל הגוף. אשרי שיאחז בו ויעורר לבו כדי שחמימות זו שכל באי עולם נכספים לה תתפשט בעולם.

For the moment, let us read this internal quoted monologue as an artificially rendered dialogue.[30] The text of the original quoted monologue appears in italics as "*Ḥ*" and the imagined dialogic other as "Ḥ'."

Ḥ: He said to himself, "As long as I will be staying with them, I will direct my attention to enlightening their souls with vitality and divine joy."

Ḥ': Including Gershom?

Ḥ: "Especially Gershom whose importance is equivalent to a whole group of Jews."

Ḥ': But wouldn't this be the case for any Jew? Aren't all Jews equal before God?

Ḥ: "There is, of course, no difference between one Jew and another as the entire Jewish people is part of divinity."

Ḥ': So then all Jews are indeed equal. There is in fact no difference between them.

Ḥ: "But there is, however, a difference between souls, since there are different types, levels, and aspects of Jewish souls."

Ḥ': How so?

Ḥ: "There are souls whose source is taken from the 'head' and there are souls whose only source of sustenance is from the 'heel.'"

Ḥ' So where does Gershom's soul fit in to this?

Ḥ: "Gershom's soul is great because it [corresponds to] the aspect of the heart, which warms the entire body."

Ḥ': So what do heart and body signify with regard to Gershom?

Ḥ: "Happy is he who gets a hold of him and ignites his passion so that this warmth, for which all people on earth yearn, will be scattered throughout the world."

Ḥ': So Gershom will influence many others.

Important here is the concern with the differences and likenesses between Jews and between the souls of individual Jews.[31] As if the *Ḥozer* addresses an interlocutor, he tries to explain why Gershom carries a disproportional spiritual weight, despite there being no differences in the value of individual Jews. The reader is left to interpret this apparent contradiction as the narrator does not simply objectify a monolithic perspective of the *Ḥozer*. There would be no need for the *Ḥozer*'s explanations of the distinction between a Jew and a Jewish soul, nor would there be a need to explain the different levels of souls, were it not for an assumed dialogic interlocutor who is asking questions. Nor is this simply the narrator's effort to explain this distinction directly. The narrator, rather, is refracting these distinctions through the *Ḥozer*'s internal narrated monologue. Equally important, each "voice" in this interlocutory dialogue reflects a larger, normative, societal view. Suggestive of a kind of Talmudic argument, the conversation appeals to competing normative principles in its effort to reconcile the universal divine quality of all Jews, on the one hand, with distinctions between the spiritual levels of Jewish souls, on the other.

These then are clear illustrations of interlocutory double-voiced discourse. The discursive appeal to a double voice of normative principles (communal, hermeneutic, theological, or ethical) and the contrapuntal challenge to those principles represent an important difference between the discourse of *"Hanidaḥ"* and that of Agnon's earlier work, as I will show below.

Microdialogue

A second type of polyphonic discourse is "microdialogue." In this type of narrative "hybridity," a dialogic relationship exists on the levels of "whole utterances" or of "any signifying part of an utterance, even toward an individual word."[32] This kind of dialogue is possible when a given word, phrase, sentence, or broader utterance is read not as an objective "impersonal word of language," an expression or reference to a single definitive "semantic position," but rather "as the representative of another person's utterance." We thus hear two voices within a single utterance or thought.[33] Microdialogue is a "hybrid construction"—"an utterance that belongs, by its grammatical (syntactic) and compositional markers, to a single speaker, but that actually contains mixed within it two utterances, two speech manners, two styles, two 'languages,' two semantic and axiological belief systems."[34] Its distinction is in constituting more than one ideational and semantic framework within a single word or phrase.

This second type of double-voiced discourse occurs repeatedly in "*Hanidaḥ*," particularly in the voice of the narrator. In the following example, it is a function of the narrative's depiction of the town, Shibush, as a differentiated collective.

The anticipation of the rebbe's visit to Shibush is refracted through multiple voices. This multiplicity is reinforced in a microdialogue comprised of at least three separate but converging levels of interest in the Rebbe's arrival.

> With dawn, the few *ḥasidim* went to the outskirts of the town to greet and welcome this tsadik. Some of the men of Shibush tagged along with them to watch him make his entrance, noting that, if he is indeed a tsadik, the entrance of a *tsadik* brings about the fear of heaven. And everyone who was still wavering in his faith in tsadiks [באמונת צדיקים] became more steadfast, saying that, if people long to see him, this is a sign that the divine presence rests upon him. And so some Jews were standing to see him. As they gazed out, a cart wheel started grinding in the town's street. The entire place filled with joy, "The rebbe is coming. The rebbe is coming!" (10)

כיון שהאיר היום יצאו החסידים המועטים אל מחוץ לעיר לקדם פניו של אותו צדיק. נטפלו להם כמה מאנשי שבוש לראות בכניסתו. אמרו אם צדיק הוא כניסתם של צדיקים מביאה לידי יראת שמים. וכל מי שעדיין לבו רופף באמונת צדיקים מתחזק ואומר, מי שמשתוקקים לראותו סימן שהשכינה שורה עליו, והרי כמה מישראל עומדים לראותו. עד שעיניהם נשואות התחיל גלגל של עגלה מנסר והולך ברחובה של עיר. נתמלא כל המקום שמחה, הרבי בא הרבי בא.

In this passage, three collectives, each of whom has a distinctive behavior and rationale, are noted: (1) "the few *ḥasidim*" who want to welcome their tsadik, (2) "some men of Shibush," who want "to watch him make his entrance" because doing so might enhance their "fear of heaven," and (3) "everyone whose faith in tsadiks is still wavering" who are "standing to see him" because, if people are indeed longing to see him, "this is a sign that the divine presence rests upon him." This microdialogic narrator is assembling three different groups, behaviors, and rationales that interpenetrate each other, merging within the collective voice at the end of the paragraph, "The rebbe is coming! The rebbe is coming!" The narrator here thus refracts this plurality of perspectives and motivations through this converging exclamation.

Heteroglossia

The third type of double-voice discourse, "heteroglossia" (literally, "multispeechedness"), is what Bakhtin describes as multiple, interactive styles. Diverse linguistic forms, artistically situated in dynamic interaction, create a tension between a dominant, totalizing language and the multiplicity of language styles of groups and individuals. Heteroglossia contributes to a narrative's dialogic, double-voiced quality by structuring "distinctive links and interrelationships between utterances and languages . . . and speech types." This type of polyphonic discourse is distinct from interlocutory dialogue and microdialogue in that it accentuates tensions and discourse between "the social and historical voices populating language" and between these voices and a story's characters, including the narrator.[35] So, for Bakhtin, heteroglossia includes such styles as "the eloquence of the court," "forms used by reporters in newspaper articles," "the dry business language of the City," "the pedantic speech of scholars," "high epic style, Biblical style, or the style of the hypocritical moral sermon or finally the way . . . the subject of the story, happens to speak."[36] Heteroglossia thus refers not simply to different historical linguistic epochs nor solely to differences between formal and informal speech. Within any moment in time, a society may employ multiple types of daily speech; this stylistic plurality reflects a particular community's discourse.

That Agnon's fiction draws consistently on traditional rabbinic, kabbalistic, and biblical Hebrew should not preclude us from recognizing this quality of heteroglossia in his discourse. To be sure, the language style throughout

"*Hanidaḥ*" is traditional—rabbinic and kabbalistic. Within its unity of Hebrew style, nevertheless, multiple forms of discourse emerge: a letter, a curse, liturgical recitations, internal monologues, naturalistic description, speculations, non-verbal sighs and gestures, depictions of mystical experiences, personal introductions, laments, supplications, quoted speech, "objective" depictions, and evaluative explanations. What is significant, for our purposes, is that both within and among these types of discourse, contradictory understandings, perspectives, and aspirations are expressed. Below, I will illustrate Agnon's heteroglossia in his later work and in my discussion of the problematic nature of this story's ending.

Double-Voice Prior to *"Hanidaḥ"*

"Interlocutory" and "microdialogic" double-voiced discourse are scarce in Agnon's earlier stories, prior to his completing "*Hanidaḥ*." Examples of heteroglossia do exist in these early works, although less subtle and more explicitly self-conscious. To be sure, there are multiple examples of individual internal struggles and displays of psychological ambivalence in Agnon's fiction from its beginnings—during his "Palestinian" and subsequent "German" period before 1919. Yet the narratives of these tensions are, for the most part, single-voiced, monophonic. Polyphonic discourse requires the interpenetration of language styles and psychological dispositions, a relationship to multiple social contexts, conflicting belief systems, individual or collective breaks with social or religious norms, and most importantly, the allusive invocation of a real or imagined dialogic "other." Bakthin's notion of dialogue, then, is not to be equated with interpersonal exchange and expressions of internal conflict. Rather, it requires a presence of broader, conflicting, normative, revolutionary, communitarian, and individualistic understandings as background or prominent foreground. Here I will provide three examples from these earlier works.

In his mythic religious tale, "*Agunot*" (1908), despite the emotional anguish of its characters, there is an absence of double-voiced discourse. We can, in fact, consider this absence to contribute to its characters' figurative "*'aginut*"—what Nehama Aschkenasy felicitously characterizes as "a spiritual sense of separation and existential loneliness."[37] In "*Agunot*," we search in vain for double-voice within individual consciousnesses. The internal monologues call to an "other" who does not answer. This is evident, for example, in the voice of the story's principal feminine character, Dina: "'Mother, Mother!' her heart cries out. But there is no answer."[38] At times of greatest conflict and ambivalence, there is no dialogue; there is an absence of discursive recognition of an internal "other": "Dinah heard his song and did not know her heart." Even as she confesses her sin to the rabbi as her wedding day approaches there is no dialogic partner—neither internal nor external.

There is only silence: "The rabbi stood mute." When the rabbi does respond to Dina's confession, he assures her, in a long monophonic address, that "on the day of their marriage, the Holy One, blessed be He, pardons their sins" and that "absolution" comes in "the rearing of children in the ways of the Lord." But as to the substance of her confession, the rabbi closes off the possibility of dialogue: "And when the rabbi came to the matter of the ark, he intimated that silence would be seemly." Like the marriage of Dina to Rabbi Ezekiel in this story, all possibility of dialogue is annulled.

The protagonist, Ne'eman, in Agnon's story, "*Tishre*" (1911), struggles between aversion, compassion, and erotic-romantic attraction toward his student, Yael.[39] This story illustrates how expressions of internal psychological, emotional struggles are not to be confused with double-voice. The latter is linked to contradictory societal norms to which the individual is dialogically engaged. In this story, the implicated alterity is a vague discomfort rather than societal or normative meanings and principles:

> Ne'eman agreed to teach Torah to her, that fair lass; and he was quite surprised about this. Now, two years after the tumult, late in his life, he is occupied with things like this. Afterwards, finding it to be one of his secret personal enigmas, being irresolvable, he was somewhat more at ease; it became clear in his mind, which is common when one recognizes what is beyond oneself and realizes that these kinds of things exceed comprehension.[40]

To be sure, Ne'eman struggles between a desire to understand himself and resignation. Yet sustained dialogue is preempted as the struggle is fundamentally, ultimately "irresolvable."[41]

Yael, the object of Ne'eman's confused and conflicted affections, also displays contradictory inclinations and desires: "Yael Hayyut recoiled. She want to leave, but her desire to stay overpowered her."[42] Yet this type of ambivalence can be contrasted, for example, to that of Gershom in "*Hanidaḥ*," as he enters the hasidic *kloyz*:[43]

> But when . . . he heard them reciting "We will sanctify you (*nakdishekha*)," he realized that he had entered "the sect's" domain. He jumped up from his place as if a snake had bitten him. But the pleasing melody of the prayer captivated him so he did not leave. (38)

> כיון שהגיעו לקדושת השם ושמע שהם אומרים נקדישך הכיר שנכנס לרשות של ה"כת." קפץ ממקומו כאילו נשכו נחש. אבל נעימה של התפילה הקיפה את לבו ולא יצא.

Though both texts express a dynamic of "recoiling" and an acquiescence of reason to desire, in this latter excerpt, the struggle is set against the background of two systems of thought, two axiological religiosocial frameworks. Gershom's double-voice can only fully be understood in relation to the broader conflicts between the discourses of "*nakdishekha*" and "*nikadesh*" (between the hasidic and mitnagdic liturgical formulations of the "*kedushah*" prayer) as they interpenetrate each other in this dramatic dialogic moment.[44]

In Agnon's novella-length work, "The Crooked Shall Become Straight" (והיה העקוב למישור) (1912), there are also examples of dialogue, but very different from that of "*Hanidaḥ*":

> Surely, it is decreed that our lives and needs will depend on others; if it is so decreed we much accept it. And essentially, there is no harm done, God forbid. What is essential is the deed and thus having faith deep in our hearts in the Creator, blessed by He . . . When we have enough, we will return the money to the poor many times over . . . all hope is actually lost already and a sharp sword is resting our necks . . . When the end was nearing, they recognized that this was not the time to debate endlessly with hunger and passively to do nothing.[45]

In this monologue we hear one perspective. Menasheh Ḥayyim and his wife, Kreindal, are together, rationalizing a decision to ask for handouts. The justification is not based on a dialogue between two different sets of beliefs or even two distinct points of view. Rather, it is based on the fact that there is nothing to have a dialogue about. It is a *gezeirah*, a "divine decree," that they must resort to asking for handouts. It is not a choice, it is the only choice.[46] Any competing voice must be reconciled to nonnegotiable divine demand; there is no room for dialogue, even as, in making this decision, they are overcome with anguish and sorrow.[47]

Double-Voice after *"Hanidaḥ"*

Many examples of double-voiced discourse appear in Agnon's later writing. And, to be sure, it is widely known that his literary discourse is fraught with multiple meanings, ironic contradictions, and layers of semantic allusions. What I am arguing here is that understanding some of these features as double-voice can illuminate developments of this type of discourse in Agnon's fiction, the beginnings of which are significant in "*Hanidaḥ.*" Equally important, as we will see in this chapter's final section, this understanding of double-voice has significant import for education.

In his novel *A Guest for the Night*, a conversation between a child, his mother, and the first-person narrator constitutes a double-voiced microdialogue regarding the meanings of "story" and "to tell a story":

> His father said to the child, "Ask the gentleman to tell you a nice story." The child said to me, "If you can tell stories, so tell me what Grandpa is doing just now." Said Erela, "that isn't in the category of stories." "Well what is it?" said the child. "When you learn the theory of literature, you will know what is a story and what isn't a story," said Erela. "And if someone doesn't learn the

> theory of literature, doesn't he know what a story is?" said the child. "Certainly he doesn't know," replied Erela. "So why don't you know how to tell stories?" said the child. "You've learned the theory of literature, haven't you?" Said Erela, "But I know what is a story and what isn't a story." "And what Grandpa is doing isn't a story?" said the child. "No," said Erela, "That isn't a story." "And what is it?" "That is in the category of information," said Erela, "so long as it is important, but if it isn't important, it's nothing at all." "Well," said the child, "let the gentleman tell me the story of nothing at all." Erela turned her spectacles on the child and said in surprise, "What do you mean 'nothing'? If there is nothing, there isn't anything to tell." Said the child, "Grandpa is doing some thing, so there is something to tell. Tell me what my grandfather is doing just now, sir."
>
> I passed my hand over my forehead and said, "At this moment your grandfather is sitting in the courtyard, in front of the little house—no, in front of a large house, with his head bowed in thought, and he is saying, 'Wonder of wonders, it is not yet Passover and already it is warm in the open, just as in the days of spring.'"[48]

Reflecting different narrative theories, a child's and his mother's understandings of "story" and "to tell a story" diverge and converge, traversing fictional construction, imaginative vision, and delivery of "information." With the first person narrator's passing his hand over his forehead, the different axiological assumptions converge microdialogically, as he begins "to tell a story" that brings together the father's, the child's, and perhaps even the mother's understandings into his discourse.

And it is well known that tensions between dissonant or dialogic heteroglossia are central to Agnon's literary project in his particular usages of invocations, allusions, and digressions in the forms of letters, speeches, folktales, parables, maxims, legal declarations, biblical and rabbinic prooftexts, midrashic expositions, poetry, and modernist narrative styles. More often than not, there is no clearly marked border between these stylistic usages. An important example, however, of an exemplary demarcation of types of discourse is in *Only Yesterday,* which goes as far as narrating the "excommunication" of secularized Hebrew from its sacred, sacramental usage, thus closing out dialogue between the two.[49] This is thus a banishment of dialogue itself, expressed metaphorically in the treatment of the figure of Balak, the "mad dog." That section of the novel opens with a normative rabbinic precedent:

> When our Rabbis in the Land of Israel would excommunicate a person, they would tie notes to the tails of black dogs, writing on them, So-and-So, son of So-and-So is excommunicated, and they would send them throughout the city to warn the people to stay away from him.[50]

The narrative then returns to a present, unprecedented act of writing: "But to write on the skin of a dog no man had ever done." This assertion of unprecedentedness is followed by a contradictory claim, a generalization concerning the constancy of precedent and repetition, supported by an historical example.

> But there is nothing new under the sun, everything man does and will do has already been done before him and before that. And Jerusalem still recalls that once they excommunicated a wise man who wanted to correct the *Yishuv*[51] against the will of the Keepers of the Walls, and they brought a pack of dogs and wrote on their skin, Heretic, Banned and Excommunicated.[52]

This fate is borne by Balak as he runs frantically through an ultra-orthodox Jerusalem neighborhood, making a plea using biblical, liturgical discourse: "The dog shouted, 'Where is Heaven? Your sons have sinned and I am beaten.'" This is to no avail. Banishment is the sentence: "When he shouted, all the men, women, and children hid in their houses and locked their doors. Meah She`arim emptied and there wasn't a creature left outside, aside from that dog."[53]

This setting of linguistic boundaries and proscriptions is itself narrated in a progression of heteroglossia—a statement of authoritative rabbinic practice (including a ritual recitation), a characterization of the current moment as unprecedented, a contradictory generalization claiming the constancy of precedent and repetition, supposed historical proof to support this generalization, liturgical supplication, and episodic narration of current communal response. Agnon thus arranges a seemingly cacophonous array of discursive styles into a narrative heteroglossia depicting a recurring dissonance and figurative separation between secular and sacred language. But, importantly, the multivoiced heteroglossia leaves the situation unresolved as the dog is "left outside" alone, yet with no monophonic finality.

Like heteroglossia, dialogic interlocutors are also ubiquitous in Agnon's writing. In *The Bridal Canopy*,[54] the variations of style and R. Yudel's comic, ironic, indecisive ruminations are well known:

> The Hassid hesitated whether to take the road, since travel diminishes the study of the Torah and prayer with the congregation as well as disturbing a man's customary ways. Nonetheless he did not dismiss the matter, for it is a duty to hearken to the words of the wise. So he applied to himself the saying of the sage, When your daughter attains puberty free your slave; that is, free yourself, for you are one of the slaves of the Blessed Creator.[55]

The double-voiced quality of R. Yudel's discourse in the form of an internal dialogue—between the voice of remaining in place and the voice of travelling elsewhere—suggests a tension between endearing comic innocence and absurd comic reasoning. Significantly, his internal dialogue shows his effort to reconcile his own desires, societal norms, and religious standards ("study of Torah," "prayer with the congregation," "a duty to hearken to the words of the wise") and creative (comic) interpretation ("free yourself").

We hear double-voices in the discourse of Hirshl, Tsirl, Baruch Meir, and the narrator throughout *A Simple Story*[56] as well. Trying to deal with what he considers to be Blume's "silent treatment," Hirshl—who "had eyes only for Blume, who had just curtly left the dining room"—speculates: "I see you're keeping accounts, thought Hirshl. If you mean to give me the silent treatment, believe me, two can play at that game: I can be as silent as you . . . Blume's eyes looked so anguished that he simply had to say something, and so he followed her back to her room."[57] Hirshl, in a sense, reveals two voices discussing different interpretations of Blume's silence (that she is "keeping accounts" in being silent and that she is "so anguished") and differing responses to that silence (being "as silent as you" and having "to say something").[58]

Ethics of Alterity

Bakhtin considered aesthetic, linguistic, and ethical dimensions of discourse inseparable. In this mode of discursive analysis and in its recognition of multivocality, there is an implicit ethics of alterity. For dialogic discourse is "to affirm someone else's 'I' not as an object but as another subject."[59] Reducing an individual to a type, or purporting to be able to explain a person fully, objectifies that individual, denying the reality that "there is always something that only he himself can reveal." This deference to the other is intersubjective in that "every word is directed toward an answer and cannot escape the profound influence of the answering word that it anticipates, even if unknown."[60] The unethical alternative "at its extreme, denies the existence outside itself of another consciousness with equal rights and equal responsibilities, another I with equal rights (thou)."[61]

In "*Hanidaḥ*," this ethics of alterity is expressed, in part, through counterexamples—efforts to presume a unified, understood other, efforts that objectify rather than subjectify. Throughout "*Hanidaḥ*," characters reveal distorted perspectives and oversimplifications of Gershom's struggles and responses. Gershom is rarely, if ever, viewed as an authentic "other" in the story. No character seems to recognize in him what Booth would call "the actual polyphony of his own inner chorus."[62] He is treated as one who is always on the receiving end of discourse. The *Ḥozer* considers him "ready to *receive* purification" (33) (מוכשר לקבל טהרה). The laymen, seeing his behavior, point to him as the "*imprint*" (רושם) of the tsadik's curse (32). Finally, at the story's conclusion,[63] the narrator reveals his own unreliable oversimplification, what Bakhtin would call his "pseudo-objective motivation,"[64] in his attempt to conceal alternative understandings of the story's causal relations. As was later to be the case in stories such as "Two Scholars Who Were in Our Town," these concealments of difference are in tension with the polyphonic discourse within and among the story's characters and groups.

This effort to conceal the multiple, to eclipse dialogue, is most evident in the narrator's awkward attempt at closure—a significant, abiding issue for Agnon. Immediately prior to offering an explanation for Gershom's death, the narrator describes the young man's ecstatic mystical "ascent":

> Lifting his head, he began reciting Song of Songs with terrifying ecstasy and awesome power, continuing until he reached the verse, "Draw me near to you and we will run." When he reached the verse, "Draw me near to you and we will run," his soul went out unblemished. His lips then whispered, "the king has brought me into his chambers," as his soul departed. (56)[65]

> הוציא את ראשו והתחיל קורא בשיר השירים בהתלהבות איומה ובגבורה נוראה. והיה קורא והולך עד שהגיע לפסוק משכני אחריך נרוצה. וכיון שהגיע לפסוק משכני אחריך נרוצה יצתה נשמתו בטהרה. ועדיין שפתיו מרחשות הביאני המלך חדריו. נפשו יצאה בדברו.

Explaining Gershom's death following his mystical fervor, the narrator offers a simplified, singular explanation: "Thus, Gershom, grandson of R. Avigdor, died because R. Avigdor had struggled with R. Uriel and fought the *ḥasidim*" (56) (ככה מת גרשום נכד רבי אביגדור, כי שרה רבי אביגדור עם רבי אוריאל ועם חסידים רב). Gershom would have met his death, then, on account of his grandfather's excessive battling against the *tsadik* and his followers. Read thus, Gershom's death and the manner in which he died are due to external conditions and events (such as his grandfather's provoking the tsadik's curse) that affected his capacity to continue living.

To be sure, R. Avigdor's harsh and strident battle against the *ḥasidim* and their *tsadik* serves a cardinal function in the story. Yet the narrator dissimulates by presenting this explanation as the sole or primary cause of Gershom's death. His terse explanation is questionable as it gives the appearance of resolution and finality. Indeed, the narrator's *post hoc* confusion of causality and sequence in explaining Gershom's death seems to be a parody of itself against the background of the story as a whole. The narrator's explanation simplifies an event, the causes of which—even if explainable—are multiple. Like the metaphorical and literal function of the abundance of snowfall at the story's opening, the narrator's characterization of R. Avigdor's battling the *ḥasidim* as the cause of Gershom's death blurs distinctions and causal relations, ignoring the impact of the story's multivocal dimensions.

Presenting a unitary perspective, the narrator posits a point of view that, in Bakthin's language, is exposed as "narrowly rationalistic, inadequate to reality."[66] The narrator's submergence of difference is enhanced by an abrupt discursive shift, characteristic of a number of Agnon's narrators' attempts at closure. The heteroglossia conclusion's transitions from description of the ecstatic "ascent" of Gershom's soul (i.e., his death) to "logical" explanation for its cause. The narrator refocalizes the reader's perspective with a sweeping explanation that seeks to situate that experience within the context of R. Avigdor's battle against the *ḥasidim*. This deceptively seamless (ככה—"thus," "in this way," "this is why") transition achieves the result of what Bakhtin would call the narrator's becoming "unmasked and destroyed as something false, hypocritical, greedy, limited, narrowly rationalistic."[67] While perhaps this is too harsh a characterization of Agnon's narrator, the concluding sentence does suggest a "pseudo-objective" explanation. Bakhtin notes that revealing this attempt at concealment is "characteristic of novel style since it is one of the manifold forms for concealing another's speech in hybrid constructions."[68] Furthermore, he notes that "[s]ubordinate conjunctions and link words ('thus,' 'because,' 'for the reason that,' 'in spite of' and so forth), as well as words used to maintain a logical sequence ('therefore,' 'consequently,' etc.) lose their direct authorial intention."[69] Description with subordinate explanation create a "hybrid construction" in which there are two sources of speech: the witness to the event of Gershom's spiritual ascent and the subjective explanatory narrator. As heteroglossia, there is a struggle between objective, determinate "cause-of-death" language and the narrative of surreal ambiguity, as "thus Gershom died" responds to "his soul went out unblemished." The narrator's discourse of "cause of death" strives to overshadow the discourse of spiritual ascent.

A novice ecstatic kabbalist, Gershom dies when he engages in an ecstatic mystical ascent. His death takes place in the context of a complex matrix of relationships, psychic conditions, and personal loss, even as it takes place within the framework of this intense hasidic-mitnagdic struggle. Equally important is Gershom's untimely or misguided use of ecstatic experience. The risks of mystical ascent were indeed alluded to earlier in the story as R. Uriel had to "cool himself off" in order to prevent his leaving his corporeality forever. The actions of the *Ḥozer*, who guided Gershom into mystical experience and who, with Gershom, was engaging in an ecstatic recitation of Song of Songs immediately prior to Gershom's fatal experience, cannot be overlooked when considering causes for Gershom's death in an fervor of ascent.

We also need to consider that Gershom is both the least stable figure in the story and the most objectified by the narrator and by the other characters. He has no "sublimity of freed perspectives," to use Booth's language.[70] His experience of the sublime is dominated by the discourse of others—specifically of the *ḥasidim*, the *Ḥozer,* and his mitnagdic grandfather's discourse—without a "personalized persuasive discourse" of his own. Describing Bakhtin's linguistic narrative theory, Booth notes the distinction between language's "centrifugal" and "centripetal" claims on the individual:

> There is a "centrifugal" force dispersing us outward into an ever greater variety of "voices," outward into a seeming chaos that presumably only a God could encompass. And there are various "centripetal" forces preserving us from overwhelming fluidity and variety.[71]

If one can speak of "causes" for Gershom's death in Bakhtin's terminology, we would have to include the overwhelming imbalance between "centrifugal" and "centripetal" discursive forces and the lack of what Bakhtin calls "personally persuasive discourse." Gershom's objectification by all of the story's figures, his being an empty vessel to be filled with competing types of wisdom and religious experience, his emptiness in the wake of his mother's death, his being discursively "imprinted" with the tsadik's curse—all these efforts to shape and objectify him—overwhelm any discourse that could anchor him or free him. Without the necessary balance between the authoritative and personal discourses, between the centripetal and centrifugal forces, discourse becomes an "overwhelming fluidity," casting him out from the world. Whereas the tsadik, in his mystical ascent, reverses direction with his own experienced, balanced between authoritative and "personally persuasive" sensibilities, Gershom has no such recourse.

Equally important in understanding Gershom's death is the marked contrast between double-voiced discourse within individual consciousnesses and a dominating background of interpersonal objectification. What Agnon demonstrates in the story is that without intersubjectivity, discursive communication ends. Wayne Booth, in his explication of Bakhtin, would provide a helpful perspective on Gershom's fate: "To be means to communicate dialogically. When dialogue ends, everything ends."[72] The imbalance between the objectification of Gershom by others (including the narrator), his very limited capacity for interior or interpersonal intersubjectivity, and his being overwhelmed by centrifugal language, could be said to lead to his fatal ascent. Ultimately dialogue is submerged. As an outcast, *the* outcast, Gershom is dismissed dialogically. He is not a legitimate interlocutor or "other." As a "*nidaḥ*," he is "cast out" of the dialogic loop as the narrator explains his death by a single, external cause.

Anticipating his later literary works in his artistic use of double-voice, Agnon makes known the presence and narrative capacities of what Bakhtin calls "the speaking person and his discourse."[73] Important to understanding the significance of "*Hanidaḥ*" is its sustained tension between a seemingly simplified exterior, on the one hand, and an unmasked polyphonic interior, on the other. Exposing this interior, revealing its transcendence of typicality, we hear an "other" even as the narrator at times seeks to conceal it. As Agnon exposes this other voice, we become interlocutors of whose presence the narrator becomes aware, a silent voice to which he responds. The implied author wants us to challenge the narrative surface and to discover the substrata of dialogic engagement in which we too participate. In challenging us, Agnon lets us hear overtures to a discursive style that he later mastered.

CONVERSATION PARTNER 2: EDUCATIONAL THEORY

I have offered this Bakhtinian analysis of Agnon as an invitation for conversation between educational inquiry and literary interpretation. So when introducing educational theory as a partner in this conversation, I invite educators to consider the ethical nuances and pedagogical possibilities of their theories and practices. So let us consider the educational issues that appear to emerge in our reading of "*Hanidaḥ*."

Explicit assertions about education in the story are scarce. Consistent with the theme of this book, this scarcity allows us to consider a work as a whole rather than limiting ourselves to any specific references to education. Ethical, pedagogical issues emerge in the narrative's sustained intersubjectivity, in the contrapuntal responses to an other. Thus, here we look at the educational import of the work on two levels: First we consider the educational issues implicit in the narrative's theme and plot. And second we will consider how the story's double-voiced discourse raises pedagogical problems and ways of interpreting them.

Pedagogical Issues: Theme and Plot

As mentioned in our analysis of the story's ending, the actions of the *Ḥozer* are educationally and ethically questionable. Miseducation is an apparent cause of Gershom's fatal ascent. The student, Gershom, is consistently considered an object, rather than subject. He is cast as the one who will "receive" or "accept" rather than decide. His active pursuits are preempted by this singular role to which the *Ḥozer* relegates him—as one who is "ready to accept spiritual purification."

The teacher, the *Ḥozer*, hides his true intentions and dissimulates as a means to what he considers to be a greater end. He thus presents himself as someone whom he is not and rationalizes his conduct, noting that "Gershom's soul is great [and one who] gets a hold of him [will provide something] for which all people on earth yearn" (53).[74] This teacher also provides little sustained vigilance. Gershom's "readiness" for certain types of mystical experience is neither fully understood nor monitored. He is thus misread. This, despite the fact that his anguished countenance and disposition were evident. Even the usually insensitive R. Avigdor "sensed this change." But the *Ḥozer* maintains "that he has not seen any change. . .everything is going along as usual. But R. Avigdor was not at ease with this."[75] (הרגיש רבי אביגדור

בשינוי זה. היה מתיירא שמא גרמה המחלה היא הנקראת פעימת הלב שמתה בו אמו עליה השלום. שאל רבי אביגדור את החוזר מה לו לגרשום? אמר לו החוזר לרבי אביגדור שאינו רואה שום שינוי. עוסקים הם בתורה והכל נוהג כשורה. לא נחה דעתו של רבי אביגדור.)

The *Ḥozer* makes no distinction between a student's longings and his needs, apparently leading Gershom to further alienation from his family and community, even from himself. Gershom was a "forlorn soul" who was "longing for something much, much higher," (וכיסופים שלא זכו להם אנשי שבוש התחילו מבצבצים ועולים מתוך לבו ומתנוצצים מתוך עיניו העמלות בתורה ומבקשים מה למעלה, למעלה). Gershom isolated himself, with the *Ḥozer*'s help, "groping in darkness" and becoming filled with "a kind of black bitterness" that was visible externally as his faced developed "wrinkles and blemishes" as he "would sit on the ground and put his head between his knees." (אבל אצבעותיו סמויות היו והיו מגששות בחללו של עולם כאשר יגשש העור באפלה. מכאן ואילך נשתפכה בו מעין מרה שחורה ויגונו של עולם עשה עיטוף ועיטור לנועם פניו).

These elements in the story, of course, raise more educational questions than they answer: In what ways do we treat students as objects? When and how do we provide opportunities for them to see themselves as subjects of their intentional learnings? When and to what extent does teaching demand full disclosure of educational aspirations? What level of risk is appropriate in employing means to achieve desirable ends? How ought we to respond when there is substantial dissonance between our educational aspirations and the spiritual, cultural, familial milieu in which a student lives? What are the warning signs in a student that call for intervention or adjustment? Are there certain ways we should conduct ourselves differently toward the more vulnerable student? How do we make the distinction between a student's yearnings and a student's needs? When, if ever, should a teacher "pretend" while concealing this pretention from the student? More generally, when, if ever, is it right to recruit young, impressionable religious adherents into a particular normative and discursive framework while concealing one's aspirations for them? Though beyond the scope of this chapter, each of these questions requires careful consideration and are important subjects for educational inquiry.

The central educational and ethical question in the story is reflected in the story's title; there are different ways that individuals are "cast out." R. Uriel is banished from the town and Gershom is on the path to being disowned by his mitnagdic grandfather and by the established communal authority. But Gershom is also cast out from life to death in his mystical ascent. In the process, he is cast out by his teacher, the *Ḥozer*, who unwittingly but recklessly takes Gershom beyond his readiness and need. The story thus calls on us to consider how we educators may respond to the biblical promise "to not make one an outcast" "לְבִלְתִּי יִדַּח מִמֶּנּוּ נִדָּח" (2 Samuel 14:14).

Pedagogical Issues: Discursive Style

I turn now to the discourse in "*Hanidaḥ*" as a source for understanding educational and ethical issues. Interpretation and teaching of fiction call for consideration of the relationship between and within different narrative voices, showing how an appearance of unity gives way to a prevailing multiplicity, even in a single consciousness or utterance. Let us consider, then, what this Bakhtinian analysis suggests for the discerning reader and for the perceptive, responsive teacher.

First, I suggest that pursuit of a life in conversation with others is an educational value as much as an interpretive mode. As Booth affirms: "Polyphony, the miracle of our 'dialogical' lives together, is thus both a fact of life and, in its higher reaches, a value to be pursued endlessly."[76] We therefore seek to create learning spaces in which human discourse is neither suppressed nor "outcast" by a supposedly sovereign discourse of authority.

Moreover, as Bakhtin argues, in addition to ethics, "[o]ur motif [of the speaking person and his discourse] carries even greater weight in the realm of religious thought and discourse." [77] Ethics and religion—and here I would add education—wrestle with the enduring possibility of "a twofold approach to another's word when it is treated as something we seek to understand."[78] The first option is that

> The word can be perceived purely as an object (something that is, in its essence, a thing) . . . In such a word-object even meaning becomes a thing: there can be no dialogic approach to such a word of the kind immanent to any deep and actual understanding. Understanding, so conceived, is inevitably abstract: it is completely separated from the living, ideological power of the word to mean—from its truth or falsity, its significance or insignificance, beauty or ugliness. Such a reified word-thing cannot be understood by attempts to penetrate its meaning dialogically: there can be no conversing with such a word.[79]

In the second option, on the other hand, we assume "a *sharpened dialogic relationship to the word* that in turn uncovers fresh aspects within the word: Precisely such an approach is needed . . . where objectivity of understanding is linked with dialogic vigor and a deeper penetration into discourse itself."[80]

As educators, then, we may come to recognize the intersubjectivity within our own discourse and that of our students. In doing so we do not "treat the word neutrally, as if it were a thing."[81] Rather, we would seek first to evaluate the potential double-voiced interiority of the word and then to respond. Taking discourse seriously, then, involves recognizing the idiosyncratic, personal voices within and between students, teachers, and texts, responding to multiplicity rather than to unitary meanings. An educational question then becomes: How can the discourse of an "other" become part of what Booth would call the "polyphony" of the student's "own inner chorus"?[82] While a decisive answer to this question is beyond the scope of this study, the following considerations may serve as a guide for some initial steps.

As we have seen in our analysis of "*Hanidaḥ*," Gershom's sources for expression and communication are limited to those of the "authoritative discourses" of the warring socioreligious camps, leaving him bereft of what Bakhtin would call "personally persuasive discourse."[83] Engagement between the personal and authoritative dimensions of discourse takes place in a "zone of contact" in which the individual engages in a "struggle against various kinds and degrees of authority."[84] Educational settings surely constitute such contact zones. Often formal education tends to emphasize official discourse that represents a source of authority. But in addition to this formal, "authoritative discourse," Bakhtin notes the importance of its being balanced with "internally persuasive" discourse that is uniquely the student's own:[85]

> [A]n individual's becoming . . . is characterized precisely by a sharp gap between these two categories: in one, the authoritative word (religious, political, moral; the word of a father, of adults and of teachers, etc.) that does not know internal persuasiveness, in the other internally persuasive word that is denied all privilege, backed up by no authority at all, and is frequently not even acknowledged in society (not by public opinion, nor by scholarly norms, nor by criticism), not even in the legal code. The struggle and dialogic interrelationship of these categories of ideological discourse are what usually determine the history of an individual ideological consciousness.[86]

As we have seen in the example of Gershom, the teacher could play a critical role in seeking to understand his discursive tension and to assist the student in achieving some sense of provisional equilibrium between discursive groundedness and a freed personal perspective to recognize, navigate, and appropriate the diversity of discourses that seek to claim him. What a Bakhtinian theory of discourse offers is the opportunity to cultivate a pedagogical disposition toward the student that recognizes that he or she "is not the site of one unitary language but rather of multiple competing languages."[87] Seeing the effort to navigate such multiplicity, the teacher recognizes that, in the classroom, the camp, the trip abroad, indeed in any educational event, the student is involved in a struggle. If we neither acknowledge nor encourage such a struggle, if we overemphasize "unconditional allegiance" to the authoritative side of discourse, education becomes uncompromising and inert—obstructing the student's "free appropriation and assimilation of the word itself that authoritative discourse seeks to elicit from us."[88]

What "is constitutive" of "the internally persuasive word . . . is a special conception of listeners, readers, perceivers,"[89] and, I would add, of students. What Bakhtin says here of discourse can also apply to education and teaching: "Every discourse presupposes a special conception of the listener: of his apperceptive background and the degree of his responsiveness; it presupposes a specific distance."[90] The task of education is not to eliminate this distance, but to respect it, engage it, giving the student a "subliminity of freed perspectives" to navigate the claims of discursive multiplicity. For authoritative discourse alone eliminates "free stylistic development. It is by its very nature incapable of being double-voiced; it cannot enter into hybrid constructions."[91] To embrace the notion of polyphonic discourse in educational settings, the teacher needs to create spaces for "contradictory emotion," for "an agitated and cacophonous dialogic life."[92]

One educational theorist, invoking Bakhtin, helpfully suggests that teachers support students to become "critical appraisers" of the texts they study.[93] Students could learn to "talk back" to what they read and hear, resisting the either-or choice of acceptance or rejection of authoritative narratives. They would thus come to experience texts, even sacred texts, in part, as "living traces of conversations among people who came before us, progenitors whose struggles and whose language thread throughout the words and deeds of all of us today."[94] Another educational researcher suggests that a Bakhtinian approach to reading occurs when "students question the author, mark up and talk back to the text" in "a constant interaction between meanings."[95] Similarly, students can be encouraged to express "narratives of rethinking" in order to "express their own evolving interpretations dialogically, often juxtaposing several different perspectives in the process."[96]

One teacher relates how she decided to teach students questioning as an integral part of their reading:

> In the past, I've approached reading assignments by asking students to respond to my questions. There has always been that feeling like I'm feeding it to them, or that they've responded in a somewhat stifled way to the questions because they're expecting that I'm looking for a particular answer.[97]

Elaborating on this teacher's efforts, an educational researcher notes:

> Carla created a classroom in which students were invited to take on new roles as readers, as question askers and conversational partners, as discussion leaders, and as thinkers, rather than merely as responders to the teachers' questions.[98]

Another example of taking multivoiced discourse seriously relates to the types of work assigned:

> Students are introduced to the text, work with it in a variety of ways, and produce an original work in response. Their final performance, which is presented publicly to an audience, incorporates sections of the core text, other relevant texts, and their own original work, combined and organized to respond to a central theme.[99]

We also can consider the import of polyphonic discourse for teachers as they reflect on the process of developing their own educational theories. Sperling argues that:

> [T]eachers' shifting theories reveal the multiple and sometimes conflicting realities of their dialogic existence in the world of school or, put another way, their shifting identities as they relate to one another, to students inside the classroom, and to outside others, such as policy makers, who influence classroom life.[100]

When we consider that the teacher's implicit and explicit discourses change—become multiple, not only over time, but at any given moment of time—the teacher can be considered akin to an implied author, responding to contradictions, internal and external struggles, dilemmas, and the unpredictability of certain outcomes. For what Bakhtin maintains of "the word" can also reflect the words and gestures of the teacher as well as those of the student. The analogy between the word and pedagogy suggests the dynamic nature of teaching, embodying the multiple and even the contradictory. When we consider teaching to be more than a separate "thing," more than the process of conveying word-objects, we begin to see the teacher's voice too as multiple and as internally responsive to its own and others' alterities.

NOTES

1. J. Hillis Miller, *The Ethics of Reading* (New York: Columbia University Press, 1987). J. Hillis Miller, "The Ethics of Narration" in *The J. Hillis Miller Reader,* Julian Wolfreys, ed. (Stanford, California: Stanford University Press, 2005), 38–44.
2. See part 2, note 12.
3. Landy, 2004, p. 91. On "implied author" see part 2, note 12.
4. Agnon, "*Hanidaḥ*." The first edition was published in 1919. All references are to the 1953 edition. All translations of *Hanidaḥ* and of its criticism are my own unless otherwise indictated.
5. Weiser, 54, 56 and Werses, 309.
6. Shaked, *Shmuel Yosef Agnon*, 22. Also see Moked, 208.
7. Alter, "*Hishtalshelut ha-olamot*," 13.
8. Band, *Nostalgia and Nightmare*, 96.
9. Miron, 5–6, 22. Also see Aberbach, *At the Handles of the Lock,* 85–87; Krojanker, 85–89; Laor, *Heibatim Hadashim*, 5.
10. To be sure, these earlier stories anticipate other important aspects of Agnon's later work and are remarkable literary achievements in their own right.
11. Bakthin, "Discourse in the Novel," 300.
12. Bakthin's work focuses on the development of the novel. If, for the purpose of our analysis, we accept Miron's view that Agnon's short stories and novellas "must . . . be seen as achieved against the background of Agnon's "ongoing novelistic enterprise," then we may consider the development of qualities of Agnon's fiction, more generally, as informed by a Bakhtinian notion of dialogue. Miron, "Agnon's Transactions," 1.
13. והמתנגדים נלחמים בחסידים, ויגרשו החסידים איש מבית חותנו ואת נשיהם הוציאו מחיקם. את חלונותיהם שברו ואת ציציותיהם טינפו וגם בבית תפילבם שלחו ידיהם (50).

14. For the purpose of this analysis, it is important to note that among the characteristic qualities of ḥasidism, the wide-spread religious movement that began in eighteenth century Eastern Europe, are ecstatic prayer, allegiance to charismatic rabbis who are considered holy men (*tsadikim*), treating a *tsadik*'s tales and his interpretations as sacred "Torah," and certain mystical experiences. With its dramatic growth, the popular movement presented a major communal and religious challenge to the rabbinic establishment and its loyalists, the *mitnagdim* ("opponents"). Frequently the two parties would publicly renounce each other and make accusations to regional authorities, at times leading to banishment from certain towns or imprisonment. A *tsadik* was thought to possess extraordinary spiritual powers to create mystical connections to the divine and to influence God's beneficence.

15. See 2 Sam. 14:14. "לְבִלְתִּי יִדַּח מִמֶּנּוּ נִדָּח." "that he that is banished be not an outcast from him."

16. On this kind of spiritual malaise that often led young mitnagdic scholars to hasidism, see Dynner, 2006, 176 and Maimon, 1888, 154.

17. A "*ḥozer*" (lit. "returnee" or "reviewer") is responsible for representing the hasidic rebbe, reviewing and recapitulating his lessons.

18. Song of Songs 1:4

19. Mikhail Bakhtin, *Problems of Dostoevsky's Poetics*. (Minneapolis, MN: University of Minnesota Press, 1984), 184.

20. Bakhtin, *Problems of Dostoevsky's Poetics*, 32.

21. Bakhtin, "Discourse in the Novel," 284.

22. Dentith, 163.

23. See, for example, Band, *Nostalgia and Nightmare*. I wish here to demonstrate how this tension is expressed discursively in Agnon's polyphonic narration.

24. "Heavy snow descended in a heavenly stream to the earthly realm that entire week. The black earth whitened and the sky remained dark as people entered their houses to huddle near their stoves. There was no coming and going in the town. But on Thursday, by divine grace, the snow began to melt as the sun shined on the land. Women went out to the market to buy meat and people came by horse and carriage from surrounding villages. So life's ebb and flow began again as if its vitality had never ceased." (9)

> שלג רב ירד כל אותו השבוע בנתיב עליון כלפי העולם השפל. האדמה השחורה הלבינה והשמים עמדו בכהיונם ובני אדם נתכנסו לבתיהם בין התנור ולכירים ובעיר אין יוצא ואין בא. אבל בחמישי בשבת נתגברה מדת החסד. השמש זרחה על הארץ והשלג התחיל מתמסה. נשים יצאו לשוק לקנות בשר ודגים ומן הכפרים אשר מסביב באו בקרונות ובסוסים. ושוב שופעים צנורות החיים כאילו לא נפסק השפע מעולם.

25. Bakhtin, *Problems of Dostoevsky's Poetics*, 10.

26. Here R. Avigdor uses a Talmudic reference almost verbatim (with a characteristically Agnonic twist). See *Babylonian Talmud*, Sanhedrin 95a.

27. Noticeable here, too, are dissonant depictions of the *tsadik*. Why would his "holiness's heart" give way to "natural inclination" and release such a primal "vigorous curse"?

28. Booth, "Introduction" to Bakhtin, *Problems of Dostoevsky's Poetics*, xxv.

29. כִּי חֵלֶק יְהוָה עַמּוֹ יַעֲקֹב חֶבֶל נַחֲלָתוֹ. (Deut. 32:9) "For the Lord's portion is his people; Jacob is the lot of his inheritance."

30. Bakhtin uses this "translation to dialogue" technique, asserting that, in the novel, "all the truly essential self-utterances could also be turned into dialogues." Bakhtin, *Problems of Dostoevsky's Poetics*, 210.

31. This distinction is espoused by R. Shneur Zalman of Lyady in his *Tanya*.

32. Bakhtin, *Problems of Dostoevsky's Poetics*, 75.

33. It is important to note that, from a narratological perspective, utterances and thoughts are intimately connected and, at times, one and the same. For example, "quoted monologue" is a character's directly quoted mental verbal discourse. A "narrated monologue" is a presentation of a character's verbal narration through the narrator's paraphrasing. "Psychonarration" is a narrative of a character's point of view or state of mind without quoting or paraphrasing the character's thoughts. See Shires, 111 and Cohn, 9–17.

34. Bakhtin, "Discourse in the Novel," 304.
35. Bakthin, "Discourse in the Novel," 300.
36. Bakthin, "Discourse in the Novel," 301.
37. Nehama Aschkenasy, *Eve's Journey,* 65.
38. S. Y. Agnon, "*Agunot*," 40.
39. S. Y. Agnon, "*Tishre*," *Ha-po'el ha-tsa'ir*, 1912.
40. Agnon, "*Tishre*". This type of dialogue is an important theme in this story and in its later revisions as "The Hill of Sand" (first published in 1919).
41. Agnon, "*Tishre*," translated portion from "Hill of Sand," Hillel Halkin, trans. in Mintz and Hoffman, 91. From "*Tishre*," 10. Translation modified.
42. Agnon, "*Tishre*."
43. A *kloyz* refers to a hasidic self-made synagogue, often unauthorized.
44. In Agnon's revisions of "*Tishre*" into "Hill of Sand" we do begin to see the introduction of this type of broader societal background that informs individual dialogues.
45. Agnon, "The Crooked Shall Be Made Straight," 29–30.
46. אבל מה נעשה. גזירה היא, ומי יודע מה שיסבב השי"ת והצדיק עליו את הדין.
47. Not insignificant, however, is this story's being comprised of heteroglossia, albeit within a somewhat narrow range: Sermonic epigrams, biblical proof texts, rabbinic aphorisms, a traditional letter of recommendation, "illustrative" or "reassuring" (misdirecting) folktales and hasidic tales. While not dialogic, these different styles create ironic counterpoints in the story. On the narrator's use of these styles for the purpose of misdirecting the reader, see Nitza Ben-Dov, *Agnon's Art of Indirection.*
48. Agnon, *A Guest for the Night*, 246–247.
49. On this issue see Hasak-Lowy, 167–198.
50. Agnon, *Only Yesterday*, 287.
51. The *yishuv* refers to the Jewish population and settlements in the Land of Israel prior to 1947.
52. Agnon, *Only Yesterday*, 287.
53. Agnon, *Only Yesterday*, 289.
54. Agnon, *The Bridal Canopy.*
55. Agnon, *Bridal Canopy*, p. 5.
56. Agnon, *A Simple Story.*
57. Agnon, *A Simple Story* , 33.
58. See the analysis of Agnon's word systems in Edna Aphek, Y. Tobin, *Word systems in modern Hebrew* and Baruch Kurzweil on the dual meaning of "*mikhtav*" as "letter" and "divine commandment" ("*mitzvah*") in *Essays in the Writings on S. Y. Agnon.*
59. Dentith, *Bakhtinian Thought*, 41.
60. Bakhtin, *The Dialogic Imagination*, 280.
61. Bakhtin, *Problems of Dostoevsky's Poetics*, 293.
62. Booth, "Introduction," xxii.
63. Miron notes that the modern novel's particular issues of open-ended closure are evident in Agnon's sustained artistic struggle with this "obtrusive difficulty" of the novel form. Also see Shaked, "By a Miracle: Agnon's Literary Representation of Social Dramas," 138.
64. Bakhtin, "Discourse in the Novel," 305
65. See Song of Songs.
66. Bakthtin, "Discourse in the Novel," 311–12.
67. Bakthtin, "Discourse in the Novel," 311–12.
68. Bakthtin, "Discourse in the Novel," 305.
69. Bakthtin, "Discourse in the Novel," 305.
70. Booth, Introduction to Bakhtin, *Problems of Dostoevsky's*, xx. Booth here is referring to "Longinus's" "On the Sublime."
71. Booth, "Introduction," xxi.
72. Bakhtin, *Problems of Dostoevsky's Poetics*, 252.
73. Bakhtin, "Discourse in the Novel," 332.

74. We should note, however, that the idea that a spiritual inductee or "seeker" as part of a milieu that is distorted, false, and in need of redemption is a fundamental tenet of Bratslav hasidism. See Roskies, 2002, 84.

75. Solitude is also a function of mystical practice. The Hebrew "*hitbodedut*" can mean both "solitude and mental concentration," Idel, 1995, 55. (It is also important to recognize here the practice of R. Nahman's ideal of *hitbodedut* as a prerequisite for achieving unity with the God. Gershom's actions of isolation and loss of "selfhood" may also be considered part of this mystical practice of self-negation ("*bitul*"). See Wiskind-Elper, 1998, 134.

76. Booth, "Introduction," xxi.

77. Bakhtin, "Discourse in the Novel," 351.

78. Bakhtin, "Discourse in the Novel," 352.

79. Bakhtin, "Discourse in the Novel," 352.

80. Bakhtin, "Discourse in the Novel," 352.

81. Bakhtin, "Discourse in the Novel," 353.

82. Booth, "Introduction," xxii.

83. Landay, "Performance," 109.

84. Bakhtin, as quoted in Sarah Warshauer Freedman and Arnetha F. Ball "Ideological Becoming: Bakhtinian Concepts to Guide the Study of Language, Literacy, and Learning," in Ball and Freedman.

85. Bakhtin, *Discourse in the Novel*, 342.

86. Bakhtin, *Discourse in the Novel*, 342.

87. Landay, "Performance as the Foundation for a Secondary School Literacy Program: A Bakhtinian Perspective," 107, 111.

88. Bakhtin, "Discourse in the Novel," 353.

89. Bakhtin, "Discourse in the Novel," 346.

90. Bakhtin, "Discourse in the Novel," 346.

91. Bakhtin, "Discourse in the Novel," 344.

92. Bakhtin, "Discourse in the Novel," 344.

93. Dressman, "Dewey and Bakhtin in Dialogue from Rosenblatt to a Pedagogy of Literature as Social, Aesthetic Practice," 35.

94. Dressman, "Dewey and Bakhtin in Dialogue," 34, 35.

95. Landay, "Performance as the Foundation," 107, 112.

96. Knoeller, "Narratives of Rethinking the Inner Dialogue of Classroom Discourse and Student Writing," 148–49.

97. Greenleaf and Katz, "Ever Newer Ways to Mean Authoring Pedagogical Change in Secondary Subject-Area Classrooms," 172, 195.

98. Greenleaf and Katz, "Ever Newer Ways to Mean Authoring Pedagogical Change in Secondary Subject-Area Classrooms," 172, 196.

99. Landay, 115.

100. Sperling, "Is Contradiction Contrary?" 232.

Afterword

The Legacy of Conversation

Continuing . . .

This book's premise is that the relationship between Jewish studies and education is in need of further philosophical articulation and conceptual development. Though these fields constitute essential, combined dimensions of a number of higher education programs, there are many lost opportunities for interdiscursive engagement. The respective discourses tend to function in parallel rather than interactively. In addition, the recent growth of scholarship that combines education and Jewish studies discourses invites more extensive consideration of the nature and purposes of their relationships. In this book I have intended to continue, differentiate, and expand these fields' interdiscursivity.

In the academy, interdiscursivity emerges when there is communication and deliberation in a multiplicity of styles and disciplinary frameworks. In this process, different discourses present their conversability, creating a sensitivity to what Oakeshott calls "the presence of ideas of another order." Each field, then, avoids having "an exclusive concern with its own utterance, which may result in its identifying the conversation with itself and its speaking as if it were speaking only to itself."[1]

This book's meta-theme has been that of a transversal conversation between Jewish studies and educational theory. Throughout these studies, I have sought what Bakhtin calls an "interaction between meanings, all of which have the potential of conditioning others."[2] As a conversation, disparate and dissonant voices are admitted even when, at the outset, there is no transparent connection between them. When the voices are engaged interdiscursively, the conversation's agenda is not limited to points of overlap or intersection, nor does it constitute a mere cacophonous assemblage. As transversal, the conversation seeks what Schrag calls a "convergence without coincidence,"[3] an interaction without absorption, and respect for discursive and disciplinary boundaries, as we noted in chapter 1. Yet we have also seen how, paradoxically, these very boundaries point to areas that they do not specifically contain.

I have tried to show how the relationship between Jewish studies and education might function in a variety of ways. First, it functions as what Dewey calls a "source" for educational theory. Thus, for example, in chapter 3, we considered the import for educational theory of R. Ḥayyim's interpretation of Genesis 1:26–27. As we saw, R. Ḥayyim's interpretation of God's having created human beings in His image suggests notions of human empowerment, extensive responsibility, and contingency. His interpretation thus illuminates the transcendent dimensions of Nussbaum's notion of "the narrative imagination" in education and Dewey's conception of "the infinite reach of an act."

As explained in chapter 2, I have sought to demonstrate what Buchler calls "transordinal, coordinative query." Buchler's notion informs how the tensions we have encountered cut across the full range of complexes and discourses that we have considered and, specifically, how these tensions are present in educational experience: tensions between the nomian and the antinomian (chapter 3), historical time and messianic time (chapter 4), the ideal as context and the ideal as goal (chapter 5), traditional storytelling and modern narration (chapter 6), authoritative and personal discursive forces (chapter 7). Indeed, we could say that, for Buchler, these tensions—as articulated in Jewish studies disciplines and educational theory—reflect relationships among these different "complexes" or "orders." Thus, this book has shown the potential of "transordinal," "coordinative" inquiry across the different discourses.

It is also significant that each of the texts in this set of studies shares what Buchler would call conceptual and axiological "traits."[4] Across the discourses, these texts express an emphasis on contingency and enduring possibility; each, in its own language, calls for sustained vigilance, a provisionality of conclusions, and a positive interdependence between desire, thought, and action in education. All point to the dangers of complacency when we feel satisfied with current attainments or frameworks. And all express the value of an interactive discursive heterogeneity that evokes interpretation, regard for difference, and thinking beyond habituated frames of reference.

Oakeshott, too, has been an ever-present interlocutor in what he would call a conversation among different discourses. Considering Jewish texts as social practices and as living discourses, I have tried to demonstrate how reading these texts in conversation with the social and discursive practices of education can reveal powerful affinities and possibilities for further kinds of engagement. Thus, for example, I have suggested how an interpretation of narrative voices in Agnon's fiction might "converse" with pedagogical issues regarding inclusion and exclusion.

The type of relationship we have illustrated is not simply utilitarian; it has a performative quality that invites scholars, students, and practitioners into a meaningful conversation that traverses differences, shows connections, and assembles multiple discourses in dynamic interaction, revealing intricately entangled sets of phenomena. Thus, I have engaged ethical, ontological, literary, hermeneutic, and educational questions and discourses together, rather than subordinating one to another or isolating but one aspect. In the process, I have suggested that educational experience has an intricately textured, transphenomenal quality that benefits from being explored and articulated interdiscursively.

This conversation, at times, displaces fixed boundaries around particular discourses and disciplines. Yet it is important to note that this displacement is achieved not by the creation of a new amalgam, a newly integrated whole. What is displaced is the assumption of incommensurability that would preclude sustained conversation. What is emplaced are new kinds of beneficial conversations and new possible contexts. As soon as we engage two or more discourses into conversation, the original context of each discourse is displaced; new problems and questions emerge that cut across them. Each discourse is somewhat transformed in the process, as its boundaries show a porousness and as the multiple language games converse. Thus, I have sought to appeal to the fields of Jewish studies and educational theory to reconsider the qualities and effects of their boundaries. Such reconsideration would not be for the purpose of expanding or extending these boundaries, not to claim more territory. Rather, the purpose is to reconceive these disciplines' demarcations in order to transcend the roles of containment, definition, separation, and exclusion, to revise the presumption of the disciplinary boundaries' stasis and stability, and to recognize their dynamics and fault lines.[5]

To apply a "deconstructive pragmatics"[6] to the boundaries of professional, disciplinary, and discursive categories, then, we are not seeking a kind of universalization of discourses and disciplines. What we are suggesting is a rethinking of the features of boundaries as both containment and openness, enabling a conversation between and among disciplinary discourses.

As mentioned in chapter 1, this alternative interdiscursive paradigm can be characterized as "transversal." Calvin Schrag is helpful in tempering some of the more radical, anarchic postmodern perspectives on transversality in his formulation of it as a "discourse and action" that realizes "communicative achievement," though not synthesis or consensus. For Schrag, the key to transversality is communication and dialogue across various disciplines and groups, engendering a recognition of alterity that resists synthesis but converses, circumventing both "the synchronic verticality of totalitarian hegemony and the diachronic horizontality of anarchic multiplicity." Using his language, we are thus neither pursuing "pure consensus," nor "pure dissensus":[7]

> There is no undivided, solidified, hermetically sealed chunks of either commensurable or incommensurable discourse, of either consensus or dissensus. The vocabulary of 'either/or' remains pecularily impoverished for dealing with the mixed discourse that is at issue here.[8]

Despite this openness to "mixed discourse," Schrag adds an important caveat. When presented with two fields, it is important "to acknowledge that each displays their [*sic*] own genres of discourse, knowledge regimes, and peculiar constellations of disciplinary practices. The task is to fathom the claims of reason that are tranversally operative between the two."[9] In other words, we need to do two things: First, we need to consider the particularity of one field's discourse, as we have done in our analyses of R. Ḥayyim of Volozhin and Agnon within the framework of Jewish studies fields. Second, we need to consider how these different discourses can converse with each other. For every conversation reveals both "converging and diverging gestalts."[10] We have pursued this conversation in a transversal engagement that suggests and augments new possible understandings of educational, philosophical, literary, and linguistic phenomena.

Deleuze's notion of interdisciplinarity is also helpful for this project, though, as defined in chapter 1, I suggest his concept is more akin to transversality and interdiscursivity. Claire Colebrook here paraphrases Deleuze:

> Being inter-disciplinary does not just mean combining literary insights with philosophy, or using anthropology to enhance psychology; it means accounting for all the different ways in which thought produces order out of chaos . . . thinking globally: not remaining within any one discipline, and not just combining disciplines, but crossing from discipline to discipline, to continually open and renew the very medium or 'milieu' within which we think.[11]

So, for Deleuze, transversality involves an "assemblage" of interactions and connections. This active movement is open-ended and dialogic. Bakhtin, again, aptly describes this kind of open dialogue when he characterizes it as happening when one's "discourse enters into the . . . fabric of . . . the world symposium."[12] In this symposium, we seek not a unity, but "a dialogic concordance of unmerged twos and multiples."[13]

Perhaps asking for sustained conversation between the academy's Jewish studies and education discourses is informed by one of chapter 6's Talmudic epigrams:

> When two scholars go for a walk together without exchanging Torah insights, they might as well be consumed by fire.[14]

In this book, we take this exchange to include different forms of scholarship and discourse, including, to be sure, matters of Torah. Notwithstanding the disturbing, hyperbolic quality of the above aphorism, what could potentially become lost are the opportunities for transversal conversation, for interdiscursive exchange. We recognize these possibilities in both the integrity of the other and in the value of walking and talking together.

NOTES

1. Oakeshott, "Voice of Poetry," 492.
2. Bakhtin, *Speech Genres*, 95.
3. Calvin O. Schrag, *The Resources of Rationality: A Response to the Postmodern Challenge* (Indianapolis: Indiana University Press, 1992), 158–159.
4. See chapter 1.
5. Morris, "Placing and Displacing Jewish Studies."
6. See chapter 1 and Weber, *Institution and Interpretation*, 32.
7. Schrag, *Resources of Rationality*, 135.
8. Schrag, *Resources of Rationality*, 135.
9. Schrag, *Resources of Rationality*, 147.
10. Schrag, *Resources of Rationality*, 152.
11. Colebrook, *Understanding Deleuze*, 80.
12. Bakhtin, *Problems of Dostoevsky's Poetics*, 293.
13. Bakhtin, *Problems of Dostoevsky's Poetics*, 289.
14. Babylonian Talmud, *Sotah*, 49a.

Bibliography

Aberbach, David. *At the Handles of the Lock: Themes in the Fiction of S. J. Agnon*. New York: Oxford University Press, 1984.
Ackerman, Ari. "'Creating a Shared Spiritual Language': David Hartman's Philosophy of Jewish Education." *Studies in Jewish Education* 13 (2008/2009): 51–74.
Ackerman, Walter. "The Americanization of Jewish Education." *Judaism* 24, no. 4 (1974): 420–435.
Addy, Tracie Marcella. "Epistemological Beliefs and Practices of Science Faculty with Education Specialties: Combining Teaching Scholarship and Interdisciplinarity." Dissertation. North Carolina State University, Raleigh, North Carolina, 2011.
Adler, Rachel. *Engendering Judaism: An Inclusive Theology and Ethics*. Boston: Beacon Press, 1999.
Aphek, Edna and Tobin, Yishai. *Word Systems in Modern Hebrew*. New York: Brill, 1988.
Agnon, S. Y. "*Agunot*." Translated by Baruch Hochman. In *A Book That Was Lost and Other Stories*. Edited by Alan Mintz and Anne Golomb Hoffman. New York: Schocken, 1995.
———. "*Aliyat ha'neshanah*" ("Ascent of the Soul"). *Hashilo'aḥ* 21 (1909): 443–445.
———. "*Giv'at ha-ḥol*" ("Hill of Sand"). Translated by Hillel Halkin. In *A Book That Was Lost and Other Stories*. Edited by Alan Mintz and Anne Golomb Hoffman. New York: Schocken, 1995.
———. "*Hanidaḥ*." ("The Outcast"). *Hatekufah* 4 (1919): 1–54; Revised in *Me'az Ume'atah, Kol kitvei Shmuel Yosef Agnon*. First Edition, 9–69. Berlin: 1931; Final revision in *Elu ve'elu, Kol kitvei Shmuel Yosef Agnon*. Second Edition, 9–56. Tel Aviv: Schocken, 1953.
———. "*Shnei talmidei ḥakhamim she-hayu be-'irenu*" ("Two Scholars Who Were in Our Town.")(Hebrew). *Kol sipurav shel Shmu'el Yosef Agnon* 6, *Samukh ve-nir'eh*. Jerusalem and Tel Aviv: Schocken, 1979.
———. "Tehila." In *'Ad Hena*. Translated by Walter Lever. In *Firstfruits: A Harvest of 24 Years of Israeli Writing*. Edited by James A. Michener. Greenwich, CT: Fawcett, 1973.
———. "Tishre." *Ha-po'el ha-tsa'ir* (1912).
———. *T'mol shilshom*. (*Only Yesterday*). Translated by Barbara Harshav. Tel Aviv: Schocken, 2000.
———. "*Vehayah he'akov li-mishor*" ("The Crooked Shall Be Made Straight"). Berlin: Jüdishcer Verlag, 1919.
———. *Hakhnasat kallah* (*The Bridal Canopy*). Translated by I.M. Lask. New York: Doubleday, Doran & Company, 1937.
———. *Oreah natah la-lun* (*A Guest for the Night*). Translated by Misha Louvish. New York: Schocken, 1968.
———. *Shira*. Translated by Zeva Shapiro. New York: Schocken, 1989.

———. *Sipur Pashut* (*A Simple Story*). Translated by Hillel Halkin. New York: Schocken, 1985.

Alexander, Hanan A. *Reclaiming Goodness: Education and the Spiritual Quest.* Notre Dame: University of Notre Dame Press, 2001.

Alter, Robert. "*Hishtalshelut ha-olamot be-'Ha-nidah' le-Sh. Y. Agnon,*" *Proceedings of the Fifth World Congress of Jewish Studies* 5 (1969).

———. "What Jewish Studies Can Do," *Commentary* (Oct. 1974): 71–76.

Aphek, Edna and Y. Tobin. *Word Systems in Modern Hebrew: Implications and Applications.* New York: Brill, 1988.

Arbel, Michal. "Societal and Strategic Closure Dilemmas: Two Scholars Who Were in Our Town," (Hebrew) ("*Dilemot ḥevratiyot ve-'estragegiyot shel siyum: Shnei talmidei ḥakhamim she-hayu be-'irenu*"). In *Literature and Society in Modern Hebrew Culture: Papers in Honor of Gershon Shaked* (Hebrew), edited by Judith Bar-el, Yigal Schwartz and Tamar S. Hess. Keter and Ha-kibutz Hameuchad: Tel Aviv, 2000.

———. *Sof Ma'aseh: Al ofane hasiyum beyitsirator shel S. Y. Agnon.* ("The Tale's End: Styles of Closure in the Work of S. Y. Agnon"). (Hebrew) Hebrew University, 1999.

———. *Tam ve'nishlam? Al darkhe hasiyum basiporet* (*The End? Closure in the Short Story*) (Hebrew). Kibbutz Hame'uhad, 2008

Arnold, Matthew. "The Function of Criticism at the Present Time." In *Selections from the Prose Works of Matthew Arnold*, edited by William Savage Johnson. Boston, New York, Chicago, San Francisco: Houghton Mifflin, 1913.

Aron, Isa. "Deweyan Deliberation as a Model for Decision-Making in Jewish Education." *Studies in Jewish Education* 2 (1984): 136–149.

———. "What Is the Philosophy of Jewish Education?" Review of *Roads to the Palace: Jewish Texts and Teaching*, by Michael Rosenak. *Religious Education* 94, no. 1 (1999): 126–132.

Asaf, S. "The Altshul Family Tree." *Reshumot*. New Edition 4 (1946–1947).

Aschkenasy, Nehama. *Eve's Journey: Feminine Images in Hebraic Literary Tradition.* Philadelphia: University of Pennsylvania Press, 1986.

ASHE. "Special Issue: Understanding Interdisciplinary Challenges and Opportunities in Higher Education" 35, no. 2 (2009).

Auerbach, Efraim. "Two Scholars Who Were in Our Town: Sources and Commentary" (Hebrew). In *On Judaism and Education* (Hebrew), edited by Efraim A. Auerbach, 162–79. Jerusalem: Hebrew University School of Education and the Department of Education and Culture, 1966.

Bakthin, Mikhail. "Discourse in the Novel." In *The Dialogic Imagination*, translated by Michael Holquist, edited by Caryl Emerson and Michael Holquist, 259–422. Austin, TX: University of Texas Press, 1981.

———. *Problems of Dostoevsky's Poetics*. Edited and translated by Caryl Emerson. Minneapolis: University of Michigan Press, 1984.

———. *Speech Genres and Other Late Essays*. Edited by C. Emerson and M. Holquist. Translated by C. Emerson, M. Holquist, and V. W. McGee. Austin, TX: University of Texas Press, 1986.

Ball, Arnetha F., and Sarah Warshauer Freedman, eds. *Bakhtinian Perspectives on Language, Literacy and Learning*. Cambridge, UK: Cambridge University Press, 2004.

Band, Arnold F. *Nostalgia and Nightmare: A Study in the Fiction of S. Y. Agnon*. Los Angeles, University of California Press, 1968.

Barlett, S. and D. Burton. "The Evolution of Education Studies in Higher Education in England." *Curriculum Journal* 17, no. 4 (2006): 383–396.

Barnett, Ronald. "Recapturing the Universal in the University." *Educational Philosophy and Theory* 37, no. 6 (2005).

Baskin, Judith R. "Academic Jewish Studies in North America." In *International Handbook of Jewish Education*, edited by Helena Miller, Lisa Grant, and Alex Pomson. Dordrecht, New York: Springer, 2011.

Ben-Dov, Nitza. *Agnon's Art of Indirection: Uncovering Latent Content in the Fiction of S. Y. Agnon*. Leiden: Brill, 1993.

Ben-Horin, Meir. "John Dewey and Jewish Education." *Religious Education* 55 (1960): 201–202.
Benjamin, Walter. "The Storyteller: Reflections on the Works of Nikolai Leskov." In Walter Benjamin, *Illuminations: Essays and Reflections,* translated by Harry Zohn, edited by Hannah Arendt, 83–109. New York: Schocken Books, 1968.
Berkson, Isaac. "John Dewey's Philosophy: Ethical and Religious Aspects." *Judaism* 3, no. 3 (1954): 209–220.
———. "John Dewey's Philosophy of Religion: Its Pragmatist Background." *Judaism* 3, no. 2 (1954): 132–141.
Booth, Wayne C. Introduction to *Problems of Dostoevsky's Poetics*, by Mikhail Bakhtin, edited and translated by Caryl Emerson, xiii. Minneapolis: University of Michigan Press, 1984.
———. *The Company We Keep: An Ethics of Fiction.* Berkeley: University of California Press, 1988.
———. *The Rhetoric of Fiction.* Chicago: University of Chicago Press, 1961.
Brandeis University, Mandel Center for Studies in Jewish Education. "Bridging Scholarship and Pedagogy in Jewish Studies." Last modified August 15, 2011. http://www.brandeis.edu/mandel/projects/bridging/index.html.
Brill, Alan. "Judaism in Culture: Beyond the Bifurcation of Torah and Madda." *The Edah Journal* 4, no. 1 (2004).
Buchler, Justus. *The Concept of Method.* New York: Columbia University Press, 1961.
———. *The Main of Light: On the Concept of Poetry.* New York: Oxford University Press, 1974.
———. *The Metaphysics of Natural Complexes.* New York: Columbia University Press, 1966.
———. *Nature and Judgment.* New York: Columbia University Press, 1955.
———. *Toward a General Theory of Human Judgment.* New York: Columbia University Press, 1951.
Bush, Andrew. *Jewish Studies: A Theoretical Introduction.* Piscataway, NJ: Rutgers University Press, 2011.
Caputo, John D. *Deconstruction in a Nutshell: A Conversation with Jacques Derrida.* New York: Fordham University Press, 1997.
———. *The Prayers and Tears of Jacques Derrida: Religion without Religion.* Bloomington: Indiana University Press, 1997.
Chatman, Seymour. "Defense of the Implied Author." In *Coming to Terms: The Rhetoric of Narrative in Fiction and Film.* Edited by Seymour Chatman. 74–90. Ithaca, NY: Cornell University Press, 1990.
Cohen, Jonathan. "Hartman, Rosenak and Schweid on Maimonides' Introduction to Helek: The Beginnings of a Tradition in the Philosophy of Jewish Education." *Studies in Jewish Education* 13 (2008/2009): 15–46.
———. "Jewish Thought for Jewish Education: Sources and Resources." In *International Handbook of Jewish Education*, edited by Helena Miller, Lisa Grant, and Alex Pomson. Springer, 2011. http://www.springerlink.com.ilsprod.lib.neu.edu/content/m37707861l470749/.
Cohn, Dorrit. *Transparent Minds: Narrative Modes for Presenting Consciousness in Fiction.* Princeton, NJ: Princeton University Press, 1978.
Colebrook, Claire. *Understanding Deleuze.* Crows Nest, NSW, Australia: Allen & Unwin, 2002.
Conant, J., and U. Zeglen, eds. *Hilary Putnam: Pragmatism and Realism.* New York: Routledge, 2002.
Curren, R. R. *Aristotle on the Necessity of Public Education.* Lanham, MD: Rowman and Littlefield, 2000.
Darby, David. "Form and Context: An Essay in the History of Narratology." *Poetics Today* 22, no. 4 (2001): 829–852.
Dentith, Simon. *Bakhtinian Thought.* Florence, KY: Routledge, 1994.
Derrida, Jacques. "Le Parergon" in Jacques Derrida. *The Truth in Painting.* Translated by Geoff Bennington and Ian McLeod. Chicago: University of Chicago Press, 1987.
———. *Positions.* Translated by Alan Bass. London: Athlone Press, 1981.

———. "The Principle of Reason: The University in the Eyes of Its Pupils." *Diacritics* 13, no. 3 (Autumn, 1983): 2–20.

———. "Structure, Sign, and Play in the Discourse of the Human Sciences." Translated by Alan Bass. In *Jacques Derrida, Writing and Difference.* Chicago, University of Chicago Press, 1978.

Dewey, John. *Art as Experience.* New York: Minton, Balch, and Company, 1934.

———. *Democracy and Education.* The Pennsylvania State University, Electronic Classics Series, Jim Manis, Faculty Editor, Hazleton, PA, 2001.

———. *Experience and Nature.* New York: Dover, 1925/1958.

———. *Human Nature and Conduct: An Introduction to Social Psychology.* New York: Holt, 1922.

———. *Outlines of a Critical Theory of Ethics.* Ann Arbor, Michigan: Register, 1891.

———. *The Sources of a Science of Education.* New York: Horace Liveright, 1929.

———. *Theory of the Moral Life.* New York: Holt, Rinehart, Winston, 1908/1932.

Dinur, Benzion. "*Wissenschaft des Judentums.*" In *Encyclopaedia Judaica.* Edited by Michael Berenbaum and Fred Skolnik. 2nd ed. Vol. 21. Detroit: Macmillan Reference USA, 2007. 105–114.

Dressman, Mark. "Dewey and Bakhtin in Dialogue." In *Bakhtinian Perspectives on Language, Literacy, and Learning*, edited by Arnetha F. Ball and Sarah Warshauer Freedman, 34–52. Cambridge, UK: Cambridge University Press, 2004.

Dynner, Glenn. *Men of Silk: The Hasidic Conquest of Polish Jewish Society.* Cary, NC: Oxford University Press, 2006.

Eisenman, Esther. "The Structure and Content of R. Ḥayyim of Volozhin's *Nefesh Ha-Ḥayyim.*" (Hebrew). In *The Vilna Gaon and His Disciples* (Hebrew), edited by M. Hallamish, Y. Rivlin, & R. Shuchat, 185–196. Ramat Gan: Bar-Ilan University Press, 2003.

Eliach, D. *Father of Yeshivot* (Hebrew). Jerusalem: Mekhon Moreshet ha-yeshivot, 1990.

Elijah Gaon of Vilna. "Introduction to the Secret of *Tsimtsum*" (Hebrew). In *The GRA's Commentary on Sifra Ditsniuta.* Ha'almanah veha'ahim re'im: Vilna, 1912.

———. "Introduction to *Tikkune Zohar* with the GRA's Commentary" (Hebrew). In *Selections on the Zohar*, unnumbered pages, 2nd edition, Bilorta b'avnin.

Etkes, Immanuel. "Ḥayyim of Volozhin's Response to Hasidism." In *The Vilna Gaon and His Image*, edited by Immanuel Etkes, translated by J. M. Green, 151–208. Berkeley and Los Angeles: University of California Press, 2002.

———. "The Ideology and Activity of R. Ḥayyim of Volozhin as an Anti-Hasidic Response to Hasidism." (Hebrew). *Proceedings of the American Academy of Jewish Research* 40 (1972): 1–45.

Ellenson, David. "An Ideology for the Liberal Jewish Day School: A Philosophical-Sociological Investigation." *Journal of Jewish Education* 74 (2008): 245–263.

Ezrahi, Sidra DeKoven. *Booking Passage: Exile and Homecoming in the Modern Jewish Imagination.* Berkeley and Los Angeles: University of California Press, 2000.

Finkenthal, Michael. *Complexity, Multi-Disciplinarity, and Beyond.* New York: Peter Lang, 2008.

Fludernik, Monika. *Towards a "Natural" Narratology.* London: Routledge, 1996.

Fox, Everett, trans. *The Five Books of Moses: A New Translation with Introductions, Commentary, and Notes.* New York: Schocken, 1995.

Fox, Seymour and Geraldine Rosenfield, eds. *From the Scholar to the Classroom: Translating Jewish Tradition into Curriculum.* New York: Melton Research Center for Jewish Education, Jewish Theological Seminary of America, 1977.

Fox, Seymour, Israel Scheffler, Daniel Marom, eds. *Visions of Jewish Education.* New York: Cambridge University Press, 2003.

Fuchs, Esther. *Cunning Innocence: On S. Y. Agnon's Irony.* (Hebrew). *('Omanut ha-hitamemut: 'al ha-ironiah shel Agnon).* Tel Aviv: Tel Aviv University: 1985.

———. "Ironic Characterization in the Works of S. Y. Agnon," *AJS Review* 7 (1982): 101–128.

Garrison, James W. *Dewey and Eros: Wisdom and Desire in the Art of Teaching.* New York: Teachers College Press, 1997.

Goldberg, Leah. "S. Y. Agnon: The Author and His Hero." (Hebrew). *("Shai Agnon: Ha-sofer ve-giburo")*. In *Le-Agnon Shai: Devarim al ha-sofer u-sefarav*, edited by Dov Sadan and A. A. Orbach, 47–61. Jerusalem: Hotsaat Ha-Sefarim shel Ha-Sokhnut Ha-Yahadut, 1966.

Gordon, M., ed. *Hannah Arendt and Education: Renewing Our Common World*. Boulder, CO: Westview Press, 2001.

Greenleaf, Cynthia L. and Katz, Mira-Lisa. "Ever Newer Ways to Mean: Authoring Pedagogical Change in Secondary Subject-Area Classrooms." In *Bakhtinian Perspectives on Language, Literacy and Learning*, edited by Arnetha, F. Ball and Sarah Warshauer Freedman. Cambridge, UK: Cambridge University Press, 2004. 172–202.

Gross, B. "Rabbi Ḥayyim of Volozhin's Philosophical View." (Hebrew). *Annual of Bar-Ilan University, Studies in Judaica and the Humanities*. 22–23 (1987): 151–152.

Hartman, Geoffrey H. "The Work of Reading." In *Criticism in the Wilderness: The Study of Literature Today*, edited by Geoffrey Hartman, 161–88. New Haven and London: Yale University Press, 1980.

Hartman, Geoffrey H. and Budick, Sandord. *Midrash and Literature*. New Haven: Yale University Press, 1986.

Hasak-Lowy, Todd. "A Mad Dog's Attack on Secularized Hebrew: Rethinking Agnon's *Temol shilshom*," *Prooftexts* 24, no. 2 (Spring 2004): 167–198.

Ḥayyim of Volozhin. *Hut ha-meshulash: she'elot u-teshuvot*. Brooklyn, NY: A. Kohn, 1956.

———. "Introduction to the Vilna Gaon's Commentary on Sifra di-tsiniuta." (Hebrew). In *Shivi'at ha-me'orot* (*The Book of Seven Light Sources*), unnumbered pages, section 6. Vilna: Ha-almanah veha-ahim rom, 1913.

———. "Letter to Lithuanian Communities." *Ha-Peles* 3 (1912): 140–143 (1912).

———. *Nefesh Ha-Ḥayyim*. Edited by Isasskhar Dov Rubin. B'nai B'rak: Makhon l'arichat s'farim torani'im, 1988.

———. *Ruaḥ Ḥayyim*: *Be'ur Al Masekhet Avot*. Jerusalem: Makhon Or ha-ner, 2000.

———. "Sermon for Selihot 1812." In *Nefesh Ha-Ḥayyim*, edited by Isasskhar Dov Rubin. B'nai B'rak: Machon l'arichat s'farim torani'im, 1988.

Heller, Scott. "The New Jewish Studies: Defying Tradition and Easy Categorization." *Chronicle of Higher Education* (January 29, 1999).

Heschel, Abraham J. "The Values of Jewish Education," *Proceedings of the Rabbinical Assembly of America* 26 (1962): 83–100.

Holtz, Barry W. "Across the Divide: What Might Jewish Educators Learn from Jewish Scholars?" *Journal of Jewish Education* 72 (2006): 5–28.

———. "Bible: Teaching the Bible in Our Times." In *International Handbook of Jewish Education*, edited by Helena Miller, Lisa Grant and Alex Pomson. New York: Springer, 2011. http://www.springerlink.com.ilsprod.lib.neu.edu/content/p287138r8311670w/.

Holzer, Elie. "Educational Aspects of Hermeneutical Activity in Text Study." *Studies in Jewish Education* 13 (2008/2009): 205–239.

———. "What Connects 'Good' Teaching, Text Study and Hevruta Learning? A Conceptual Argument." *Journal of Jewish Education* 72 (2006): 183–204.

Idel, Moshe. *Ascensions on High in Jewish Mysticism: Pillars, Lines, Ladders*. New York, NY, USA: Central European University Press, 2005.

———. *Hasidism: Between Ecstasy and Magic* (Albany: State University of New York Press, 1995) 1–30.

Jacobs, Benjamin M. "Socialization into a Civilization: The Dewey-Kaplan Synthesis in American Jewish Schooling in the Early 20th Century." *Religious Education* 104, no. 2 (2009): 149–165.

The Jewish Quarterly Review 97, no. 4, (2007), special issue, twenty-fifth anniversary of the first publication of Yosef Hayim Yerushalmi's *Zakhor*.

Kalani, E. "The Educational Ideal in the Thought of R. Ḥayyim of Volozhin and Its Practical Actualization." (Hebrew). In *Al derekh ha-avot: Shloshim shana le-mikhlelet Yaacov Herzog le-yad Yeshivat Har Etzion*, edited by A. Bazak, M Munitz, and S. Wygoda, 177–204. Alon Shevut: Tevunot, 2000, 5761.

Kamuf, Peggy. *The Division of Literature, or, The University in Deconstruction*. Chicago: The University of Chicago Press, 1997.

Kestenbaum, Victor. *The Grace and the Severity of the Ideal: John Dewey and the Transcendent*. Chicago and London: University of Chicago Press. 2002.

———. *The Phenomenological Sense of John Dewey: Habit and Meaning.* Atlantic Highlands, NJ: Humanities Press, 1977.

Klein, Julie T. *Interdisciplinarity: History, Theory, and Practice.* Detroit: Wayne State University Press, 1990.

———. *Humanities, Culture, and Interdisciplinarity: The Changing American Academy.* Albany: State University of New York, 2005.

———. *Crossing Boundaries: Knowledge, Disciplinarities, and Interdisciplinarities.* University Press of Virginia, 1996.

———. "Education." In *Handbook of Transdisciplinary Research,* edited by G. Hirsch Hadorn, et al. Springer, 2008.

———. "A Taxonomy of Interdisciplinarity." In *The Oxford Handbook of Interdisciplinarity,* edited by Robert Frodeman, Julie Thompson Klein, and Carl Mitcham. Oxford: Oxford University Press, 2010: 15–30.

———. *Creating Interdisciplinary Campus Cultures: A Model for Strength and Sustainability.* Hoboken, NJ: Jossey-Bass, 2010.

Knoeller, Christian. "Narratives of Rethinking: The Inner Dialogue of Classroom Discourse and Student Writing." In *Bakhtinian Perspectives on Language, Literacy and Learning*, edited by Arnetha, F. Ball and Sarah Warshauer Freedman. Cambridge, UK: Cambridge University Press, 2004.

Krojanker, Gustav. *Yetsirato shel Sh. Y. Agnon.* ("Agnon's Writings"). Translated to Hebrew by Jacob Gottschalk. Jerusalem: Bialik Institute, 1991.

Kronish, Ronald. "John Dewey's Influence on Jewish Educators: The Case of Alexander M. Dushkin. *Teachers College Record* 83, no. 3 (1982): 419–433.

Kurzweil, Baruch. *Essays in the Writings on S. Y. Agnon.* (Hebrew). Tel-Aviv: Schocken, 1965.

Lamm, Norman. "The Phase of Dialogue and Reconciliation." In *Tolerance and Movements of Religious Dissent in Eastern Europe*, edited by Béla K. Király, 115–129. New York: Columbia University Press, 1975.

———. *Torah Lishmah: Torah for Torah's Sake in the Works of Rabbi Ḥayyim of Volozhin and His Contemporaries*. Hoboken, NJ: Ktav, 1989.

Laor, Dan. *S. Y. Agnon: Hebatim hadashim.* (*S. Y. Agnon: New Perspectives*). (Hebrew). Tel Aviv: Sifriat Poalim, 1995.

Landay, Eileen. "Performance as the Foundation for a Secondary School Literacy Program: A Bakhtinian Perspective." In Ball, Arnetha, F. and Freedman, Sarah Warshauer Freedman, Eds. *Bakhtinian Perspectives on Language, Literacy and Learning*. Cambridge, UK: Cambridge University Press, 2004. 107–128.

Landy, Joshua. "Proust, His Narrator, and the Importance of the Distinction." *Poetics Today* 25, 1 (2004): 91–135.

Laron, Dinah and Shkedi, Asher. "Between Two Languages: Student-Teachers Teach Jewish Content," *Religious Education* 102, no. 2 (Spring 2007).

Lattuca, Lisa Rose. "Envisioning Interdisciplinarity: Processes, Contexts, Outcomes," Ph.D. Dissertation. University of Michigan, 1996.

Lattuca, Lisa R. "Learning Interdisciplinarity: Sociocultural Perspectives on Academic Work." *The Journal of Higher Education* 73, no. 6 (November/December 2002): 711–739.

Levinas, Emmanuel. "'In the Image of God' According to Rabbi Ḥayyim Volozhiner." In *Beyond the Verse: Talmudic Readings and Lectures*, edited by Emmanuel Levinas, translated by G. D. Mole, 151–167. Bloomington and Indianapolis: Indiana University Press, 1994.

———. "Judaism and Kenosis." In *The Time of the Nations*, edited by Emmanuel Levinas, translated by M. B. Smith, 114–132. London: Athlone, 1994.

Levingston, Judd Kruger. "The Moral Mishnah: How Can Teachers of Rabbinics Use the Mishnah for Moral Education?" The Initiative on Bridging Scholarship and Pedagogy in Jewish Studies, Brandeis University Mandel Center for Studies in Jewish Education, Working Paper No. 21 (April 2010).

Levisohn, Jon. "What Is Bridging Scholarship and Pedagogy?" The Initiative on Bridging Scholarship and Pedagogy, Brandeis University, Mandel Center for Studies in Jewish Education. Working Paper 1 (Revised September 2006).

Lewis, H. M. "The Jewish Studies Professor as Communal Leader." *Shofar: An Interdisciplinary Journal of Jewish Studies* 24, no. 3 (2006): 131–132.

Losche, D. "What Do Abelam Images Want from Us?: Plato's Cave and Kwatbil's Belly." *The Australian Journal of Anthropology* 8, no. 1 (1997).

Lukinsky, Joseph. "Law in Education: A Reminiscence with Some Footnotes to Robert Cover's Nomos and Narrative." *Yale Law Journal* 96 (1986–1987): 1836–1859.

Magid, Shaul. "Deconstructing the Mystical: The Anti-Mystical Kabbalism in Rabbi Ḥayyim of Volozhin's Nefesh Ha-Ḥayyim." *Journal of Jewish Thought and Philosophy* 9, no. 1 (1999): 21–67.

Maimon, Solomon. *Solomon Maimon: An Autobiography.* Translated by J. C. Murray. Boston: Cupples and Kurd, 1888.

Mansilla, Veronica Boix. "Assessing Student Work at Disciplinary Crossroads." *Change* 37, no. 1 (January/February 2005): 14–21.

———. "Learning to Synthesize: A Cognitive-Epistemological Foundation for Interdisciplinary Learning." http://www.pz.harvard.edu/interdisciplinary/pdf/VBM_Synthesize_2009.pdf.

Marom, Daniel. "Who's Afraid of Horace Kallen? Cultural Pluralism and Jewish Education," *Studies in Jewish Education* 13: 283–337.

Menand, Louis. *The Marketplace of Ideas: Reform and Resistance in the American University.* New York: Norton, 2010.

Meyer, Michael A. "Toward a Definition of Jewish Studies." *Association for Jewish Studies Newsletter* 24 (March 1979): 1–2.

Merleau-Ponty, Maurice. *Signs.* Translated by R. C. McCleary. Evanston, IL: Northwestern University Press, 1964.

Miller, J. Hillis. *The Ethics of Reading.* New York: Columbia University Press, 1987.

———. "The Ethics of Narration." In *The J. Hillis Miller Reader*. Edited by Julian Wolfreys. Stanford, California: Stanford University Press, 2005. 38–44.

Miller, Raymond. "Varieties of Interdisciplinarity Approaches in the Social Sciences." *Issues in Integrative Studies* 1 (1982): 1–17.

Mintz, Alan and Hoffman, Anne Golomb. *A Book That Was Lost and Other Stories*. New York: Schocken, 1995.

Miron, Dan. "Domesticating a Foreign Genre: Agnon's Transactions with the Novel." *Prooftexts* 7, no. 1 (Jan. 1987).

———. "The Literary Image of the Shtetl." *Jewish Social Studies* 1, no.3 (Spring 1995): 1–43.

Moked, Gavriel. "Revadei mashma'ut shonim be'tekhnikah shel 'Ha-nidah'" (Different levels of meaning in the technique of "The Outcast"). (Hebrew). *Moznayim* 27, nos. 3–4 (1968).

Moran, Joe. *Interdisciplinarity*.Second Edition. New York: Routledge, 2010.

Morgenstern, Arie. "Dispersion and the Longing for Zion, 1240–1840." *Azure* 12 (Winter 5762 / 2002).

———. "Messianic Concepts and Settlement in the Land of Israel." In *Vision and Conflict in the Holy Land*, edited by Richard I. Cohen. Jerusalem: Yad Izhak Ben-Zvi and New York: St. Martin's, 1985.

———. "The Place of the Ten Tribes in the Redemption Process" (Hebrew). In *The Vilna Gaon and His Disciples*, edited by Moshe Hallamish, Yosef Rivlin, and Raphael Shuchat, 217–225. Ramat Gan: Bar-Ilan University Press, 2003.

———. *Mysticism and Messianism: From Luzzatto to the Vilna Gaon.* Jerusalem: Keter, 1999.

Morris, Leslie. "How Jewish Is German Studies? How German Is Jewish Studies? *The German Quarterly* 82, no. 3 (Summer 2009): vii–xii.

———. "Placing and Displacing Jewish Studies: Notes on the Future of a Field." *PMLA*. 125, no. 3 (2010): 764–773.

Murphy, Lisa, Emmanuel Mufti, and Derek Kassem. *Education Studies: An Introduction.* Berkshire, GBR: Open University Press, 2008.

Nadler, Alan. *The Faith of the Mithnagdim: Rabbinic Responses to Hasidic Rapture*. Baltimore and London: John Hopkins University Press, 1997.

National Academies. Committee on Facilitating Interdisciplinary Research, Committee on Science, Engineering, and Public Policy. *Facilitating Interdisciplinary Research.* Washington, DC: National Academy of Sciences, National Academy of Engineering, and Institute of Medicine, National Academies Press, 2004.

Neuhaus, Richard John. "The Public Square: The American Mind." *First Things: A Monthly Journal of Religion and Public Life* 118, no. 1 (2001).

New York University, Steinhardt School of Culture, Education and Human Development (2011). The Department of Humanities and Social Sciences in the Professions. "Ph.D. in Education and Jewish Studies." Accessed August 15, 2011. http://steinhardt.nyu.edu/humsocsci/jewish/doctoral#phd.

Noblit, George W. "The Walls of Jericho: The Struggle for an American Educational Studies Association." *Educational Studies* 333, no.1 (2002): 6–83.

Norich, Anita. "Under Whose Sign? Hebraism and Yiddishism as Paradigms of Modern Jewish Literary History." *Publications of the Modern Language Association of America* 125, no. 3 (2010): 774–784.

Nussbaum, Martha. *Cultivating Humanity: A Classical Defense of Reform in Liberal Education*. Cambridge: Harvard University Press, 1997.

———. "Education and Democratic Citizenship: Capabilities and Quality Education." *Journal of Human Development* 7, no. 3 (2006): 385–395.

———. "Education for Profit, Education for Freedom." *Liberal Education* 95, no. 3 (2009): 6–13.

———. "Political Soul-making and the Imminent Demise of Liberal Education." *Journal of Social Philosophy* 37, no. 2 (2006): 301–313.

———. "Skepticism About Practical Reason in Literature and the Law." *Harvard Law Review* 107, no. 3 (1994): 714–744.

———. "On Moral Progress: A Response to Richard Rorty." *The University of Chicago Law Review* 74, no. 3 (2007): 939–960.

———. *The Clash Within: Democracy, Religious Violence, and India's Future*. Cambridge, MA: Harvard University Press, 2007.

———. *The Therapy of Desire: Theory and Practice in Hellenistic Ethics*. Princeton: Princeton University Press, 1994.

———. *Upheavals of Thought: The Intelligence of Emotions.* Cambridge: Cambridge University Press, 2001.

Oakeshott, Michael. "The Idea of a University." In *The Voice of Liberal Learning: Michael Oakeshott on Education*, edited by T. Fuller. New Haven: Yale University Press, 1975/1989.

———. "A Place for Learning." In *The Voice of Liberal Learning: Michael Oakeshott on Education*, edited by T. Fuller. New Haven: Yale University Press, 1975/1989.

———. "Learning and Teaching." In *The Voice of Liberal Learning: Michael Oakeshott on Education*, edited by T. Fuller. New Haven: Yale University Press, 1975/1989.

———. "The Study of Politics in a University." In *Rationalism in Politics and Other Essays*, edited by T. Fuller. Indianapolis: The Liberty Fund, 1962/1991.

———. "The Voice of Poetry in the Conversation of Mankind." In *Rationalism in Politics and Other Essays*, edited by T. Fuller. Indianapolis: The Liberty Fund, 1962/1991.

Orlitzky, Kerry. "The Impact of John Dewey on Jewish Education." *Religious Educa*tion 81, no. 1 (1986): 5–18.

Ozick, Cynthia. "An Interview with Cynthia Ozick." *Contemporary Literature* 34, no. 3 (Fall 1993).

Pachter, Mordechai. "Between Acosmism and Theism: R. Ḥayyim of Volozhin's Concept of God." (Hebrew). In *Studies in Jewish Thought*, edited by Sarah O. Heller-Willensky and Moshe. Idel, 139–157. Jerusalem: Magnes Press, 1989.

———. "The Gaon's Kabbalah from the Perspective of Two Traditions." (Hebrew). In *The Vilna Gaon and His Disciples*, edited by Moshe Hallamish, Yosef Rivlin, and Raphael Shuchat, 119–136. Ramat Gan: Bar-Ilan University Press, 2003.

Palaiologou, Ioanna. "The Death of a Discipline or the Birth of a Transdiscipline: Subverting Questions of Disciplinarity within Undergraduate Courses." *Education Studies* 36, no. 3 (July 2010): 269–282.

Peters, Michael A., ed. *Heidegger, Education, and Modernity*. New York: Rowman and Littlefield, 2002.

Phillips, Jr., Alan G. "John Dewey and His Religious Critics." *Religion and Education* 29, no. 1 (2002).

Propp, Vladimir J. *Morphology of the Folktale*. Translated by Laurence Scott. Second revised edition. Austin, Texas and London: University of Texas Press, 1968.

———. *Theory and History of Folklore.* Translated by Ariadna Y. Martin and Richard P. Martin. Edited by Anatoly Liberman. Minneapolis, MN: University of Minnesota Press, 1984.

Putnam, Hilary. "Pragmatism and Non-scientific Knowledge." In *Hilary Putnam: Pragmatism and Realism*, edited by James Conant and Urszula M. Zeglen, 14–24. New York: Routledge, 2002.

Putnam, Ruth Anna. "Taking Pragmatism Seriously." In *Hilary Putnam: Pragmatism and Realism*, edited by James Conant and Urszula M. Zeglen, 7–11. New York: Routledge, 2002.

Ravitzky, Aviezer. "The Land of Israel: Longing and Trembling in Jewish Literature." (Hebrew). In *Freedom Inscribed: Diverse Voices in Jewish Religious Thought.* (Hebrew), 11–48. Tel Aviv: Am Oved, 1999.

———. "Messianic Agitation: Between Historical Calamity and Prosperity." (Hebrew). In *Freedom Inscribed: Diverse Voices in Jewish Religious Thought.* (Hebrew). 90–114. Tel Aviv: Am Oved, 1999.

———. *Messianism Zionism and Jewish Religious Radicalism*. Translated by Michael Swirsky and Jonathan Chipman. Chicago and London: University of Chicago, 1991.

Readings, Bill. *The University in Ruins*. The Estate of Bill Readings, 1996.

Ricoeur, Paul. *Interpretation Theory: Discourse and the Surplus of Meaning*. Fort Worth: Texas Christian University Press, 1976.

Rorty, Richard. *Consequences of Pragmatism (Essays: 1972–1980).* Minneapolis: University of Minnesota, 1982.

———. *Contingency, Irony, and Solidarity*. Cambridge, UK: Cambridge University Press, 1989.

Rosenak, Avinoam. "The Concept of 'Image'—Between Philosophy and Kabbalah, Education and Thought: A Response to Moshe Meir's Article. *Studies in Jewish Education* 13 (2008/2009).

———. "Styles of Halakhic Ruling: A Mapping in Light of Joseph Schwab's Philosophy of Education." *Journal of Jewish Education* 73 (2007): 81–106.

Rosenak, Michael. *Commandments and Concerns: Jewish Religious Education in Secular Society*. New York: Jewish Publication Society, 1987.

———. "From Strength to Strength: Dewey and Religious Jewish Education." *Courtyard: A Journal of Research and Thought in Jewish Education* 1 (1999–2000): 66–80.

———. "Philosophy of Jewish Education: Some Thoughts." In *International Handbook of Jewish Education*, edited by Helena Miller, Lisa Grant, and Alex Pomson, 237–46. New York: Springer, 2011.

———. *Roads to the Palace: Jewish Texts and Teaching*. New York: Berghahn Books, 1995.

———. *Tree of Life, Tree of Knowledge: Conversations with the Torah*. Boulder, CO: Westview, 2003.

———. "Zelophehad's Daughters, Religion, and Jewish Religious Education." *Journal of Jewish Education* 71 (2005): 3–21.

Rosenak, Michael and Rosenak, Avinoam. "Rabbi Joseph B. Soloveitchik and Aspects of Jewish Educational Philosophy: Explorations in his Philosophical Writings." *Journal of Jewish Education* 75 (2009): 114–129.

Rosenberg, Shalom. "Kabbalistic Doctrine in the Nefesh Ha-Ḥayyim." (Hebrew). *Analysis and Theory* 5 (2001): 5–21.

Rosenblatt, Samuel. "Olam Ha-Ba." In *Encyclopaedia Judaica*, edited by Michael Berenbaum and Fred Skolnik. 2nd ed. Vol. 15, 399–400. Detroit: Macmillan Reference USA, 2007.
Roskies, David G. "The Task of the Jewish Translator: A Valedictory Address." *Prooftexts* 24, no. 3 (Fall 2004).
Ross, Tamar. "Two Interpretations of the Doctrine of Tsimtsum: Ḥayyim of Volozhin and Shneur Zalman of Lyadi." (Hebrew). *Jerusalem Studies in Jewish Thought* 2 (1981): 153–69.
Rothstein, Gidon. "Motivation Before Method: Helping Students Get a Foot in the Door Through the Use of Academic Scholarship in the Teaching of Rabbinic Texts." The Initiative on Bridging Scholarship and Pedagogy in Jewish Studies, Brandeis University, Mandel Center for Studies in Jewish Education and Jewish Studies, Working Paper No. 22 (November 2009).
Rubenstein, Jeffrey L. "From History to Literature: The Pedagogical Impliications of Shifting Paradigms in the Study of Rabbinic Narratives." The Initiative on Bridging Scholarship and Pedagogy in Jewish Studies, Brandeis University, Mandel Center for Studies in Jewish Education and Jewish Studies, Working Paper No. 26 (April 2010).
Saito, Naoko. *The Gleam of Light: Moral Perfectionism and Education in Dewey And Emerson*. New York: Fordham University Press, 2005.
Sartre, Jean-Paul "What Is Literature?" Translated by Bernard Freedman. London: 1981.
Schachter, Allison. "The Shtetl and the City: The Origins of Nostalgia in *Ba-yamim ha-hem and Shloyme reb khayims*," *Jewish Social Studies* 12, no. 3 (2006).
Scheffler, Israel. "The Concept of the Educated Person: With Some Applications to Jewish Education." In *Visions of Jewish Education*, edited by Seymour Fox, Israel Scheffler, and Daniel Marom. Cambridge University Press, 2003.
Scholem, Gershom. *Major Trends in Jewish Mysticism*. New York: Schocken Books, 1995.
———. *The Messianic Idea in Judaism and Other Essays on Jewish Spirituality*. New York: Schocken, 1971.
———. *On the Mystical Shape of the Godhead: Basic Concepts in the Kabbalah*. Translated by J. Neugroschel. New York: Schocken Books, 1991.
———. "Reflections on Modern Jewish Studies." In *On the Possibility of Jewish Mysticism in Our Time and Other Essays*. Edited by Avraham Shapira, Translated by Jonathan Chipman. Philadelphia: Jewish Publication Society, 1997.
Schrag, Calvin O. *Communicative Praxis and the Space of Subjectivity*. Bloomington and Indianapolis: Indiana University Press, 1986.
———. *Radical Reflection and the Origin of the Human Sciences*. West Lafayette, IN: Purdue University Press, 1980.
———. *The Resources of Rationality: A Response to the Postmodern Challenge*. Indianapolis: Indiana University Press, 1992.
———. *The Self after Postmodernity*. New Haven and London: Yale University Press, 1999.
Shaked, Gershon. "By a Miracle: Agnon's Literary Representation of Social Dramas." In *The Shadows Within: Essays on Modern Jewish Writers*," by Gershon Shaked. Philadelphia: Jewish Publication Society, 1987.
———. *The New Tradition: Essays on Modern Hebrew Literature*. Cincinnati: Hebrew Union College Press, 2006.
———. *Shmuel Yosef Agnon: A Revolutionary Traditionalist*. Translated by Jeff M. Green. New York: New York University Press, 1989.
Shapiro, Harvey. "Cultivating a Viable Relationship Between North American Jews and Israel." Ph.D. Dissertation. Los Angeles: Hebrew Union College—Jewish Institute of Religion, 1996.
Shires, Linda M. *Telling Stories: A Theoretical Analysis of Narrative Fiction*. Florence, KY: Routledge, 1988.
Shuchat, Raphael. "Messianic and Mystical Elements Associated with the Study of Torah According to the Gaon and His Disciples." (Hebrew). In *The Vilna Gaon and His Disciples*, edited by Moshe Hallamish, Yosef Rivlin, and Raphael Shuchat, 155–172. Ramat Gan: Bar-Ilan University Press, 2003.

Shulman, Lee. S. "Pedagogies of Interpretation, Argumentation, and Formation: From Understanding to Identity in Jewish Education." *Journal of Jewish Education* 74 (October 2008): 1–20.

Singer, Beth. "Systematic Nonfoundationalism: The Philosophy of Justus Buchler." *The Journal of Speculative Philosophy* 7, no. 3 (1993): 191–205.

Smith, Angela Marie. "Fiery Constellations: Winterson's Sexing the Cherry and Benjamin's Materialist Historiography." *College Literature* 32, no. 3 (2005).

Smith, Barry, et. al. *The Times.* London: May 9, 1992. *Internationale Akademie für Philosophie.*

Smith, Barry with Jeffrey Sims. "Revisiting the Derrida Affair with Barry Smith." *Sophia* 138, no. 2 (September-October, 1999): 142–168.

Sperling, "Is Contradiction Contrary?" In *Bakhtinian Perspectives on Language, Literacy and Learning*, edited by Arnetha F. Ball and Sarah Warshauer Freedman. Cambridge, UK: Cambridge University Press, 2004.

Stampfer, Shaul. *The Lithuanian Yeshiva* (Hebrew). Jerusalem: Zalman Shazar Center for Jewish History, 1995.

Stanford University, School of Education. 2011 "Jim Joseph Chair in Education and Jewish Studies." Accessed August 15, 2011. http://ed.stanford.edu/faculty/jobs/jim-joseph-chair-education-and-jewish-studies.

Stember, Marilyn. "Advancing the Social Sciences through the Interdisciplinary Enterprise." *Social Science Journal* 28, no. 1 (1991).

Stern, David. *Midrash and Theory: Ancient Jewish Exegesis and Contemporary Literary Studies.* Evanston, Illinois: Northwestern University Press, 1996.

Taylor, Charles. "Comparison, History, Truth." In *Philosophical Arguments*, edited by Charles Taylor, 146–164. Cambridge: Harvard University Press, 1995.

———. "Ethics and Ontology." *The Journal of Philosophy* 100, no. 6 (2003): 305–320.

———. "What Is Pragmatism?" In *Pragmatism, Critique, Judgment: Essays for Richard J. Bernstein*, edited by Seyla Benhabib and Nancy Fraser, 73–92. Cambridge and London: MIT Press, 2004.

Tishby, Isaiah. "The Messianic Idea and Messianic Trends in the Growth of Hasidism." (Hebrew). *Zion* 32 (1967): 1–45.

Tsimerman, David. "'On Two Scholars Who Were in Our Town,' of S. Y. Agnon: Comments and Insights from a Reader." (Hebrew). *Al-siaḥ* 12–13–14: 177–189.

Wallace, Kathleen A. "Justus Buchler." In *Dictionary of Literary Biography.* Thomson Gale, 2005–2006.

Weber, Samuel. "The Limits of Professionalism," *Oxford Literary Review* 5, nos.1–2 (1982): 59–74.

———. "The Future of the Humanities: Experimenting." *Culture Machine* 2 (2000). http://www.culturemachine.net/index.php/cm/rt/printerFriendly/311/296.

Weiser, Raphael. "S. Y. Agnon's Letters to Y. H. Brenner." (Hebrew). In *S. Y. Agnon: Studies and Documents*, edited by S. Shaked and R. Weiser. Jerusalem: Bialik Institute, 1978.

Weiss, Hillel. *Commentary on Five Stories of S. Y. Agnon*: 'Two Scholars Who Were in Our Town,' 'The Kershief,' 'Tehila,' 'The Crooked Shall Become Straight,' and 'A Tale on Rabbi Tori Zahav.' (Hebrew). (*Parshanut la-ḥamishah mi-sipurei Shai 'Agnon: shnei talmidei ḥakhamim she-hayu be-'irenu, ha-miṭpaḥat, tehilah, ve-hayah ha-'aḳov le-mishor, ma'aśeh be-Rav Ṭori Zahav*), Tel-Aviv: 'Aḳad, 1974.

Welch, James Lee. "Interdisciplinarity and the History of Ideas." Ph.D. Dissertation. The University of Texas at Dallas (August 2009).

Werses, Shmuel. *Shai Agnon kif'shuto: Keri'ah bi-khtavav.* (Hebrew). ("Shai Agnon taken literally: Reading his correspondence") Jerusalem: Bialik Institute, 2000.

Whitehead, Alfred North. *Science and the Modern World.* Cambridge: Cambridge University Press, 1953.

———. "Understanding." Lecture Three in *Modes of Thought.* New York: Macmillan, 1938.

Wigzell, Faith. "Folklore and Russian literature." In *Routledge Companion to Russian Literature,* edited by Neil Cornwell. London: Routledge, 2001.

Wiskind-Elper, Ora. *Tradition and Fantasy in the Tales of Reb Nahman of Bratslav.* Albany, NY: State University of New York Press, 1988.

Wisse, Ruth R. *The Modern Jewish Canon: A Journey Through Language and Culture.* Chicago: University of Chicago Press, 2000.

Wortham, Simon . "'To Come Walking': Reinterpreting the Institution and the Work of Samuel Weber." *Cultural Critique* 48 (Spring, 2001): 164–199.

Yerushalmi, Yosef Hayim. *Zakhor: Jewish History and Jewish Memory.* Seattle: University of Washington Press, 1989.

Zeldin, Michael. "Integration and Interaction in the Jewish Day School." In *The Jewish Educational Leader's Handbook*, edited by Robert E. Tornberg. Denver: A.R.E. Publishing, 1998.

Index

Agnon, S. Y., 103–152n58
ascent of the soul, 80n7, 131, 132, 142, 143, 144

Bakhtin, Mikhail, 16, 17, 127
bitul hayesh, 79, 83n67–83n68, 152n72
Bledstein, Burton, 12, 13
Booth, Wayne C., 106, 107n12, 122n35, 132, 141, 143, 144, 147
borders. *See* limits
boundaries. *See* limits
Buchler, Justus, 23, 27–34
Bush, Andrew, 5, 6, 7

centripetal and centrifugal discourse, 17, 61, 143, 144
closure, 105, 114, 119, 124n62, 142
Cohen, Jonathan, 19n31, 32, 37, 40n32, 42n107

deconstruction, 14, 15, 157
Derrida, Jacques, 13–14, 15, 21n67, 21n84
devekut , 75–76, 77, 79, 82n52, 82n57, 89, 92, 93, 94, 98, 100n25
Dewey, John, 23–27, 48–52, 54, 56–57, 60, 67, 85–88, 90–92, 99, 101n49
discourse, 9, 15–16, 17, 125–126, 147–150
double-voiced discourse ("polyphony"), 128–144

education studies, 7–8
ethics of alterity, 141–150

Fox, Seymour, 3
Fuchs, Esther, 114, 115

GRA. *See* Vilna Gaon

"*Hanidaḥ*" "The Outcast", 125–152n66
hasidism, 46n11, 52, 60, 67, 68, 81n32, 82n57, 83n67, 89, 93, 100n25, 127–128, 129, 130, 134, 137, 142, 143–144, 151n14, 151n16, 151n17, 152n43, 152n71; opposition to hasidism. *See* mitnagdism

interdisciplinarity, 2, 3, 8, 9, 10, 11, 19n36, 20n58; resistance to, 11, 21n63
interdiscursivity, 2, 9, 17, 155–159
interillumination, 2, 16

kabbalah, 46n6, 52–54, 64n31, 70, 78–79, 81n18, 83n63
Kestenbaum, Victor, 54, 88, 91

Levinas, Emmanuel, 58, 68
limits, boundaries, borders, 2, 12, 13, 14, 15, 2, 7, 24, 7, 17, 28, 34–155, 157
Lukinsky, Joseph, 38

means, ends, and ideals, 67, 75–79, 85–101n54

About the Author

Harvey Shapiro is associate professor of education at Northeastern University in Boston. He earned his Ph.D. in Jewish education from Hebrew Union College in 1996. At that time he was appointed as dean of the Shoolman Graduate School of Jewish Education at Hebrew College, where he also served as associate professor of Jewish education until 2008. Prior to his academic appointments, he was a Jewish day school headmaster for ten years and a camp director for four years. His scholarly work presently focuses on philosophy of education in both secular and Jewish contexts. His most recent articles are on John Dewey's theory of reflective practice and Jacques Derrida's theory of iterability in education. He and his wife, Abby, live in Needham, Massachusetts. They have three sons.